ISBN 0-8373-0707-4

C-707   CAREER EXAMINATION SERIES

This is your
PASSBOOK® for...

Senior Clerk

Test Preparation Study Guide

Questions & Answers

NATIONAL LEARNING CORPORATION

PASSBOOK®
NOTICE

This book is SOLELY intended for, is sold ONLY to, and its use is RESTRICTED to *individual*, bona fide applicants or candidates who qualify by virtue of having seriously filed applications for appropriate license, certificate, professional and/or promotional advancement, higher school matriculation, scholarship, or other legitimate requirements of educational and/or governmental authorities.

This book is NOT intended for use, class instruction, tutoring, training, duplication, copying, reprinting, excerption, or adaptation, etc., by:

(1) Other publishers

(2) Proprietors and/or Instructors of "Coaching" and/or Preparatory Courses

(3) Personnel and/or Training Divisions of commercial, industrial, and governmental organizations

(4) Schools, colleges, or universities and/or their departments and staffs, including teachers and other personnel

(5) Testing Agencies or Bureaus

(6) Study groups which seek by the purchase of a single volume to copy and/or duplicate and/or adapt this material for use by the group as a whole without having purchased individual volumes for each of the members of the group

(7) Et al.

Such persons would be in violation of appropriate Federal and State statutes.

PROVISION OF LICENSING AGREEMENTS. — Recognized educational commercial, industrial, and governmental institutions and organizations, and others legitimately engaged in educational pursuits, including training, testing, and measurement activities, may address a request for a licensing agreement to the copyright owners, who will determine whether, and under what conditions, including fees and charges, the materials in this book may be used by them. In other words, a licensing facility exists for the legitimate use of the material in this book on other than an individual basis. However, it is asseverated and affirmed here that the material in this book *CANNOT* be used without the receipt of the express permission of such a licensing agreement from the Publishers.

NATIONAL LEARNING CORPORATION
212 Michael Drive
Syosset, New York 11791

Inquiries re licensing agreements should be addressed to:
The President
National Learning Corporation
212 Michael Drive
Syosset, New York 11791

PASSBOOK® SERIES

THE *PASSBOOK® SERIES* has been created to prepare applicants and candidates for the ultimate academic battlefield – the examination room.

At some time in our lives, each and every one of us may be required to take an examination – for validation, matriculation, admission, qualification, registration, certification, or licensure.

Based on the assumption that every applicant or candidate has met the basic formal educational standards, has taken the required number of courses, and read the necessary texts, the *PASSBOOK® SERIES* furnishes the one special preparation which may assure passing with confidence, instead of failing with insecurity. Examination questions – together with answers – are furnished as the basic vehicle for study so that the mysteries of the examination and its compounding difficulties may be eliminated or diminished by a sure method.

This book is meant to help you pass your examination provided that you qualify and are serious in your objective.

The entire field is reviewed through the huge store of content information which is succinctly presented through a provocative and challenging approach – the question-and-answer method.

A climate of success is established by furnishing the correct answers at the end of each test.

You soon learn to recognize types of questions, forms of questions, and patterns of questioning. You may even begin to anticipate expected outcomes.

You perceive that many questions are repeated or adapted so that you can gain acute insights, which may enable you to score many sure points.

You learn how to confront new questions, or types of questions, and to attack them confidently and work out the correct answers.

You note objectives and emphases, and recognize pitfalls and dangers, so that you may make positive educational adjustments.

Moreover, you are kept fully informed in relation to new concepts, methods, practices, and directions in the field.

You discover that you are actually taking the examination all the time: you are preparing for the examination by "taking" an examination, not by reading extraneous and/or supererogatory textbooks.

In short, this PASSBOOK®, used directedly, should be an important factor in helping you to pass your test.

SENIOR CLERK

DUTIES

As a Senior Clerk, you would do responsible office work requiring the exercise of independent judgment and, in many cases, supervise the work of a small group of subordinates in routine office work. You would plan work assignments and maintain desired standards of quality and output; keep complex office records; collect information to be used to as a basis for reports; and review applications and other forms for correctness and completeness in cases calling for judgment as to compliance with prescribed requirements. In addition, you would dictate correspondence and memoranda, set up time schedules and be responsible for discipline in the unit.

An employee in this class performs a variety of difficult and responsible clerical functions. The incumbent may supervise clerical workers or may perform complex clerical work involving intricate procedures and the exercise of a high degree of independent judgment. Work is performed within the framework of established practices and procedures and is usually reviewed for achievement of desired results. Does related work as required.

SCOPE OF THE EXAMINATION

The written test will cover knowledge, skills and/or abilities in such areas as:
1. Understanding and interpreting written material;
2. English usage, grammar, punctuation and spelling;
3. Office practices / record keeping;
4. Clerical abilities;
5. Name and number checking;
6. Coding; and
7. Arithmetic reasoning.

HOW TO TAKE A TEST

I. YOU MUST PASS AN EXAMINATION

A. *WHAT EVERY CANDIDATE SHOULD KNOW*

Examination applicants often ask us for help in preparing for the written test. What can I study in advance? What kinds of questions will be asked? How will the test be given? How will the papers be graded?

As an applicant for a civil service examination, you may be wondering about some of these things. Our purpose here is to suggest effective methods of advance study and to describe civil service examinations.

Your chances for success on this examination can be increased if you know how to prepare. Those "pre-examination jitters" can be reduced if you know what to expect. You can even experience an adventure in good citizenship if you know why civil service exams are given.

B. *WHY ARE CIVIL SERVICE EXAMINATIONS GIVEN?*

Civil service examinations are important to you in two ways. As a citizen, you want public jobs filled by employees who know how to do their work. As a job seeker, you want a fair chance to compete for that job on an equal footing with other candidates. The best-known means of accomplishing this two-fold goal is the competitive examination.

Exams are widely publicized throughout the nation. They may be administered for jobs in federal, state, city, municipal, town or village governments or agencies.

Any citizen may apply, with some limitations, such as the age or residence of applicants. Your experience and education may be reviewed to see whether you meet the requirements for the particular examination. When these requirements exist, they are reasonable and applied consistently to all applicants. Thus, a competitive examination may cause you some uneasiness now, but it is your privilege and safeguard.

C. *HOW ARE CIVIL SERVICE EXAMS DEVELOPED?*

Examinations are carefully written by trained technicians who are specialists in the field known as "psychological measurement," in consultation with recognized authorities in the field of work that the test will cover. These experts recommend the subject matter areas or skills to be tested; only those knowledges or skills important to your success on the job are included. The most reliable books and source materials available are used as references. Together, the experts and technicians judge the difficulty level of the questions.

Test technicians know how to phrase questions so that the problem is clearly stated. Their ethics do not permit "trick" or "catch" questions. Questions may have been tried out on sample groups, or subjected to statistical analysis, to determine their usefulness.

Written tests are often used in combination with performance tests, ratings of training and experience, and oral interviews. All of these measures combine to form the best-known means of finding the right person for the right job.

II. HOW TO PASS THE WRITTEN TEST

A. NATURE OF THE EXAMINATION

To prepare intelligently for civil service examinations, you should know how they differ from school examinations you have taken. In school you were assigned certain definite pages to read or subjects to cover. The examination questions were quite detailed and usually emphasized memory. Civil service exams, on the other hand, try to discover your present ability to perform the duties of a position, plus your potentiality to learn these duties. In other words, a civil service exam attempts to predict how successful you will be. Questions cover such a broad area that they cannot be as minute and detailed as school exam questions.

In the public service similar kinds of work, or positions, are grouped together in one "class." This process is known as *position-classification*. All the positions in a class are paid according to the salary range for that class. One class title covers all of these positions, and they are all tested by the same examination.

B. FOUR BASIC STEPS

1) Study the announcement

How, then, can you know what subjects to study? Our best answer is: "Learn as much as possible about the class of positions for which you've applied." The exam will test the knowledge, skills and abilities needed to do the work.

Your most valuable source of information about the position you want is the official exam announcement. This announcement lists the training and experience qualifications. Check these standards and apply only if you come reasonably close to meeting them.

The brief description of the position in the examination announcement offers some clues to the subjects which will be tested. Think about the job itself. Review the duties in your mind. Can you perform them, or are there some in which you are rusty? Fill in the blank spots in your preparation.

Many jurisdictions preview the written test in the exam announcement by including a section called "Knowledge and Abilities Required," "Scope of the Examination," or some similar heading. Here you will find out specifically what fields will be tested.

2) Review your own background

Once you learn in general what the position is all about, and what you need to know to do the work, ask yourself which subjects you already know fairly well and which need improvement. You may wonder whether to concentrate on improving your strong areas or on building some background in your fields of weakness. When the announcement has specified "some knowledge" or "considerable knowledge," or has used adjectives like "beginning principles of…" or "advanced … methods," you can get a clue as to the number and difficulty of questions to be asked in any given field. More questions, and hence broader coverage, would be included for those subjects which are more important in the work. Now weigh your strengths and weaknesses against the job requirements and prepare accordingly.

3) Determine the level of the position

Another way to tell how intensively you should prepare is to understand the level of the job for which you are applying. Is it the entering level? In other words, is this the position in which beginners in a field of work are hired? Or is it an intermediate or advanced level? Sometimes this is indicated by such words as "Junior" or "Senior" in the class title. Other jurisdictions use Roman numerals to designate the level – Clerk I, Clerk II, for example. The word "Supervisor" sometimes appears in the title. If the level is not indicated by the title,

2

check the description of duties. Will you be working under very close supervision, or will you have responsibility for independent decisions in this work?

4) Choose appropriate study materials

Now that you know the subjects to be examined and the relative amount of each subject to be covered, you can choose suitable study materials. For beginning level jobs, or even advanced ones, if you have a pronounced weakness in some aspect of your training, read a modern, standard textbook in that field. Be sure it is up to date and has general coverage. Such books are normally available at your library, and the librarian will be glad to help you locate one. For entry-level positions, questions of appropriate difficulty are chosen – neither highly advanced questions, nor those too simple. Such questions require careful thought but not advanced training.

If the position for which you are applying is technical or advanced, you will read more advanced, specialized material. If you are already familiar with the basic principles of your field, elementary textbooks would waste your time. Concentrate on advanced textbooks and technical periodicals. Think through the concepts and review difficult problems in your field.

These are all general sources. You can get more ideas on your own initiative, following these leads. For example, training manuals and publications of the government agency which employs workers in your field can be useful, particularly for technical and professional positions. A letter or visit to the government department involved may result in more specific study suggestions, and certainly will provide you with a more definite idea of the exact nature of the position you are seeking.

III. KINDS OF TESTS

Tests are used for purposes other than measuring knowledge and ability to perform specified duties. For some positions, it is equally important to test ability to make adjustments to new situations or to profit from training. In others, basic mental abilities not dependent on information are essential. Questions which test these things may not appear as pertinent to the duties of the position as those which test for knowledge and information. Yet they are often highly important parts of a fair examination. For very general questions, it is almost impossible to help you direct your study efforts. What we can do is to point out some of the more common of these general abilities needed in public service positions and describe some typical questions.

1) General information

Broad, general information has been found useful for predicting job success in some kinds of work. This is tested in a variety of ways, from vocabulary lists to questions about current events. Basic background in some field of work, such as sociology or economics, may be sampled in a group of questions. Often these are principles which have become familiar to most persons through exposure rather than through formal training. It is difficult to advise you how to study for these questions; being alert to the world around you is our best suggestion.

2) Verbal ability

An example of an ability needed in many positions is verbal or language ability. Verbal ability is, in brief, the ability to use and understand words. Vocabulary and grammar tests are typical measures of this ability. Reading comprehension or paragraph interpretation questions are common in many kinds of civil service tests. You are given a paragraph of written material and asked to find its central meaning.

3) Numerical ability

Number skills can be tested by the familiar arithmetic problem, by checking paired lists of numbers to see which are alike and which are different, or by interpreting charts and graphs. In the latter test, a graph may be printed in the test booklet which you are asked to use as the basis for answering questions.

4) Observation

A popular test for law-enforcement positions is the observation test. A picture is shown to you for several minutes, then taken away. Questions about the picture test your ability to observe both details and larger elements.

5) Following directions

In many positions in the public service, the employee must be able to carry out written instructions dependably and accurately. You may be given a chart with several columns, each column listing a variety of information. The questions require you to carry out directions involving the information given in the chart.

6) Skills and aptitudes

Performance tests effectively measure some manual skills and aptitudes. When the skill is one in which you are trained, such as typing or shorthand, you can practice. These tests are often very much like those given in business school or high school courses. For many of the other skills and aptitudes, however, no short-time preparation can be made. Skills and abilities natural to you or that you have developed throughout your lifetime are being tested.

Many of the general questions just described provide all the data needed to answer the questions and ask you to use your reasoning ability to find the answers. Your best preparation for these tests, as well as for tests of facts and ideas, is to be at your physical and mental best. You, no doubt, have your own methods of getting into an exam-taking mood and keeping "in shape." The next section lists some ideas on this subject.

IV. KINDS OF QUESTIONS

Only rarely is the "essay" question, which you answer in narrative form, used in civil service tests. Civil service tests are usually of the short-answer type. Full instructions for answering these questions will be given to you at the examination. But in case this is your first experience with short-answer questions and separate answer sheets, here is what you need to know:

1) Multiple-choice Questions

Most popular of the short-answer questions is the "multiple choice" or "best answer" question. It can be used, for example, to test for factual knowledge, ability to solve problems or judgment in meeting situations found at work.

A multiple-choice question is normally one of three types—
- It can begin with an incomplete statement followed by several possible endings. You are to find the one ending which *best* completes the statement, although some of the others may not be entirely wrong.
- It can also be a complete statement in the form of a question which is answered by choosing one of the statements listed.

- It can be in the form of a problem – again you select the best answer.

Here is an example of a multiple-choice question with a discussion which should give you some clues as to the method for choosing the right answer:

When an employee has a complaint about his assignment, the action which will *best* help him overcome his difficulty is to
- A. discuss his difficulty with his coworkers
- B. take the problem to the head of the organization
- C. take the problem to the person who gave him the assignment
- D. say nothing to anyone about his complaint

In answering this question, you should study each of the choices to find which is best. Consider choice "A" – Certainly an employee may discuss his complaint with fellow employees, but no change or improvement can result, and the complaint remains unresolved. Choice "B" is a poor choice since the head of the organization probably does not know what assignment you have been given, and taking your problem to him is known as "going over the head" of the supervisor. The supervisor, or person who made the assignment, is the person who can clarify it or correct any injustice. Choice "C" is, therefore, correct. To say nothing, as in choice "D," is unwise. Supervisors have and interest in knowing the problems employees are facing, and the employee is seeking a solution to his problem.

2) True/False Questions

The "true/false" or "right/wrong" form of question is sometimes used. Here a complete statement is given. Your job is to decide whether the statement is right or wrong.

SAMPLE: A roaming cell-phone call to a nearby city costs less than a non-roaming call to a distant city.

This statement is wrong, or false, since roaming calls are more expensive.

This is not a complete list of all possible question forms, although most of the others are variations of these common types. You will always get complete directions for answering questions. Be sure you understand *how* to mark your answers – ask questions until you do.

V. RECORDING YOUR ANSWERS

Computer terminals are used more and more today for many different kinds of exams.

For an examination with very few applicants, you may be told to record your answers in the test booklet itself. Separate answer sheets are much more common. If this separate answer sheet is to be scored by machine – and this is often the case – it is highly important that you mark your answers correctly in order to get credit.

An electronic scoring machine is often used in civil service offices because of the speed with which papers can be scored. Machine-scored answer sheets must be marked with a pencil, which will be given to you. This pencil has a high graphite content which responds to the electronic scoring machine. As a matter of fact, stray dots may register as answers, so do not let your pencil rest on the answer sheet while you are pondering the correct answer. Also, if your pencil lead breaks or is otherwise defective, ask for another.

Since the answer sheet will be dropped in a slot in the scoring machine, be careful not to bend the corners or get the paper crumpled.

The answer sheet normally has five vertical columns of numbers, with 30 numbers to a column. These numbers correspond to the question numbers in your test booklet. After each number, going across the page are four or five pairs of dotted lines. These short dotted lines have small letters or numbers above them. The first two pairs may also have a "T" or "F" above the letters. This indicates that the first two pairs only are to be used if the questions are of the true-false type. If the questions are multiple choice, disregard the "T" and "F" and pay attention only to the small letters or numbers.

Answer your questions in the manner of the sample that follows:

32. The largest city in the United States is
   A. Washington, D.C.
   B. New York City
   C. Chicago
   D. Detroit
   E. San Francisco

1) Choose the answer you think is best. (New York City is the largest, so "B" is correct.)
2) Find the row of dotted lines numbered the same as the question you are answering. (Find row number 32)
3) Find the pair of dotted lines corresponding to the answer. (Find the pair of lines under the mark "B.")
4) Make a solid black mark between the dotted lines.

VI. BEFORE THE TEST

Common sense will help you find procedures to follow to get ready for an examination. Too many of us, however, overlook these sensible measures. Indeed, nervousness and fatigue have been found to be the most serious reasons why applicants fail to do their best on civil service tests. Here is a list of reminders:

- Begin your preparation early — Don't wait until the last minute to go scurrying around for books and materials or to find out what the position is all about.
- Prepare continuously — An hour a night for a week is better than an all-night cram session. This has been definitely established. What is more, a night a week for a month will return better dividends than crowding your study into a shorter period of time.
- Locate the place of the exam — You have been sent a notice telling you when and where to report for the examination. If the location is in a different town or otherwise unfamiliar to you, it would be well to inquire the best route and learn something about the building.
- Relax the night before the test — Allow your mind to rest. Do not study at all that night. Plan some mild recreation or diversion; then go to bed early and get a good night's sleep.
- Get up early enough to make a leisurely trip to the place for the test — This way unforeseen events, traffic snarls, unfamiliar buildings, etc. will not upset you.
- Dress comfortably — A written test is not a fashion show. You will be known by number and not by name, so wear something comfortable.

- Leave excess paraphernalia at home – Shopping bags and odd bundles will get in your way. You need bring only the items mentioned in the official notice you received; usually everything you need is provided. Do not bring reference books to the exam. They will only confuse those last minutes and be taken away from you when in the test room.
- Arrive somewhat ahead of time – If because of transportation schedules you must get there very early, bring a newspaper or magazine to take your mind off yourself while waiting.
- Locate the examination room – When you have found the proper room, you will be directed to the seat or part of the room where you will sit. Sometimes you are given a sheet of instructions to read while you are waiting. Do not fill out any forms until you are told to do so; just read them and be prepared.
- Relax and prepare to listen to the instructions
- If you have any physical problem that may keep you from doing your best, be sure to tell the test administrator. If you are sick or in poor health, you really cannot do your best on the exam. You can come back and take the test some other time.

VII. AT THE TEST

The day of the test is here and you have the test booklet in your hand. The temptation to get going is very strong. Caution! There is more to success than knowing the right answers. You must know how to identify your papers and understand variations in the type of short-answer question used in this particular examination. Follow these suggestions for maximum results from your efforts:

1) Cooperate with the monitor

The test administrator has a duty to create a situation in which you can be as much at ease as possible. He will give instructions, tell you when to begin, check to see that you are marking your answer sheet correctly, and so on. He is not there to guard you, although he will see that your competitors do not take unfair advantage. He wants to help you do your best.

2) Listen to all instructions

Don't jump the gun! Wait until you understand all directions. In most civil service tests you get more time than you need to answer the questions. So don't be in a hurry. Read each word of instructions until you clearly understand the meaning. Study the examples, listen to all announcements and follow directions. Ask questions if you do not understand what to do.

3) Identify your papers

Civil service exams are usually identified by number only. You will be assigned a number; you must not put your name on your test papers. Be sure to copy your number correctly. Since more than one exam may be given, copy your exact examination title.

4) Plan your time

Unless you are told that a test is a "speed" or "rate of work" test, speed itself is usually not important. Time enough to answer all the questions will be provided, but this does not mean that you have all day. An overall time limit has been set. Divide the total time (in minutes) by the number of questions to determine the approximate time you have for each question.

5) Do not linger over difficult questions

If you come across a difficult question, mark it with a paper clip (useful to have along) and come back to it when you have been through the booklet. One caution if you do this — be sure to skip a number on your answer sheet as well. Check often to be sure that you have not lost your place and that you are marking in the row numbered the same as the question you are answering.

6) Read the questions

Be sure you know what the question asks! Many capable people are unsuccessful because they failed to *read* the questions correctly.

7) Answer all questions

Unless you have been instructed that a penalty will be deducted for incorrect answers, it is better to guess than to omit a question.

8) Speed tests

It is often better NOT to guess on speed tests. It has been found that on timed tests people are tempted to spend the last few seconds before time is called in marking answers at random — without even reading them — in the hope of picking up a few extra points. To discourage this practice, the instructions may warn you that your score will be "corrected" for guessing. That is, a penalty will be applied. The incorrect answers will be deducted from the correct ones, or some other penalty formula will be used.

9) Review your answers

If you finish before time is called, go back to the questions you guessed or omitted to give them further thought. Review other answers if you have time.

10) Return your test materials

If you are ready to leave before others have finished or time is called, take ALL your materials to the monitor and leave quietly. Never take any test material with you. The monitor can discover whose papers are not complete, and taking a test booklet may be grounds for disqualification.

VIII. EXAMINATION TECHNIQUES

1) Read the general instructions carefully. These are usually printed on the first page of the exam booklet. As a rule, these instructions refer to the timing of the examination; the fact that you should not start work until the signal and must stop work at a signal, etc. If there are any *special* instructions, such as a choice of questions to be answered, make sure that you note this instruction carefully.

2) When you are ready to start work on the examination, that is as soon as the signal has been given, read the instructions to each question booklet, underline any key words or phrases, such as *least, best, outline, describe* and the like. In this way you will tend to answer as requested rather than discover on reviewing your paper that you *listed without describing*, that you selected the *worst* choice rather than the *best* choice, etc.

3) If the examination is of the objective or multiple-choice type – that is, each question will also give a series of possible answers: A, B, C or D, and you are called upon to select the best answer and write the letter next to that answer on your answer paper – it is advisable to start answering each question in turn. There may be anywhere from 50 to 100 such questions in the three or four hours allotted and you can see how much time would be taken if you read through all the questions before beginning to answer any. Furthermore, if you come across a question or group of questions which you know would be difficult to answer, it would undoubtedly affect your handling of all the other questions.

4) If the examination is of the essay type and contains but a few questions, it is a moot point as to whether you should read all the questions before starting to answer any one. Of course, if you are given a choice – say five out of seven and the like – then it is essential to read all the questions so you can eliminate the two that are most difficult. If, however, you are asked to answer all the questions, there may be danger in trying to answer the easiest one first because you may find that you will spend too much time on it. The best technique is to answer the first question, then proceed to the second, etc.

5) Time your answers. Before the exam begins, write down the time it started, then add the time allowed for the examination and write down the time it must be completed, then divide the time available somewhat as follows:
   • If 3-1/2 hours are allowed, that would be 210 minutes. If you have 80 objective-type questions, that would be an average of 2-1/2 minutes per question. Allow yourself no more than 2 minutes per question, or a total of 160 minutes, which will permit about 50 minutes to review.
   • If for the time allotment of 210 minutes there are 7 essay questions to answer, that would average about 30 minutes a question. Give yourself only 25 minutes per question so that you have about 35 minutes to review.

6) The most important instruction is to *read each question* and make sure you know what is wanted. The second most important instruction is to *time yourself properly* so that you answer every question. The third most important instruction is to *answer every question*. Guess if you have to but include something for each question. Remember that you will receive no credit for a blank and will probably receive some credit if you write something in answer to an essay question. If you guess a letter – say "B" for a multiple-choice question – you may have guessed right. If you leave a blank as an answer to a multiple-choice question, the examiners may respect your feelings but it will not add a point to your score. Some exams may penalize you for wrong answers, so in such cases *only*, you may not want to guess unless you have some basis for your answer.

7) Suggestions
   a. Objective-type questions
      1. Examine the question booklet for proper sequence of pages and questions
      2. Read all instructions carefully
      3. Skip any question which seems too difficult; return to it after all other questions have been answered
      4. Apportion your time properly; do not spend too much time on any single question or group of questions

5. Note and underline key words – *all, most, fewest, least, best, worst, same, opposite,* etc.
6. Pay particular attention to negatives
7. Note unusual option, e.g., unduly long, short, complex, different or similar in content to the body of the question
8. Observe the use of "hedging" words – *probably, may, most likely,* etc.
9. Make sure that your answer is put next to the same number as the question
10. Do not second-guess unless you have good reason to believe the second answer is definitely more correct
11. Cross out original answer if you decide another answer is more accurate; do not erase until you are ready to hand your paper in
12. Answer all questions; guess unless instructed otherwise
13. Leave time for review

    b. Essay questions
1. Read each question carefully
2. Determine exactly what is wanted. Underline key words or phrases.
3. Decide on outline or paragraph answer
4. Include many different points and elements unless asked to develop any one or two points or elements
5. Show impartiality by giving pros and cons unless directed to select one side only
6. Make and write down any assumptions you find necessary to answer the questions
7. Watch your English, grammar, punctuation and choice of words
8. Time your answers; don't crowd material

8) Answering the essay question

Most essay questions can be answered by framing the specific response around several key words or ideas. Here are a few such key words or ideas:

M's: manpower, materials, methods, money, management
P's: purpose, program, policy, plan, procedure, practice, problems, pitfalls, personnel, public relations
    a. Six basic steps in handling problems:
1. Preliminary plan and background development
2. Collect information, data and facts
3. Analyze and interpret information, data and facts
4. Analyze and develop solutions as well as make recommendations
5. Prepare report and sell recommendations
6. Install recommendations and follow up effectiveness

    b. Pitfalls to avoid
1. *Taking things for granted* – A statement of the situation does not necessarily imply that each of the elements is necessarily true; for example, a complaint may be invalid and biased so that all that can be taken for granted is that a complaint has been registered

2. *Considering only one side of a situation* – Wherever possible, indicate several alternatives and then point out the reasons you selected the best one
3. *Failing to indicate follow up* – Whenever your answer indicates action on your part, make certain that you will take proper follow-up action to see how successful your recommendations, procedures or actions turn out to be
4. *Taking too long in answering any single question* – Remember to time your answers properly

IX. AFTER THE TEST

Scoring procedures differ in detail among civil service jurisdictions although the general principles are the same. Whether the papers are hand-scored or graded by machine we have described, they are nearly always graded by number. That is, the person who marks the paper knows only the number – never the name – of the applicant. Not until all the papers have been graded will they be matched with names. If other tests, such as training and experience or oral interview ratings have been given, scores will be combined. Different parts of the examination usually have different weights. For example, the written test might count 60 percent of the final grade, and a rating of training and experience 40 percent. In many jurisdictions, veterans will have a certain number of points added to their grades.

After the final grade has been determined, the names are placed in grade order and an eligible list is established. There are various methods for resolving ties between those who get the same final grade – probably the most common is to place first the name of the person whose application was received first. Job offers are made from the eligible list in the order the names appear on it. You will be notified of your grade and your rank as soon as all these computations have been made. This will be done as rapidly as possible.

People who are found to meet the requirements in the announcement are called "eligibles." Their names are put on a list of eligible candidates. An eligible's chances of getting a job depend on how high he stands on this list and how fast agencies are filling jobs from the list.

When a job is to be filled from a list of eligibles, the agency asks for the names of people on the list of eligibles for that job. When the civil service commission receives this request, it sends to the agency the names of the three people highest on this list. Or, if the job to be filled has specialized requirements, the office sends the agency the names of the top three persons who meet these requirements from the general list.

The appointing officer makes a choice from among the three people whose names were sent to him. If the selected person accepts the appointment, the names of the others are put back on the list to be considered for future openings.

That is the rule in hiring from all kinds of eligible lists, whether they are for typist, carpenter, chemist, or something else. For every vacancy, the appointing officer has his choice of any one of the top three eligibles on the list. This explains why the person whose name is on top of the list sometimes does not get an appointment when some of the persons lower on the list do. If the appointing officer chooses the second or third eligible, the No. 1 eligible does not get a job at once, but stays on the list until he is appointed or the list is terminated.

X. HOW TO PASS THE INTERVIEW TEST

The examination for which you applied requires an oral interview test. You have already taken the written test and you are now being called for the interview test – the final part of the formal examination.

You may think that it is not possible to prepare for an interview test and that there are no procedures to follow during an interview. Our purpose is to point out some things you can do in advance that will help you and some good rules to follow and pitfalls to avoid while you are being interviewed.

What is an interview supposed to test?

The written examination is designed to test the technical knowledge and competence of the candidate; the oral is designed to evaluate intangible qualities, not readily measured otherwise, and to establish a list showing the relative fitness of each candidate – as measured against his competitors – for the position sought. Scoring is not on the basis of "right" and "wrong," but on a sliding scale of values ranging from "not passable" to "outstanding." As a matter of fact, it is possible to achieve a relatively low score without a single "incorrect" answer because of evident weakness in the qualities being measured.

Occasionally, an examination may consist entirely of an oral test – either an individual or a group oral. In such cases, information is sought concerning the technical knowledges and abilities of the candidate, since there has been no written examination for this purpose. More commonly, however, an oral test is used to supplement a written examination.

Who conducts interviews?

The composition of oral boards varies among different jurisdictions. In nearly all, a representative of the personnel department serves as chairman. One of the members of the board may be a representative of the department in which the candidate would work. In some cases, "outside experts" are used, and, frequently, a businessman or some other representative of the general public is asked to serve. Labor and management or other special groups may be represented. The aim is to secure the services of experts in the appropriate field.

However the board is composed, it is a good idea (and not at all improper or unethical) to ascertain in advance of the interview who the members are and what groups they represent. When you are introduced to them, you will have some idea of their backgrounds and interests, and at least you will not stutter and stammer over their names.

What should be done before the interview?

While knowledge about the board members is useful and takes some of the surprise element out of the interview, there is other preparation which is more substantive. It *is* possible to prepare for an oral interview – in several ways:

1) Keep a copy of your application and review it carefully before the interview

This may be the only document before the oral board, and the starting point of the interview. Know what education and experience you have listed there, and the sequence and dates of all of it. Sometimes the board will ask you to review the highlights of your experience for them; you should not have to hem and haw doing it.

2) Study the class specification and the examination announcement

Usually, the oral board has one or both of these to guide them. The qualities, characteristics or knowledges required by the position sought are stated in these documents. They offer valuable clues as to the nature of the oral interview. For example, if the job involves supervisory responsibilities, the announcement will usually indicate that knowledge of modern supervisory methods and the qualifications of the candidate as a supervisor will be tested. If so, you can expect such questions, frequently in the form of a hypothetical situation which you are expected to solve. NEVER go into an oral without knowledge of the duties and responsibilities of the job you seek.

3) Think through each qualification required

Try to visualize the kind of questions you would ask if you were a board member. How well could you answer them? Try especially to appraise your own knowledge and background in each area, *measured against the job sought*, and identify any areas in which you are weak. Be critical and realistic – do not flatter yourself.

4) Do some general reading in areas in which you feel you may be weak

For example, if the job involves supervision and your past experience has NOT, some general reading in supervisory methods and practices, particularly in the field of human relations, might be useful. Do NOT study agency procedures or detailed manuals. The oral board will be testing your understanding and capacity, not your memory.

5) Get a good night's sleep and watch your general health and mental attitude

You will want a clear head at the interview. Take care of a cold or any other minor ailment, and of course, no hangovers.

What should be done on the day of the interview?

Now comes the day of the interview itself. Give yourself plenty of time to get there. Plan to arrive somewhat ahead of the scheduled time, particularly if your appointment is in the fore part of the day. If a previous candidate fails to appear, the board might be ready for you a bit early. By early afternoon an oral board is almost invariably behind schedule if there are many candidates, and you may have to wait. Take along a book or magazine to read, or your application to review, but leave any extraneous material in the waiting room when you go in for your interview. In any event, relax and compose yourself.

The matter of dress is important. The board is forming impressions about you – from your experience, your manners, your attitude, and your appearance. Give your personal appearance careful attention. Dress your best, but not your flashiest. Choose conservative, appropriate clothing, and be sure it is immaculate. This is a business interview, and your appearance should indicate that you regard it as such. Besides, being well groomed and properly dressed will help boost your confidence.

Sooner or later, someone will call your name and escort you into the interview room. *This is it.* From here on you are on your own. It is too late for any more preparation. But remember, you asked for this opportunity to prove your fitness, and you are here because your request was granted.

What happens when you go in?

The usual sequence of events will be as follows: The clerk (who is often the board stenographer) will introduce you to the chairman of the oral board, who will introduce you to the other members of the board. Acknowledge the introductions before you sit down. Do not be surprised if you find a microphone facing you or a stenotypist sitting by. Oral interviews are usually recorded in the event of an appeal or other review.

Usually the chairman of the board will open the interview by reviewing the highlights of your education and work experience from your application – primarily for the benefit of the other members of the board, as well as to get the material into the record. Do not interrupt or comment unless there is an error or significant misinterpretation; if that is the case, do not hesitate. But do not quibble about insignificant matters. Also, he will usually ask you some question about your education, experience or your present job – partly to get you to start talking and to establish the interviewing "rapport." He may start the actual questioning, or turn it over to one of the other members. Frequently, each member undertakes the questioning on a particular area, one in which he is perhaps most competent, so you can expect each member to participate in the examination. Because time is limited, you may also expect some rather abrupt switches in the direction the questioning takes, so do not be upset by it. Normally, a board member will not pursue a single line of questioning unless he discovers a particular strength or weakness.

After each member has participated, the chairman will usually ask whether any member has any further questions, then will ask you if you have anything you wish to add. Unless you are expecting this question, it may floor you. Worse, it may start you off on an extended, extemporaneous speech. The board is not usually seeking more information. The question is principally to offer you a last opportunity to present further qualifications or to indicate that you have nothing to add. So, if you feel that a significant qualification or characteristic has been overlooked, it is proper to point it out in a sentence or so. Do not compliment the board on the thoroughness of their examination – they have been sketchy, and you know it. If you wish, merely say, "No thank you, I have nothing further to add." This is a point where you can "talk yourself out" of a good impression or fail to present an important bit of information. Remember, *you close the interview yourself.*

The chairman will then say, "That is all, Mr. _____, thank you." Do not be startled; the interview is over, and quicker than you think. Thank him, gather your belongings and take your leave. Save your sigh of relief for the other side of the door.

How to put your best foot forward

Throughout this entire process, you may feel that the board individually and collectively is trying to pierce your defenses, seek out your hidden weaknesses and embarrass and confuse you. Actually, this is not true. They are obliged to make an appraisal of your qualifications for the job you are seeking, and they want to see you in your best light. Remember, they must interview all candidates and a non-cooperative candidate may become a failure in spite of their best efforts to bring out his qualifications. Here are 15 suggestions that will help you:

1) Be natural – Keep your attitude confident, not cocky

If you are not confident that you can do the job, do not expect the board to be. Do not apologize for your weaknesses, try to bring out your strong points. The board is interested in a positive, not negative, presentation. Cockiness will antagonize any board member and make him wonder if you are covering up a weakness by a false show of strength.

2) Get comfortable, but don't lounge or sprawl

Sit erectly but not stiffly. A careless posture may lead the board to conclude that you are careless in other things, or at least that you are not impressed by the importance of the occasion. Either conclusion is natural, even if incorrect. Do not fuss with your clothing, a pencil or an ashtray. Your hands may occasionally be useful to emphasize a point; do not let them become a point of distraction.

3) Do not wisecrack or make small talk

This is a serious situation, and your attitude should show that you consider it as such. Further, the time of the board is limited – they do not want to waste it, and neither should you.

4) Do not exaggerate your experience or abilities

In the first place, from information in the application or other interviews and sources, the board may know more about you than you think. Secondly, you probably will not get away with it. An experienced board is rather adept at spotting such a situation, so do not take the chance.

5) If you know a board member, do not make a point of it, yet do not hide it

Certainly you are not fooling him, and probably not the other members of the board. Do not try to take advantage of your acquaintanceship – it will probably do you little good.

6) Do not dominate the interview

Let the board do that. They will give you the clues – do not assume that you have to do all the talking. Realize that the board has a number of questions to ask you, and do not try to take up all the interview time by showing off your extensive knowledge of the answer to the first one.

7) Be attentive

You only have 20 minutes or so, and you should keep your attention at its sharpest throughout. When a member is addressing a problem or question to you, give him your undivided attention. Address your reply principally to him, but do not exclude the other board members.

8) Do not interrupt

A board member may be stating a problem for you to analyze. He will ask you a question when the time comes. Let him state the problem, and wait for the question.

9) Make sure you understand the question

Do not try to answer until you are sure what the question is. If it is not clear, restate it in your own words or ask the board member to clarify it for you. However, do not haggle about minor elements.

10) Reply promptly but not hastily

A common entry on oral board rating sheets is "candidate responded readily," or "candidate hesitated in replies." Respond as promptly and quickly as you can, but do not jump to a hasty, ill-considered answer.

11) Do not be peremptory in your answers

A brief answer is proper – but do not fire your answer back. That is a losing game from your point of view. The board member can probably ask questions much faster than you can answer them.

12) Do not try to create the answer you think the board member wants

He is interested in what kind of mind you have and how it works – not in playing games. Furthermore, he can usually spot this practice and will actually grade you down on it.

13) Do not switch sides in your reply merely to agree with a board member

Frequently, a member will take a contrary position merely to draw you out and to see if you are willing and able to defend your point of view. Do not start a debate, yet do not surrender a good position. If a position is worth taking, it is worth defending.

14) Do not be afraid to admit an error in judgment if you are shown to be wrong

The board knows that you are forced to reply without any opportunity for careful consideration. Your answer may be demonstrably wrong. If so, admit it and get on with the interview.

15) Do not dwell at length on your present job

The opening question may relate to your present assignment. Answer the question but do not go into an extended discussion. You are being examined for a *new* job, not your present one. As a matter of fact, try to phrase ALL your answers in terms of the job for which you are being examined.

Basis of Rating

Probably you will forget most of these "do's" and "don'ts" when you walk into the oral interview room. Even remembering them all will not ensure you a passing grade. Perhaps you did not have the qualifications in the first place. But remembering them will help you to put your best foot forward, without treading on the toes of the board members.

Rumor and popular opinion to the contrary notwithstanding, an oral board wants you to make the best appearance possible. They know you are under pressure – but they also want to see how you respond to it as a guide to what your reaction would be under the pressures of the job you seek. They will be influenced by the degree of poise you display, the personal traits you show and the manner in which you respond.

ABOUT THIS BOOK

This book contains tests divided into Examination Sections. Go through each test, answering every question in the margin. We have also attached a sample answer sheet at the back of the book that can be removed and used. At the end of each test look at the answer key and check your answers. On the ones you got wrong, look at the right answer choice and learn. Do not fill in the answers first. Do not memorize the questions and answers, but understand the answer and principles involved. On your test, the questions will likely be different from the samples. Questions are changed and new ones added. If you understand these past questions you should have success with any changes that arise. Tests may consist of several types of questions. We have additional books on each subject should more study be advisable or necessary for you. Finally, the more you study, the better prepared you will be. This book is intended to be the last thing you study before you walk into the examination room. Prior study of relevant texts is also recommended. NLC publishes some of these in our Fundamental Series. Knowledge and good sense are important factors in passing your exam. Good luck also helps. So now study this Passbook, absorb the material contained within and take that knowledge into the examination. Then do your best to pass that exam.

———

EXAMINATION SECTION

EXAMINATION SECTION
TEST 1

DIRECTIONS: Each question or incomplete statement is followed by several suggested answers or completions. Select the one that BEST answers the question or completes the statement. *PRINT THE LETTER OF THE CORRECT ANSWER IN THE SPACE AT THE RIGHT.*

1. A supervisor may be required to help train a newly appointed clerk.
   Which of the following is LEAST important for a newly appointed clerk to know in order to perform his work efficiently?

   A. Acceptable ways of answering and recording telephone calls
   B. The number of files in the storage files unit
   C. The filing methods used by his unit
   D. Proper techniques for handling visitors

   1.____

2. In your agency you have the responsibility of processing clients who have appointments with agency representatives. On a particularly busy day, a client comes to your desk and insists that she must see the person handling her case although she has no appointment.
   Under the circumstances, your FIRST action should be to

   A. show her the full appointment schedule
   B. give her an appointment for another day
   C. ask her to explain the urgency
   D. tell her to return later in the day

   2.____

3. Which of the following practices is BEST for a supervisor to use when assigning work to his staff?

   A. Give workers with seniority the most difficult jobs
   B. Assign all unimportant work to the slower workers
   C. Permit each employee to pick the job he prefers
   D. Make assignments based on the workers' abilities

   3.____

4. In which of the following instances is a supervisor MOST justified in giving commands to people under his supervision? When

   A. they delay in following instructions which have been given to them clearly
   B. they become relaxed and slow about work, and he wants to speed up their production
   C. he must direct them in an emergency situation
   D. he is instructing them on jobs that are unfamiliar to them

   4.____

5. Which of the following supervisory actions or attitudes is MOST likely to result in getting subordinates to try to do as much work as possible for a supervisor?
   He

   A. shows that his most important interest is in schedules and production goals
   B. consistently pressures his staff to get the work out
   C. never fails to let them know he is in charge
   D. considers their abilities and needs while requiring that production goals be met

   5.____

6. Assume that a supervisor has been explaining certain regulations to a new clerk under his supervision.
The MOST efficient way for the supervisor to make sure that the clerk has understood the explanation is to

    A. give him written materials on the regulations
    B. ask him if he has any further questions about the regulations
    C. ask him specific questions based on what has just been explained to him
    D. watch the way he handles a situation involving these regulations

6._____

7. One of your unit clerks has been assigned to work for a Mr. Jones in another office for several days. At the end of the first day, Mr. Jones, saying the clerk was not satisfactory, asks that she not be assigned to him again. This clerk is one of your most dependable workers, and no previous complaints about her work have come to you from any other outside assignments.
To get to the root of this situation, your FIRST action should be to

    A. ask Mr. Jones to explain in what way her work was unsatisfactory
    B. ask the clerk what she did that Mr. Jones considered unsatisfactory
    C. check with supervisors for whom she previously worked to see if your own rating of her is in error
    D. tell Mr. Jones to pick the clerk he would prefer to have work for him the next time

7._____

8. A senior typist, still on probation, is instructed to type, as quickly as possible, one section of a draft of a long, complex report. Her part must be typed and readable before another part of the report can be written. Asked when she can have the report ready, she gives her supervisor an estimate of a day longer than she knows it will actually take. She then finishes the job a day sooner than the date given her supervisor.
The judgment shown by the senior typist in giving an overestimate of time in a situation like this is, in general,

    A. *good* because it prevents the supervisor from thinking she works slowly
    B. *good* because it keeps unrealistic supervisors from expecting too much
    C. *bad* because she should have used the time left to further check and proofread her work
    D. *bad* because schedules and plans for other parts of the project may have been based on her false estimate

8._____

9. Suppose a new clerk, still on probation, is placed under your supervision and refuses to do a job you ask him to do. What is the FIRST thing you should do?

    A. Explain that you are the supervisor and he must follow your instructions.
    B. Tell him he may be suspended if he refuses.
    C. Ask someone else to do the job and rate him accordingly.
    D. Ask for his reason for objecting to the request.

9._____

10. As a supervisor of a small group of people, you have blamed worker A for something that you later find out was really done by worker B.
The BEST thing for you to do now would be to

10._____

    A. say nothing to worker A but criticize worker B for his mistake while worker A is near so that A will realize that you know who made the mistake

    B. speak to each worker separately, apologize to worker A for your mistake, and discuss worker B's mistake with him

    C. bring both workers together, apologize to worker A for your mistake, and discuss worker B's mistake with him

    D. say nothing now but be careful about mixing up worker A with worker B in the future

11. You have just learned one of your staff is grumbling that she thinks you are not pleased with her work. As far as you're concerned, this isn't true at all. In fact, you've paid no particular attention to this worker lately because you've been very busy. You have just finished preparing an important report and *breaking in* a new clerk.   11.____
Under the circumstances, the BEST thing to do is

    A. ignore her; after all, it's just a figment of her imagination

    B. discuss the matter with her now to try to find out and eliminate the cause of this problem

    C. tell her not to worry about it; you haven't had time to think about her work

    D. make a note to meet with her at a later date in order to straighten out the situation

12. A most important job of a supervisor is to positively motivate employees to increase their work production. Which of the following LEAST indicates that a group of workers has been positively motivated?   12.____

    A. Their work output becomes constant and stable.

    B. Their cooperation at work becomes greater.

    C. They begin to show pride in the product of their work.

    D. They show increased interest in their work.

13. Which of the following traits would be LEAST important in considering a person for a merit increase?   13.____

    A. Punctuality   B. Using initiative successfully

    C. High rate of production   D. Resourcefulness

14. Of the following, the action LEAST likely to gain a supervisor the cooperation of his staff is for him to   14.____

    A. give each person consideration as an individual

    B. be as objective as possible when evaluating work performance

    C. rotate the least popular assignments

    D. expect subordinates to be equally competent

15. It has been said that, for the supervisor, nothing can beat the *face-to-face* communication of talking to one subordinate at a time.   15.____
This method is, however, LEAST appropriate to use when the

    A. supervisor is explaining a change in general office procedure

    B. subject is of personal importance

    C. supervisor is conducting a yearly performance evaluation of all employees

    D. supervisor must talk to some of his employees concerning their poor attendance and punctuality

16. While you are on the telephone answering a question about your agency, a visitor comes to your desk and starts to ask you a question. There is no emergency or urgency in either situation, that of the phone call or that of answering the visitor's question.
In this case, you should

    A. continue to answer the person on the telephone until you are finished and then tell the visitor you are sorry to have kept him waiting
    B. excuse yourself to the person on the telephone and tell the visitor that you will be with him as soon as you have finished on the phone
    C. explain to the person on the telephone that you have a visitor and must shorten the conversation
    D. continue to answer the person on the phone while looking up occasionally at the visitor to let him know that you know he is waiting

16.____

17. While speaking on the telephone to someone who called, you are disconnected.
The FIRST thing you should do is

    A. hang up but try to keep your line free to receive the call back
    B. immediately get the dialtone and continually dial the person who called you until you reach him
    C. signal the switchboard operator and ask her to re-establish the connection
    D. dial *0* for Operator and explain that you were disconnected

17.____

18. The type of speech used by an office worker in telephone conversations greatly affects the communicator.
Of the following, the BEST way to express your ideas when telephoning is with a vocabulary that consists mainly of _____ words.

    A. formal, intellectual sounding
    B. often used colloquial
    C. technical, emphatic
    D. simple, descriptive

18.____

19. Suppose a clerk under your supervision has taken a personal phone call and is at the same time needed to answer a question regarding an assignment being handled by another member of your office. He appears confused as to what he should do. How should you instruct him later as to how to handle a similar situation?
You should tell him to

    A. tell the caller to hold on while he answers the question
    B. tell the caller to call back a little later
    C. return the call during an assigned break
    D. finish the conversation quickly and answer the question

19.____

20. You are asked to place a telephone call by your supervisor. When you place the call, you receive what appears to be a wrong number.
Of the following, you should FIRST

    A. check the number with your supervisor to see if the number he gave you is correct
    B. ask the person on the other end what his number is and who he is
    C. check with the person on the other end to see if the number you dialed is the number you received
    D. apologize to the person on the other end for disturbing him and hang up

20.____

Questions 21-30.

WORD MEANING

DIRECTIONS: Each Question 21 through 30 contains a word in capitals followed by four suggested meanings of the word. For each question, choose the BEST meaning and write the letter of the best meaning in the space at the right.

21. ACCURATE   21.____
    A. correct   B. useful   C. afraid   D. careless

22. ALTER   22.____
    A. copy   B. change   C. repeat   D. agree

23. DOCUMENT   23.____
    A. outline   B. agreement   C. blueprint   D. record

24. INDICATE   24.____
    A. listen   B. show   C. guess   D. try

25. INVENTORY   25.____
    A. custom   B. discovery   C. warning   D. list

26. ISSUE   26.____
    A. annoy   B. use up   C. give out   D. gain

27. NOTIFY   27.____
    A. inform   B. promise   C. approve   D. strengthen

28. ROUTINE   28.____
    A. path   B. mistake   C. habit   D. journey

29. TERMINATE   29.____
    A. rest   B. start   C. deny   D. end

30. TRANSMIT   30.____
    A. put in   B. send   C. stop   D. go across

Questions 31-35.

READING COMPREHENSION

DIRECTIONS: Questions 31 through 35 test how well you understand what you read. It will be necessary for you to read carefully because your answers to these questions should be based SOLELY on the information given in the following paragraphs.

The recipient gains an impression of a typewritten letter before he begins to read the message. Factors which provide for a good first impression include margins and spacing that are visually pleasing, formal parts of the letter which are correctly placed according to the style of the letter, copy which is free of obvious erasures and over-strikes, and transcript that is even and clear. The problem for the typist is that of how to produce that first, positive impression of her work.

There are several general rules which a typist can follow when she wishes to prepare a properly spaced letter on a sheet of letterhead. Ordinarily, the width of a letter should not be less the four inches nor more than six inches. The side margins should also have a desirable relation to the bottom margin and the space between the letterhead and the body of the letter. Usually the most appealing arrangement is when the side margins are even and the bottom margin is slightly wider than the side margins. In some offices, however, standard line length is used for all business letters, and the secretary then varies the spacing between the date line and the inside address according to the length of the letter.

31. The BEST title for the above paragraphs would be: 31._____

    A. Writing Office Letters
    B. Making Good First Impressions
    C. Judging Well-Typed Letters
    D. Good Placing and Spacing for Office Letters

32. According to the above paragraphs, which of the following might be considered the way   32._____
in which people very quickly judge the quality of work which has been typed?
By

    A. measuring the margins to see if they are correct
    B. looking at the spacing and cleanliness of the typescript
    C. scanning the body of the letter for meaning
    D. reading the date line and address for errors

33. What, according to the above paragraphs, would be definitely UNDESIRABLE as the   33._____
average line length of a typed letter?

    A. 4"   B. 5"   C. 6"   D. 7"

34. According to the above paragraphs, when the line length is kept standard, the secretary   34._____

    A. does not have to vary the spacing at all since this also is standard
    B. adjusts the spacing between the date line and inside address for different lengths
       of letters
    C. uses the longest line as a guideline for spacing between the date line and inside
       address
    D. varies the number of spaces between the lines

35. According to the above paragraphs, side margins are MOST pleasing when they   35._____

    A. are even and somewhat smaller than the bottom margin
    B. are slightly wider than the bottom margin
    C. vary with the length of the letter
    D. are figured independently from the letterhead and the body of the letter

Questions 36-40.

CODING

DIRECTIONS:
Name of Applicant	H A N G S B R U K E
Test Code	c o m p l e x i t y
File Number	0 1 2 3 4 5 6 7 8 9

Assume that each of the above capital letters is the first letter of the name of an applicant, that the small letter directly beneath each capital letter is the test code for the applicant, and that the number directly beneath each code letter is the file number for the applicant.

In each of the following Questions 36 through 40, the test code letters and the file numbers in Columns 2 and 3 should correspond to the capital letters in Column 1. For each question, look at each Column carefully and mark your answer as follows:

If there is an error only in Column 2, mark your answer A.
If there is an error only in Column 3, mark your answer B.
If there is an error in both Columns 2 and 3, mark your answer C.
If both Columns 2 and 3 are correct, mark your answer D.

The following sample question is given to help you understand the procedure.

SAMPLE QUESTION

Column 1	Column 2	Column 3
AKEHN	otyci	18902

In Column 2, the final test code letter *i* should be *m*. Column 3 is correctly coded to Column 1. Since there is an error only in Column 2, the answer is A.

	Column 1	Column 2	Column 3	
36.	NEKKU	mytti	29987	36._____
37.	KRAEB	txlye	86095	37._____
38.	ENAUK	ymoit	92178	38._____
39.	REANA	xeomo	69121	39._____
40.	EKHSE	ytcxy	97049	40._____

Questions 41-50.

ARITHMETICAL REASONING

DIRECTIONS: Solve the following problems.

41.   If a secretary answered 28 phone calls and typed the addresses for 112 credit statements in one morning, what is the RATIO of phone calls answered to credit statements typed for that period of time?   41._____

    A. 1:4   B. 1:7   C. 2:3   D. 3:5

42. According to a suggested filing system, no more than 10 folders should be filed behind   42.___
    any one file guide, and from 15 to 25 file guides should be used in each file drawer for
    easy finding and filing.
    The MAXIMUM number of folders that a five-drawer file cabinet can hold to allow easy
    finding and filing is

    A. 550   B. 750   C. 1,100   D. 1,250

43. An employee had a starting salary of $32,902. He received a salary increase at the end   43.___
    of each year, and at the end of the seventh year, his salary was $36,738. What was his
    AVERAGE annual increase in salary over these seven years?

    A. $510   B. $538   C. $548   D. $572

44. The 55 typists and 28 senior clerks in a certain agency were paid a total of $1,943,200 in   44.___
    salaries for the year. If the average annual salary of a typist was $22,400, the AVERAGE
    annual salary of a senior clerk was

    A. $25,400   B. $26,600   C. $26,800   D. $27,000

45. A typist has been given a three-page report to type. She has finished typing the first two   45.___
    pages. The first page has 283 words, and the second page has 366 words.
    If the total report consists of 954 words, how many words will she have to type on the
    third page of the report?

    A. 202   B. 287   C. 305   D. 313

46. In one day, Clerk A processed 30% more forms than Clerk B, and Clerk C processed   46.___
    1 1/4 as many forms as Clerk A.
    If Clerk B processed 40 forms, how many MORE forms were processed by Clerk C
    than Clerk B?

    A. 12   B. 13   C. 21   D. 25

47. A clerk who earns a gross salary of $452 every week has the following deductions taken   47.___
    from her paycheck: 17 1/2% for City, State, Federal taxes, and for Social Security, $1.20
    for health insurance, and $6.10 for union dues. The amount of her take-home pay is

    A. $286.40   B. $312.40   C. $331.60   D. $365.60

48. In 2006 an agency spent $200 to buy pencils at a cost of $1 a dozen.   48.___
    If the agency used 3/4 of these pencils in 2006 and used the same number of pencils
    in 2007, how many MORE pencils did it have to buy to have enough pencils for all of
    2007?

    A. 1,200   B. 2,400   C. 3,600   D. 4,800

49. A clerk who worked in Agency X earned the following salaries: $30,070 the first year,   49.___
    $30,500 the second year, and $30,960 the third year. Another clerk who worked in
    Agency Y for three years earned $30,550 a year for two years and $30,724 the third year.
    The DIFFERENCE between the average salaries received by both clerks over a three-
    year period is

    A. $98   B. $102   C. $174   D. $282

50. An employee who works over 40 hours in any week receives overtime payment for the extra hours at time and one-half (1 1/2 times) his hourly rate of pay. An employee who earns $7.80 an hour works a total of 45 hours during a certain week.
His TOTAL pay for that week would be   50._____

   A. $312.00   B. $351.00   C. $370.50   D. $412.00

———

KEY (CORRECT ANSWERS)

1. B	11. B	21. A	31. D	41. A
2. C	12. A	22. B	32. B	42. D
3. D	13. A	23. D	33. D	43. C
4. C	14. D	24. B	34. B	44. A
5. D	15. A	25. D	35. A	45. C
6. C	16. B	26. C	36. B	46. D
7. A	17. A	27. A	37. C	47. D
8. D	18. D	28. C	38. D	48. B
9. D	19. C	29. D	39. A	49. A
10. B	20. C	30. B	40. C	50. C

———

TEST 2

DIRECTIONS: Each question or incomplete statement is followed by several suggested answers or completions. Select the one that BEST answers the question or completes the statement. *PRINT THE LETTER OF THE CORRECT ANSWER IN THE SPACE AT THE RIGHT.*

1. To tell a newly employed clerk to fill a top drawer of a four-drawer cabinet with heavy folders which will be often used and to keep lower drawers only partly filled is   1.___

    A. *good* because a tall person would have to bend unnecessarily if he had to use a lower drawer
    B. *bad* because the file cabinet may tip over when the top drawer is opened
    C. *good* because it is the most easily reachable drawer for the average person
    D. *bad* because a person bending down at another drawer may accidentally bang his head on the bottom of the drawer when he straightens up

2. If you have requisitioned a *ream* of paper in order to duplicate a single page office announcement, how many announcements can be printed from the one package of paper?   2.___

    A. 200   B. 500   C. 700   D. 1,000

3. In the operations of a government agency, a voucher is ORDINARILY used to   3.___

    A. refer someone to the agency for a position or assignment
    B. certify that an agency's records of financial transactions are accurate
    C. order payment from agency funds of a stated amount to an individual
    D. enter a statement of official opinion in the records of the agency

4. Of the following types of cards used in filing systems, the one which is generally MOST helpful in locating records which might be filed under more than one subject is the _____ card.   4.___

    A. cut   B. tickler
    C. cross-reference   D. visible index

5. The type of filing system in which one does NOT need to refer to a card index in order to find the folder is called   5.___

    A. alphabetic   B. geographic   C. subject   D. locational

6. Of the following, records management is LEAST concerned with   6.___

    A. the development of the best method for retrieving important information
    B. deciding what records should be kept
    C. deciding the number of appointments a client will need
    D. determining the types of folders to be used

7. If records are continually removed from a set of files without *charging* them to the borrower, the filing system will soon become ineffective.
   Of the following terms, the one which is NOT applied to a form used in a charge-out system is a   7.___

    A. requisition card   B. out-folder
    C. record retrieval form   D. substitution card

8. A new clerk has been told to put 500 cards in alphabetical order. Another clerk suggests   8.____
that she divide the cards into four groups such as A to F, G to L, M to R, and S to Z, and
then alphabetize these four smaller groups.
The suggested method is

    A. *poor* because the clerk will have to handle the sheets more than once and will
waste time
    B. *good* because it saves time, is more accurate, and is less tiring
    C. *good* because she will not have to concentrate on it so much when it is in smaller
groups
    D. *poor* because this method is much more tiring than straight alphabetizing

9. The term that describes the equipment attached to an office computer is   9.____

    A. interface   B. network   C. hardware   D. software

10. Suppose a clerk has been given pads of pre-printed forms   10.____
to use when taking phone messages for others in her office. The clerk is then observed
using scraps of paper and not the forms for writing her messages.
It should be explained that the BEST reason for using the forms is that

    A. they act as a checklist to make sure that the important information is taken
    B. she is expected to do her work in the same way as others in the office
    C. they make sure that unassigned paper is not wasted on phone messages
    D. learning to use these forms will help train her to use more difficult forms

11. Of the following, the one which is spelled incorrectly is   11.____

    A. alphabetization   B. reccommendation
    C. redaction   D. synergy

12. Of the following, the MAIN reason a stock clerk keeps a perpetual inventory of supplies in   12.____
the storeroom is that such an inventory will

    A. eliminate the need for a physical inventory
    B. provide a continuous record of supplies on hand
    C. indicate whether a shipment of supplies is satisfactory
    D. dictate the terms of the purchase order

13. As a supervisor, you may be required to handle different types of correspondence.   13.____
Of the following types of letters, it would be MOST important to promptly seal which
kind of letters?

    A. One marked *confidential*
    B. Those containing enclosures
    C. Any letter to be sent airmail
    D. Those in which carbons will be sent along with the original

14. While opening incoming mail, you notice that one letter indicates that an enclosure was   14.____
to be included but, even after careful inspection, you are not able to find the information
to which this refers.
Of the following, the thing that you should do FIRST is

A. replace the letter in its envelope and return it to the sender
B. file the letter until the sender's office mails the missing information
C. type out a letter to the sender informing them of their error
D. make a notation in the margin of the letter that the enclosure was omitted

15. You have been given a checklist and assigned the responsibility of inspecting certain equipment in the various offices of your agency.
Which of the following is the GREATEST advantage of the checklist?

    15.____

A. It indicates which equipment is in greatest demand.
B. Each piece of equipment on the checklist will be checked only once.
C. It helps to insure that the equipment listed will not be overlooked.
D. The equipment listed suggests other equipment you should look for.

16. Your supervisor has asked you to locate a telephone number for an attorney named Jones, whose office is located at 311 Broadway and whose name is not already listed in your files.
The BEST method for finding the number would be for you to

    16.____

A. call the information operator and have her get it for you
B. look in the alphabetical directory (white pages) under the name Jones at 311 Broadway
C. refer to the heading Attorney in the yellow pages for the name Jones at 311 Broadway
D. ask your supervisor who referred her to Mr. Jones, then call that person for the number

17. An example of material that should NOT be sent by first class mail is a

    17.____

A. carbon copy of a letter
C. business reply card
B. postcard
D. large catalogue

18. Which of the following BEST describes *office work simplification?*

    18.____

A. An attempt to increase the rate of production by speeding up the movements of employees
B. Eliminating wasteful steps in order to increase efficiency
C. Making jobs as easy as possible for employees so they will not be overworked
D. Eliminating all difficult tasks from an office and leaving only simple ones

19. The duties of a supervisor who is assigned the job of timekeeper may include all of the following EXCEPT

    19.____

A. computing and recording regular hours worked each day in accordance with the normal work schedule
B. approving requests for vacation leave, sick leave, and annual leave
C. computing and recording overtime hours worked beyond the normal schedule
D. determining the total regular hours and total extra hours worked during the week

20. Suppose a clerk under your supervision accidentally opens a personal letter while handling office mail.
Under such circumstances, you should tell the clerk to put the letter back into the envelope and

    20.____

A.   take the letter to the person to whom it belongs and make sure he understands that the clerk did not read it
B.   try to seal the envelope so it won't appear to have been opened
C.   write on the envelope *Sorry - opened by mistake,* and put his initials on it
D.   write on the envelope *Sorry - opened by mistake,* but not put his initials on it

Questions 21-25.

SPELLING

DIRECTIONS: Each Question 21 through 25 consists of three words. In each question, one of the words may be spelled incorrectly or all three may be spelled correctly. For each question, if one of the words is spelled incorrectly, write the letter of the incorrect word in the space at the right. If all three words are spelled correctly, write the letter D in the space at the right.

SAMPLE I: (A) guide   (B) departmint   (C) stranger

SAMPLE II: (A) comply   (B) valuable   (C) window

In the Sample Question I, *departmint* is incorrect.
It should be spelled *department.* Therefore, B is the
answer to Sample Question I.
In the Sample Question II, all three words are spelled correctly. Therefore, D is the answer to Sample Question II.

21.	A. argument	B. reciept	C. complain	21.____
22.	A. sufficient	B. postpone	C. visible	22.____
23.	A. expirience	B. dissatisfy	C. alternate	23.____
24.	A. occurred	B. noticable	C. appendix	24.____
25.	A. anxious	B. guarantee	C. calender	25.____

Questions 26-30.

ENGLISH USAGE

DIRECTIONS: Each Question 26 through 30 contains a sentence. Read each sentence carefully to decide whether it is correct. Then, in the space at the right, mark your answer:
(A) if the sentence is incorrect because of bad grammar or sentence structure
(B) if the sentence is incorrect because of bad punctuation
(C) if the sentence is incorrect because of bad capitalization
(D) if the sentence is correct

Each incorrect sentence has only one type of error. Consider a sentence correct if it has no errors, although there may be other correct ways of saying the same thing.

SAMPLE QUESTION I: One of our clerks were promoted
yesterday.

The subject of this sentence is *one,* so the verb should be *was promoted* instead of *were promoted.* Since the sentence is incorrect because of bad grammar, the answer to Sample Question I is A.

SAMPLE QUESTION II: Between you and me, I would prefer
not going there.

Since this sentence is correct, the answer to Sample Question II is D.

26. The National alliance of Businessmen is trying to persuade private businesses to hire youth in the summertime.   26.____

27. The supervisor who is on vacation, is in charge of processing vouchers.   27.____

28. The activity of the committee at its conferences is always stimulating.   28.____

29. After checking the addresses again, the letters went to the mailroom.   29.____

30. The director, as well as the employees, are interested in sharing the dividends.   30.____

Questions 31-40.

FILING

DIRECTIONS: Each Question 31 through 40 contains four names. For each question, choose the name that should be FIRST if the four names are to be arranged in alphabetical order in accordance with the Rules for Alphabetical Filing given below. Read these rules carefully. Then, for each question, indicate in the correspondingly numbered space at the right the letter before the name that should be FIRST in alphabetical order.

RULES FOR ALPHABETICAL FILING

Names of People

(1) *The names of people are filed in strict alphabetical order, first according to the last name, then according to first name or initial, and finally according to middle name or initial. For example: George Allen comes before Edward Bell, and Leonard P. Reston comes before Lucille B. Reston.*

(2) *When last names are the same, for example A. Green and Agnes Green, the one with the initial comes before the one with the name written out when the first initials are identical.*

(3) *When first and last names are alike and the middle name is given, for example John David Doe and John Devoe Doe, the names should be filed in the alphabetical order of the middle names.*

(4)   When first and last names are the same, a name without a middle initial comes before one with a middle name or initial. For example: John Doe comes before both John A. Doe and John Alan Doe.

(5)   When first and last names are the same, a name with a middle initial comes before one with a middle name beginning with the same initial. For example: Jack R. Herts comes before Jack Richard Hertz.

(6)   Prefixes such as De, 0', Mac, Mc, and Van are filed as written and are treated as part of the names to which they are connected. For example: Robert O'Dea is filed before David Olsen.

(7)   Abbreviated names are treated as if they were spelled out. For example: Chas. is filed as Charles and Thos. is filed as Thomas.

(8)   Titles and designations such as Dr., Mr., and Prof, are disregarded in filing.

<u>Names of Organizations</u>

(1)   The names of business organizations are filed according to the order in which each word in the name appears. When an organization name bears the name of a person, it is filed according to the rules for filing names of people as given above. For example: William Smith Service Co. comes before Television Distributors, Inc.

(2)   Where bureau, board, office or department appears as the first part of the title of a govern-mental agency, that agency should be filed under the word in the title expressing the chief function of the agency. For example: Bureau of the Budget would be filed as if written Bud-get, (Bureau of the). The Department of Personnel would be filed as if written Personnel, (Department of).

(3)   When the following words are part of an organization, they are disregarded: the, of, and.

(4)   When there are numbers in a name, they are treated as if they were spelled out. For exam-ple: 10th Street Bootery is filed as Tenth Street Bootery.

```
SAMPLE QUESTION:  (A)  Jane Earl        (2)
                  (B)  James A. Earle   (4)
                  (C)  James Earl       (1)
                  (D)  J. Earle         (3)
```

The numbers in parentheses show the proper alphabetical order in which these names should be filed. Since the name that should be filed FIRST is James Earl, the answer to the sample question is C.

31.   A.   Majorca Leather Goods   31.____
      B.   Robert Maiorca and Sons
      C.   Maintenance Management Corp.
      D.   Majestic Carpet Mills

32. A. Municipal Telephone Service   32.___
    B. Municipal Reference Library
    C. Municipal Credit Union
    D. Municipal Broadcasting System

33. A. Robert B. Pierce   B. R. Bruce Pierce   33.___
    C. Ronald Pierce   D. Robert Bruce Pierce

34. A. Four Seasons Sports Club   34.___
    B. 14 Street Shopping Center
    C. Forty Thieves Restaurant
    D. 42nd St. Theaters

35. A. Franco Franceschini   B. Amos Franchini   35.___
    C. Sandra Franceschia   D. Lilie Franchinesca

36. A. Chas. A. Levine   B. Kurt Levene   36.___
    C. Charles Levine   D. Kurt E. Levene

37. A. Prof. Geo. Kinkaid   B. Mr. Alan Kinkaid   37.___
    C. Dr. Albert A. Kinkade   D. Kincade Liquors Inc.

38. A. Department of Public Events   38.___
    B. Office of the Public Administrator
    C. Queensborough Public Library
    D. Department of Public Health

39. A. Martin Luther King, Jr. Towers   39.___
    B. Metro North Plaza
    C. Manhattanville Houses
    D. Marble Hill Houses

40. A. Dr. Arthur Davids   40.___
    B. The David Check Cashing Service
    C. A.C. Davidsen
    D. Milton Davidoff

Questions 41-45.

READING COMPREHENSION

DIRECTIONS: Questions 41 through 45 test how well you understand what you read. It will be necessary for you to read carefully because your answers to these questions should be based SOLELY on the information given in the following paragraph.

Work standards presuppose an ability to measure work. Measurement in office management is needed for several reasons. First, it is necessary to evaluate the overall efficiency of the office itself. It is then essential to measure the efficiency of each particular section or unit and that of the individual worker. To plan and control the work of sections and units, one must have measurement. A program of measurement goes hand in hand with a program of standards. One can have measurement without standards, but one cannot have work standards without measurement. Providing data on amount of work done and time expended, measure-

ment does not deal with the amount of energy expended by an individual although in many cases such energy may be in direct proportion to work output. Usually from two-thirds to three-fourths of all work can be measured. However, less than two-thirds of all work is actually measured because measurement difficulties are encountered when office work is non-repetitive and irregular, or when it is primarily mental rather than manual. These obstacles are often used as excuses for non-measurement far more frequently than is justified.

41. According to the paragraph, an office manager cannot set work standards unless he can   41._____

    A. plan the amount of work to be done
    B. control the amount of work that is done
    C. estimate accurately the quantity of work done
    D. delegate the amount of work to be done to efficient workers

42. According to the paragraph, the type of office work that would be MOST difficult to measure would be   42._____

    A. checking warrants for accuracy of information
    B. recording payroll changes
    C. processing applications
    D. making up a new system of giving out supplies

43. According to the paragraph, the actual amount of work that is measured is _____ of all work.   43._____

    A. less than two-thirds
    B. two-thirds to three-fourths
    C. less than three-sixths
    D. more than three-fourths

44. Which of the following would be MOST difficult to determine by using measurement techniques?   44._____

    A. The amount of work that is accomplished during a certain period of time
    B. The amount of work that should be planned for a period of time
    C. How much time is needed to do a certain task
    D. The amount of incentive a person must have to do his job

45. The one of the following which is the MOST suitable title for the paragraph is: 45._____

    A. How Measurement of Office Efficiency Depends on Work Standards
    B. Using Measurement for Office Management and Efficiency
    C. Work Standards and the Efficiency of the Office Worker
    D. Managing the Office Using Measured Work Standards

Questions 46-50.

INTERPRETING STATISTICAL DATA

DIRECTIONS: Answer Questions 46 through 50 using the information given in the table below.

AGE COMPOSITION IN THE LABOR FORCE IN CITY A
(1990-2000)

	Age Group	1990	1995	2000
Men	14 - 24	8,430	10,900	14,340
	25 - 44	22,200	22,350	26,065
	45+	17,550	19,800	21,970
Women	14 - 24	4,450	6,915	7,680
	25 - 44	9,080	10,010	11,550
	45+	7,325	9,470	13,180

46. The GREATEST increase in the number of people in the labor force between 1990 and   46.___
1995 occurred among

  A. men between the ages of 14 and 24
  B. men age 45 and over
  C. women between the ages of 14 and 24
  D. women age 45 and over

47. If the total number of women of all ages in the labor force increases from 2000 to 2005 by   47.___
the same number as it did from 1995 to 2000, the TOTAL number of women of all ages in
the labor force in 2005 will be

  A. 27,425   B. 29,675   C. 37,525   D. 38,425

48. The total increase in numbers of women in the labor force from 1990 to 1995 differs from   48.___
the total increase of men in the same years by being _____ than that of men.

  A. 770 less   B. 670 more   C. 770 more   D. 1,670 more

49. In the year 1990, the proportion of married women in each group was as follows: 1/5 of   49.___
the women in the 14-24 age group, 1/4 of those in the 25-44 age group, and 2/5 of those
45 and over.
How many married women were in the labor force in 1990?

  A. 4,625   B. 5,990   C. 6,090   D. 7,910

50. The 14-24 age group of men in the labor force from 1990 to 2000 increased by APPROX-   50.___
IMATELY

  A. 40%   B. 65%   C. 70%   D. 75%

KEY (CORRECT ANSWERS)

1. B	11. B	21. B	31. C	41. C
2. B	12. B	22. D	32. D	42. D
3. C	13. A	23. A	33. B	43. A
4. C	14. D	24. B	34. D	44. D
5. A	15. C	25. C	35. C	45. B
6. C	16. C	26. C	36. B	46. A
7. C	17. D	27. B	37. D	47. D
8. B	18. B	28. D	38. B	48. B
9. C	19. B	29. A	39. A	49. C
10. A	20. C	30. A	40. B	50. C

———

EXAMINATION SECTION
TEST 1

DIRECTIONS: Each question or incomplete statement is followed by several suggested answers or completions. Select the one that BEST answers the question or completes the statement. *PRINT THE LETTER OF THE CORRECT ANSWER IN THE SPACE AT THE RIGHT.*

Questions 1-2.

DIRECTIONS: Questions 1 and 2 are to be answered on the basis of the following conditions.

Assume that you work for Department A, which occupies several floors in one building. There is a reception office on each floor. All visitors (persons not employed in the department) are required to go to the reception office on the same floor as the office of the person they want to see. They sign a register, their presence is announced by the receptionist, and they wait in the reception room for the person they are visiting.

1. As you are walking in the corridor of your department on your way to a meeting in Room 314, a visitor approaches you and asks you to direct her to Room 312. She says that she is delivering some papers to Mr. Crane in that office. The MOST APPROPRIATE action for you to take is to

   A. offer to deliver the papers to Mr. Crane since you will be passing his office
   B. suggest that she come with you since you will be passing Room 312
   C. direct her to the reception office where Mr. Crane will be contacted for her
   D. take her to the reception office and contact Mr. Crane for her

1._____

2. You are acting as receptionist in the reception office on the second floor. A man enters, stating that he is an accountant from another department and that he has an appointment with Mr. Prince, who is located in Room 102 on the first floor.
The BEST action for you to take is to

   A. phone the reception office on the first floor and ask the receptionist to contact Mr. Prince
   B. advise the man to go to the reception office on the first floor where he will be further assisted
   C. contact Mr. Prince for him and ask that he come to your office where his visitor is waiting
   D. send him directly to Room 102 where he can see Mr. Prince

2._____

3. One of the employees whom you supervise complains to you that you give her more work than the other employees and that she cannot finish these assignments by the time you expect them to be completed.
Of the following, the FIRST action you should then take is to

   A. tell the employee that you expect more work from her because the other employees do not have her capabilities
   B. assure the employee that you always divide the work equally among your subordinates

3._____

    C.   review the employee's recent assignments in order to determine whether her complaint is justified

    D.   ask the employee if there are any personal problems which are interfering with the completion of the assignments

4.   Assume that a staff regulation exists which requires an employee to inform his supervisor if the employee will be absent on a particular day.
If an employee fails to follow this regulation, the FIRST action his supervisor should take is to   4._____

    A.   inform his own supervisor of the situation and ask for further instructions

    B.   ask the employee to explain his failure to follow the regulation

    C.   tell the employee that another breach of the regulation will lead to disciplinary action

    D.   reprimand the employee for failing to follow the regulation

5.   An employee tells his supervisor that he submitted an idea to the employees' suggestion program by mail over two months ago and still has not received an indication that the suggestion is being considered. The employee states that when one of his co-workers sent in a suggestion, he received a response within one week. The employee then asks his supervisor what he should do.
Which of the following is the BEST response for the supervisor to make?   5._____

    A.   "Next time you have a suggestion, see me about it first and I will make sure that it is properly handled."

    B.   "I'll try to find out whether your suggestion was received by the program and whether a response was sent."

    C.   "Your suggestion probably wasn't that good so there's no sense in pursuing the matter any further."

    D.   "Let's get together and submit the suggestion jointly so that it will carry more weight."

6.   Assume that you have been trying to teach a newly appointed employee the filing procedures used in your office. The employee seems to be having difficulty learning the procedures even though you consider them relatively simple and you originally learned them in less time than you have already spent trying to teach the new employee.
Before you spend any time trying to teach him any new filing procedures, which of the following actions should you take FIRST?   6._____

    A.   Try to teach him some other aspect of your office's work.

    B.   Tell him that you had little difficulty learning the procedures and ask him why he finds them so hard to learn.

    C.   Review with him those procedures you have tried to teach him and determine whether he understands them.

    D.   Report to your supervisor that the new employee is unsuited for the work performed in your office.

7.   There is a rule in your office that all employees must sign in and out for lunch. You notice that a new employee who is under your direct supervision has not signed in or out for lunch for the past three days. Of the following, the MOST effective action to take is to   7._____

A. immediately report this matter to your supervisor
B. note this infraction of rules on the employee's personnel record
C. remind the employee that she must sign in and out for lunch every day
D. send around a memorandum to all employees in the office telling them they must sign in and out for lunch every day

Questions 8-15.

DIRECTIONS: Questions 8 through 15 each show in Column I names written on four cards (lettered w, x, y, z) which have to be filed. You are to choose the option (lettered A, B, C, or D) in Column II which BEST represents the proper order of filing according to the rules and sample question given below. The cards are to be filed according to the following Rules for Alphabetical Filing.

RULES FOR ALPHABETICAL FILING

Names of Individuals

1.	*The names of individuals are filed in strict alphabetical order, first according to the last name, then according to first name or initial, and finally according to middle name or initial. For example: George Allen precedes Edward Bell and Leonard Reston precedes Lucille Reston.*

2.	*When last names are the same, for example, A. Green and Agnes Green, the one with the initial comes before the one with the name written out when the first initials are identical.*

3.	*When first and last names are the same, a name without a middle initial comes before one with a middle initial. For example: Ralph Simon comes before both Ralph A. Simon and Ralph Adam Simon.*

4.	*When first and last names are the same, a name with a middle initial comes before one with a middle name beginning with the same initial. For example: Sam P. Rogers comes before Sam Paul Rogers.*

5.	*Prefixes such as De , 0', Mac, Mc, and Van are filed as written and are treated as part of the names to which they are connected. For example: Gladys McTeaque is filed before Frances Meadows.*

6.	*Abbreviated names are treated as if they were spelled out. For example: Chas. is filed as Charles and Thos. is filed as Thomas.*

7.	*Titles and designations such as Dr., Mr., and Prof, are ignored in filing.*

Names of Organizations

1.	*The names of business organizations are filed according to the order in which each word in the name appears. When an organization name bears the name of a person, it is filed according to the rules for filing names of people as given above. Vivian Quinn Boutique would, therefore, come before Security Locks Inc. because Quinn comes before Security.*

2. *When numerals occur in a name, they are treated as if they were spelled out. For example: 4th Street Thrift Shop is filed as Fourth Street Thrift Shop.*

3. *When the following words are part of the name of an organization, they are ignored: on, the, of, and.*

SAMPLE

	Column I	Column II	The correct way to file the cards is:
w.	Jane Earl	A. w, y, z, x	y. James Earl
x.	James A. Earle	B. y, w, z, x	w. Jane Earl
y.	James Earl	C. x, y, w, z	z. J. Earle
z.	J. Earle	D. x, w, y, z	x. James A. Earle

The correct filing order is shown by the letters, y, w, z, x (in that sequence). Since, in Column II, B appears in front of the letters, y, w, z, x (in that sequence), B is the correct answer to the sample question.

Now answer the following questions using that same procedure.

Column I   Column II

8. w. James Rothschild   A. x, z, w, y   8.___
    x. Julius B. Rothchild   B. x, w, z, y
    y. B. Rothstein   C. z, y, w, x
    z. Brian Joel Rothenstein   D. z, w, x, y

9. w. George S. Wise   A. w, y, z, x   9.___
    x. S. G. Wise   B. x , w , y , z
    y. Geo. Stuart Wise   C. y, x, w, z
    z. Prof. Diana Wise   D. z, w, y, x

10. w. 10th Street Bus Terminal A. x, z, w, y   10.___
    x. Buckingham Travel Agency B. y, x, w, z
    y. The Buckingham Theater   C. w, z, y, x
    z. Burt Tompkins Studio   D. x, w, y, z

11. w. National Council of American   A. w, y, x, z   11.___
       Importers   B. x, z, w, y
    x. National Chain Co. of Provi-   C. z, x, w, y
       dence   D. z, x, y, w
    y. National Council on Alcoholism
    z. National Chain Co.

12. w. Dr. Herbert Alvary   A. w, y, x, z   12.___
    x. Mr. Victor Alvarado   B. z, w, x, y
    y. Alvar Industries   C. y, z, x, w
    z. V. Alvarado   D. w, z, x, y

	Column I		Column II		
13.	w. Joan MacBride	A.	w, x, z, y		13.____
	x. Wm. Mackey	B.	w, y, z, x		
	y. Roslyn McKenzie	C.	w, z, x, y		
	z. Winifred Mackey	D.	w, y , x, z		

	Column I		Column II		
14.	w. 3 Way Trucking Co.	A.	y, x, z, w		14.____
	x. 3rd Street Bakery	B.	y, z, w, x		
	y. 380 Realty Corp.	C.	x, y, z, w		
	z. Three Lions Pub	D.	x, y, w, z		
15.	w. Miss Rose Leonard	A.	z, w, x, y		15.____
	x. Rev. Leonard Lucas	B.	w, z, y, x		
	y. Sylvia Leonard Linen Shop	C.	w, x, z, y		
	z. Rose S. Leonard	D.	z, w, y, x		

Questions 16-19.

DIRECTIONS: Answer Questions 16 through 19 ONLY on the basis of the information given in the following passage.

Work measurement concerns accomplishment or productivity. It has to do with results; it does not deal with the amount of energy used up, although in many cases this may be in direct proportion to the work output. Work measurement not only helps a manager to distribute work loads fairly, but it also enables him to define work sueeess in actual units, evaluate employee performance, and determine where corrective help is needed. Work measurement is accomplished by measuring the amount produced, measuring the time spent to produce it, and relating the two. To illustrate, it is common to speak of so many orders processed within a given time. The number of orders processed becomes meaningful when related to the amount of time taken.

Much of the work in an office can be measured fairly accurately and inexpensively. The extent of wo.rk measurement possible in any given case will depend upon the particular type of office tasks performed, but usually from two-thirds to three-fourths of all work in an office can be measured. It is true that difficulty in work measurement is encountered, for example, when the office work is irregular and not repeated often, or when the work is primarily mental rather than manual. These are problems, but they are used as excuses for doing no work measurement far more frequently than is justified.

16. According to the above passage, which of the following BEST illustrates the type of information obtained as a result of work measurement? A   16.____

   A. clerk takes one hour to file 150 folders
   B. typist types five letters
   C. stenographer works harder typing from shorthand notes than she does typing from a typed draft
   D. clerk keeps track of employees' time by computing sick leave, annual leave, and overtime leave

17. The above passage does NOT indicate that work measurement can be used to help a supervisor to determine

    A. why an employee is performing poorly on the job
    B. who are the fast and slow workers in the unit
    C. how the work in the unit should be divided up
    D. how long it should take to perform a certain task

17.____

18. According to the above passage, the kind of work that would be MOST difficult to measure would be such work as

    A. sorting mail
    B. designing a form for a new procedure
    C. photocopying various materials
    D. answering inquiries with form letters

18.____

19. The excuses mentioned in the above passage for failure to perform work measurement can be BEST summarized as the

    A. repetitive nature of office work
    B. costs involved in carrying out accurate work measurement
    C. inability to properly use the results obtained from work measurement
    D. difficulty involved in measuring certain types of work

19.____

Questions 20-24.

DIRECTIONS: In each of Questions 20 through 24, there is a sentence containing one underlined word. Choose the word (lettered A, B, C, or D) which means MOST NEARLY the same as the underlined word as it is used in the sentence.

20. Mr. Warren could not attend the luncheon because he had a prior appointment.

    A. conflicting   B. official
    C. previous   D. important

20.____

21. The time allowed to complete the task was not adequate.

    A. long   B. enough   C. excessive   D. required

21.____

22. The investigation unit began an extensive search for the information.

    A. complicated   B. superficial
    C. thorough   D. leisurely

22.____

23. The secretary answered the telephone in a courteous manner.

    A. businesslike   B. friendly
    C. formal   D. polite

23.____

24. The recipient of the money checked the total amount.

    A. receiver   B. carrier   C. borrower   D. giver

24.____

25. You receive a telephone call from an employee in another agency requesting information   25.____
about a project being carried out by a division other than your own. You know little about
the work being done, but you would like to help the caller.
Of the following, the BEST action for you to take is to

    A.   ask the caller exactly what he would like to know and then tell him all you know
about the work being done
    B.   ask the caller to tell you exactly what he would like to know so that you can get the
information while he waits
    C.   tell the caller that you will have the call transferred to the division working on the
project
    D.   request that the caller write to you so that you can send him the necessary infor-
mation

KEY (CORRECT ANSWERS)

1.	C	11.	D
2.	B	12.	C
3.	C	13.	A
4.	B	14.	C
5.	B	15.	B
6.	C	16.	A
7.	C	17.	A
8.	A	18.	B
9.	D	19.	D
10.	B	20.	C

21.	B
22.	C
23.	D
24.	A
25.	C

TEST 2

DIRECTIONS: Each question or incomplete statement is followed by several suggested answers or completions. Select the one that BEST answers the question or completes the statement. *PRINT THE LETTER OF THE CORRECT ANSWER IN THE SPACE AT THE RIGHT.*

1. Which of the following actions by a supervisor is LEAST likely to result in an increase in morale or productivity?   1.___

   A. Delegating additional responsibility but not authority to his subordinates
   B. Spending more time than his subordinates in planning and organizing the office's work
   C. Giving positive rather than negative orders to his subordinates
   D. Keeping his subordinates informed about changes in rules or policies which affect their work

Questions 2-8.

DIRECTIONS: Questions 2 through 8 are based SOLELY on the information and the form given below.

The following form is a Weekly Summary of New Employees and lists all employees appointed to Department F in the week indicated. In addition to the starting date and name, the form includes each new employee's time card number, title, status, work location and supervisor's name.

DEPARTMENT F						
Weekly Summary of New Employees					Week Starting March 25	
Start-ing Date	Name Last, First	Time Card No.	Title	Status	Work Location	Supervisor
3/25	Astaire, Hannah	361	Typist	Prov.	Rm. 312	Merrill, Judy
3/25	Silber, Arthur	545	Clerk	Perm.	Rm. 532	Rizzo, Joe
3/26	Vecchio, Robert	620	Accountant	Perm.	Rm. 620	Harper, Ruth
3/26	Goldberg, Sally	373	Stenographer	Prov .	Rm. 308	Merrill, Judy
3/26	Yee, Bruce	555	Accountant	Perm.	Rm. 530	Rizzo, Joe
3/27	Dunning, Betty	469	Typist	Perm.	Rm. 411	Miller, Tony
3/28	Goldman, Sara	576	Stenographer	Prov .	Rm. 532	Rizzo, Joe
3/29	Vesquez, Roy	624	Accountant	Perm.	Rm. 622	Harper, Ruth
3/29	Browning, David	464	Typist	Perm.	Rm. 411	Miller, Tony

2. On which one of the following dates did two employees *in the same title* begin work?   2.____

   A. 3/25   B. 3/26   C. 3/27   D. 3/29

3. To which one of the following supervisors was ONE typist assigned?   3.____

   A. Judy Merrill   B. Tony Miller
   C. Ruth Harper   D. Joe Rizzo

4. Which one of the following supervisors was assigned the GREATEST number of new   4.____
   employees during the week of March 25?

   A. Ruth Harper   B. Judy Merrill
   C. Tony Miller   D. Joe Rizzo

5. Which one of the following employees was assigned *three days after another employee*   5.____
   to the same job location?

   A. Sara Goldman   B. David Browning
   C. Bruce Yee   D. Roy Vesquez

6. The title in which BOTH provisional and permanent appointments were made is   6.____

   A. accountant   B. clerk   C. stenographer   D. typist

7. The employee who started work on the SAME day and have the SAME status but DIF-   7.____
   FERENT titles are

   A. Arthur Silber and Hannah Astaire
   B. Robert Vecchio and Bruce Yee
   C. Sally Goldberg and Sara Goldman
   D. Roy Vesquez and David Browning

8. On the basis of the information given on the form, which one of the following conclusions   8.____
   regarding time card numbers appears to be CORRECT?

   A. The first digit of the time card number is coded according to the assigned title.
   B. The middle digit of the time card number is coded according to the assigned title.
   C. The first digit of the time card number is coded according to the employees' floor
       locations.
   D. Time card numbers are randomly assigned.

9. Assume that a caller arrives at your desk and states that she is your supervisor's daugh-   9.____
   ter and that she would like to see her father. You have been under the impression that
   your supervisor has only a two-year-old son.
   Of the following, the BEST way to deal with this visitor is to

   A. offer her a seat and advise your supervisor of the visitor
   B. tell her to go right in to her father's office
   C. ask her for some proof to show that she is your supervisor's daughter
   D. escort her into your supervisor's office and ask him if the visitor is his daughter

10. Assume that you answer the telephone and the caller says that he is a police officer and   10.____
    asks for personal information about one of your co-workers.
    Of the following, the BEST course of action for you to take is to

A. give the caller the information he has requested
B. ask the caller for the telephone number of the phone he is using, call him back, and then give him the information
C. refuse to give him any information and offer to transfer the call to your supervisor
D. ask the caller for his name and badge number before giving him the information

Questions 11-16.

DIRECTIONS: Questions 11 through 16 each consist of a sentence which may or may not be an example of good English usage. Consider grammar, punctuation, spelling, capitalization, awkwardness, etc. Examine each sentence, and then choose the correct statement about it from the four choices below it. If the English usage in the sentence given is better than it would be with any of the changes suggested in Options B, C, or D, choose Option A. Do not choose an option that will change the meaning of the sentence.

11. The recruiting officer said, *"There are many different goverment jobs available."*   11.____

A. This is an example of acceptable writing.
B. The word *There* should not be capitalized.
C. The word *goverment* should be spelled *government.*
D. The comma after the word *said* should be removed.

12. He can recommend a mechanic whose work is reliable.   12.____

A. This is an example of acceptable writing.
B. The word *reliable* should be spelled *relyable.*
C. The word *whose* should be spelled *who's.*
D. The word *mechanic* should be spelled *mecanic.*

13. She typed quickly; like someone who had not a moment to lose.   13.____

A. This is an example of acceptable writing.
B. The word *not* should be removed.
C. The semicolon should be changed to a comma.
D. The word *quickly* should be placed before instead of after the word *typed.*

14. She insisted that she had to much work to do.   14.____

A. This is an example of acceptable writing.
B. The word *insisted* should be spelled *incisted.*
C. The word *to* used in front of *much* should be spelled *too.*
D. The word *do* should be changed to *be done.*

15. He excepted praise from his supervisor for a job well done.   15.____

A. This is an example of acceptable writing.
B. The word *excepted* should be spelled *accepted.*
C. The order of the words *well done* should be changed to *done well.*
D. There should be a comma after the word,*supervisor*

16. What appears to be intentional errors in grammar occur several times in the passage.   16._____
    A. This is an example of acceptable writing.
    B. The word *occur* should be spelled *occurr.*
    C. The word *appears* should be changed to *appear.*
    D. The phrase *several times* should be changed to *from time to time.*

17. The daily compensation to be paid to each consultant hired in a certain agency is com-   17._____
    puted by dividing his professional earnings in the previous year by 250. The maximum
    daily compensation they can receive is $200 each. Four consultants who were hired to
    work on a special project had the following professional earnings in the previous year:
    $37,500, $44,000, $46,500, and $61,100.
    What will be the TOTAL DAILY COST to the agency for these four consultants?
    A. $932   B. $824   C. $756   D. $712

18. In a typing and stenographic pool consisting of 30 employees, 2/5 of them are typists,   18._____
    1/3 of them are senior typists and senior stenographers, and the rest are stenographers.
    If there are 5 more stenographers than senior stenographers, how many senior ste-
    nographers are in the typing and stenographic pool?
    A. 3   B. 5   C. 8   D. 10

19. There are 3330 copies of a three-page report to be collated. One clerk starts collating at   19._____
    9:00 A.M. and is joined 15 minutes later by two other clerks. It takes 15 minutes for each
    of these clerks to collate 90 copies of the report.
    At what time should the job be completed if ALL three clerks continue working at the
    SAME rate without breaks?
    A. 12:00 Noon   B. 12:15 P.M.   C. 1:00 P.M.   D. 1:15 P.M.

20. By the end of last year, membership in the blood credit program in a certain agency had   20._____
    increased from the year before by 500, bringing the total to 2500.
    If the membership increased by the same percentage this year, the TOTAL number of
    members in the blood credit program for this agency by the end of this year should be
    A. 2625   B. 3000   C. 3125   D. 3250

21. During this year, an agency suggestion program put into practice suggestions from 24   21._____
    employees, thereby saving the agency 40 times the amount of money it paid in awards.
    If 1/3 of the employees were awarded $50 each, 1/2 of the employees were awarded
    $25 each, and the rest were awarded $10 each, how much money did the agency
    SAVE by using the suggestions?
    A. $18,760   B. $29,600   C. $32,400   D. $46,740

22. Which of the following actions should a supervisor generally find MOST effective as a   22._____
    method of determining whether subordinates need additional training in performing their
    work?
    A. Compiling a list of absences and latenesses of subordinates
    B. Observing the manner in which his subordinates carry out their various tasks
    C. Reviewing the grievances submitted by subordinates
    D. Reminding his subordinates to consult him if they experience difficulty in complet-
       ing an assignment

23. Of the following types of letters, the MOST difficult to trace if lost after mailing is the _____ letter.
 23.____

    A. special delivery
    C. insured
    B. registered
    D. certified

24. Suppose that you are looking over a few incoming letters that have been put in your mail basket. You see that one has a return address on the envelope but not on the letter itself. Of the following, the BEST way to make sure there is a correct record of the return address is to
 24.____

    A. return the letter to the sender and ask him to fill in his address on his own letter
    B. put the letter back into the envelope and close the opening with a paper clip
    C. copy the address onto a 3"x5" index card and throw away the envelope
    D. copy the address onto the letter and staple the envelope to the letter

25. Although most incoming mail that you receive in an office will pertain to business matters, there are times when a letter may be delivered for your supervisor that is marked *Personal.*
Of the following, the BEST way for you to handle this type of mail is to
 25.____

    A. open the letter but do not read it, and route it along with the other mail
    B. read the letter to see if it really is personal
    C. have the letter forwarded unopened to your supervisor's home address
    D. deliver the letter to your supervisor's desk unopened

KEY (CORRECT ANSWERS)

1. A		11. C
2. B		12. A
3. A		13. C
4. D		14. C
5. A		15. B
6. D		16. C
7. D		17. D
8. C		18. A
9. A		19. B
10. C		20. C

21.	B
22.	B
23.	D
24.	D
25.	D

EXAMINATION SECTION
TEST 1

DIRECTIONS: Each question or incomplete statement is followed by several suggested answers or completions. Select the one that BEST answers the question or completes the statement. *PRINT THE LETTER OF THE CORRECT ANSWER IN THE SPACE AT THE RIGHT.*

1. A push-button telephone with six buttons, one of which is a *hold* button, is often used when more than one outside line is needed.
   If you are talking on one line of this type of telephone when another call comes in, what is the procedure to follow if you want to answer the second call but keep the first call on the line? Push the

   A. *hold* button at the same time as you push the *pickup* button of the ringing line
   B. *hold* button and then push the *pickup* button of the ringing line
   C. *pickup* button of the ringing line and then push the *hold* button
   D. *pickup* button of the ringing line and push the *hold* button when you return to the original line

   1.____

2. Suppose that you are asked to prepare a petty cash statement for March. The original and one copy are to go to the personnel office. One copy is to go to the fiscal office, and another copy is to go to your supervisor. The last copy is for your files.
   In preparing the statement and the copies, how many sheets of copy paper should you use?

   A. 3   B. 4   C. 5   D. 8

   2.____

3. Which one of the following is the LEAST important advantage of putting the subject of a letter in the heading to the right of the address?
   It

   A. makes filing of the copy easier
   B. makes more space available in the body of the letter
   C. simplifies distribution of letters
   D. simplifies determination of the subject of the letter

   3.____

4. Of the following, the MOST efficient way to put 100 copies of a one-page letter into 9 1/2" x 4 1/8" envelopes for mailing is to fold _____ into an envelope.

   A. each letter and insert it immediately after folding
   B. each letter separately until all 100 are folded; then insert each one
   C. the 100 letters two at a time, then separate them and insert each one
   D. two letters together, slip them apart, and insert each one

   4.____

5. When preparing papers for filing, it is NOT desirable to

   A. smooth papers that are wrinkled
   B. use paper clips to keep related papers together in the files
   C. arrange the papers in the order in which they will be filed
   D. mend torn papers with cellophane tape

   5.____

6. Of the following, the BEST reason for a clerical unit to have its own duplicating machine is that the unit

    A. uses many forms which it must reproduce internally
    B. must make two copies of each piece of incoming mail for a special file
    C. must make seven copies of each piece of outgoing mail
    D. must type 200 envelopes each month for distribution to the same offices

6.____

7. Several offices use the same photocopying machine.
If each office must pay its share of the cost of running this machine, the BEST way of determining how much of this cost should be charged to each of these offices is to

    A. determine the monthly number of photocopies made by each office
    B. determine the monthly number of originals submitted for photocopying by each office
    C. determine the number of times per day each office uses the photocopy machine
    D. divide the total cost of running the photocopy machine by the total number of offices using the machine

7.____

8. Which one of the following would it be BEST to use to indicate that a file folder has been removed from the files for temporary use in another office?
A(n)

    A. cross-reference card   B. tickler file marker
    C. aperture card   D. out guide

8.____

9. Which one of the following is the MOST important objective of filing?

    A. Giving a secretary something to do in her spare time
    B. Making it possible to locate information quickly
    C. Providing a place to store unneeded documents
    D. Keeping extra papers from accumulating on workers' desks

9.____

10. If a check has been made out for an incorrect amount, the BEST action for the writer of the check to take is to

    A. erase the original amount and enter the correct amount
    B. cross out the original amount with a single line and enter the correct amount above it
    C. black out the original amount so that it cannot be read and enter the correct amount above it
    D. write a new check

10.____

11. Which one of the following BEST describes the usual arrangement of a tickler file?

    A. Alphabetical   B. Chronological
    C. Numerical   D. Geographical

11.____

12. Which one of the following is the LEAST desirable filing practice?

    A. Using staples to keep papers together
    B. Filing all material without regard to date
    C. Keeping a record of all materials removed from the files
    D. Writing filing instructions on each paper prior to filing

12.____

13. Assume that one of your duties is to keep records of the office supplies used by your unit   13.____
for the purpose of ordering new supplies when the old supplies run out. The information
that will be of MOST help in letting you know when to reorder supplies is the

    A. quantity issued   B. quantity received
    C. quantity on hand   D. stock number

Questions 14-19.

DIRECTIONS: Questions 14 through 19 consist of sets of names and addresses. In each
question, the name and address in Column II should be an exact copy of the
name and address in Column I. If there is:
    a mistake *only* in the name, mark your answer A;
    a mistake *only* in the address, mark your answer B;
    a mistake in *both* name and address, mark your answer C;
    no mistake in *either* name or address, mark your answer D.

SAMPLE QUESTION

Column I
Michael Filbert
456 Reade Street
New York, N.Y. 10013

Column II
Michael Filbert
645 Reade Street
New York, N.Y. 10013

Since there is a mistake only in the address (the street number should be 456
instead of 645), the answer to the sample question is B.

COLUMN I

COLUMN II

14. Esta Wong
141 West 68 St.
New York, N.Y. 10023

Esta Wang
141 West 68 St.
New York, N.Y. 10023   14.____

15. Dr. Alberto Grosso
3475 12th Avenue
Brooklyn, N.Y. 11218

Dr. Alberto Grosso
3475 12th Avenue
Brooklyn, N.Y. 11218   15.____

16. Mrs. Ruth Bortlas
482 Theresa Ct.
Far Rockaway, N.Y. 11691

Ms. Ruth Bortlas
482 Theresa Ct.
Far Rockaway, N.Y. 11169   16.____

17. Mr. and Mrs. Howard Fox
2301 Sedgwick Ave.
Bronx, N.Y. 10468

Mr. and Mrs. Howard Fox
231 Sedgwick Ave.
Bronx, N.Y. 10468   17.____

18. Miss Marjorie Black
223 East 23 Street
New York, N.Y. 10010

Miss Margorie Black
223 East 23 Street
New York, N.Y. 10010   18.____

19. Michelle Herman
806 Valley Rd.
Old Tappan, N.J. 07675

Michelle Hermann
806 Valley Dr.
Old Tappan, N.J. 07675   19.____

Questions 20-25.

DIRECTIONS: Questions 20 through 25 are to be answered SOLELY on the basis of the information in the following passage.

Basic to every office is the need for proper lighting. Inadequate lighting is a familiar cause
of fatigue and serves to create a somewhat dismal atmosphere in the office. One requirement
of proper lighting is that it be of an appropriate intensity. Intensity is measured in foot-candles.
According to the Illuminating Engineering Society of New York, for casual seeing tasks such
as in reception rooms, inactive file rooms, and other service areas, it is recommended that
the amount of light be 30 foot-candles. For ordinary seeing tasks such as reading and work in
active file rooms and in mail rooms, the recommended lighting is 100 foot-candles. For very
difficult seeing tasks such as accounting, transcribing, and business machine use, the recommended lighting is 150 foot-candles.

Lighting intensity is only one requirement. Shadows and glare are to be avoided. For
example, the larger the proportion of a ceiling filled with lighting units, the more glare-free and
comfortable the lighting will be. Natural lighting from windows is not too dependable because
on dark wintry days, windows yield little usable light, and on sunny, summer afternoons, the
glare from windows may be very distracting. Desks should not face the windows. Finally, the
main lighting source ought to be overhead and to the left of the user.

20. According to the above passage, insufficient light in the office may cause   20.____

    A.   glare   B.   shadows
    C.   tiredness   D.   distraction

21. Based on the above passage, which of the following must be considered when planning   21.____
     lighting arrangements?
     The

    A.   amount of natural light present
    B.   amount of work to be done
    C.   level of difficulty of work to be done
    D.   type of activity to be carried out

22. It can be inferred from the above passage that a well-coordinated lighting scheme is   22.____
     LIKELY to result in

    A.   greater employee productivity
    B.   elimination of light reflection
    C.   lower lighting cost
    D.   more use of natural light

23. Of the following, the BEST title for the above passage is   23.____

    A.   Characteristics of Light
    B.   Light Measurement Devices
    C.   Factors to Consider When Planning Lighting Systems
    D.   Comfort vs. Cost When Devising Lighting Arrangements

24. According to the above passage, a foot-candle is a measurement of the   24.____
    A. number of bulbs used
    B. strength of the light
    C. contrast between glare and shadow
    D. proportion of the ceiling filled with lighting units

25. According to the above passage, the number of foot-candles of light that would be   25.____
    needed to copy figures onto a payroll is _____ foot-candles.
    A. less than 30   B. 30
    C. 100   D. 150

KEY (CORRECT ANSWERS)

1. B		11. B
2. B		12. B
3. B		13. C
4. A		14. A
5. B		15. D
6. A		16. C
7. A		17. B
8. D		18. A
9. B		19. C
10. D		20. C

21. D
22. A
23. C
24. B
25. D

TEST 2

DIRECTIONS: Each question or incomplete statement is followed by several suggested answers or completions. Select the one that BEST answers the question or completes the statement. *PRINT THE LETTER OF THE CORRECT ANSWER IN THE SPACE AT THE RIGHT.*

1. Assume that a supervisor has three subordinates who perform clerical tasks. One of the employees retires and is replaced by someone who is transferred from another unit in the agency. The transferred employee tells the supervisor that she has worked as a clerical employee for two years and understands clerical operations quite well. The supervisor then assigns the transferred employee to a desk, tells the employee to begin working, and returns to his own desk.
The supervisor's action in this situation is

1.____

   A. *proper;* experienced clerical employees do not require training when they are transferred to new assignments
   B. *improper;* before the supervisor returns to his desk, he should tell the other two subordinates to watch the transferred employee perform the work
   C. *proper;* if the transferred employee makes any mistakes, she will bring them to the supervisor's attention
   D. *improper;* the supervisor should find out what clerical tasks the transferred employee has performed and give her instruction in those which are new or different

2. Assume that you are falling behind in completing your work assignments and you believe that your workload is too heavy.
Of the following, the BEST course of action for you to take FIRST is to

2.____

   A. discuss the problem with your supervisor
   B. decide which of your assignments can be postponed
   C. try to get some of your co-workers to help you out
   D. plan to take some of the work home with you in order to catch up

3. Suppose that one of the clerks under your supervision is filling in monthly personnel forms. She asks you to explain a particular personnel regulation which is related to various items on the forms. You are not thoroughly familiar with the regulation.
Of the following responses you may make, the one which will gain the MOST respect from the clerk and which is generally the MOST advisable is to

3.____

   A. tell the clerk to do the best she can and that you will check her work later
   B. inform the clerk that you are not sure of a correct explanation but suggest a procedure for her to follow
   C. give the clerk a suitable interpretation so that she will think you are familiar with all regulations
   D. tell the clerk that you will have to read the regulation more thoroughly before you can give her an explanation

4. Charging out records until a specified due date, with prompt follow-up if they are not returned, is a

4.____

A. *good* idea; it may prevent the records from being kept needlessly on someone's desk for long periods of time
B. *good* idea; it will indicate the extent of your authority to other departments
C. *poor* idea; the person borrowing the material may make an error because of the pressure put upon him to return the records
D. *poor* idea; other departments will feel that you do not trust them with the records and they will be resentful

Questions 5-9.

DIRECTIONS: Questions 5 through 9 consist of three lines of code letters and numbers. The numbers on each line should correspond with the code letters on the same line in accordance with the table below.

Code Letter	P	L	I	J	B	O	H	U	C	G
Corresponding Number	0	1	2	3	4	5	6	7	8	9

On some of the lines, an error exists in the coding. Compare the letters and numbers in each question carefully. If you find an error or errors on
only *one* of the lines in the question, mark your answer A;
any *two* lines in the question, mark your answer B;
all *three* lines in the question, mark your answer C;
none of the lines in the question, mark your answer D.

SAMPLE QUESTION

JHOILCP   3652180
BICLGUP   4286970
UCIBHLJ   5824613

In the above sample, the first line is correct since each code letter listed has the correct corresponding number. On the second line, an error exists because code letter L should have the number 1 instead of the number 6. On the third line, an error exists because the code letter U should have the number 7 instead of the number 5. Since there are errors on two of the three lines, the correct answer is B.

5. BULJCIP   4713920   5._____
   HIGPOUL   6290571
   OCUHJBI   5876342

6. CUBLOIJ   8741023   6._____
   LCLGCLB   1818914
   JPUHIOC   3076158

7. OIJGCBPO   52398405   7._____
   UHPBLIOP   76041250
   CLUIPGPC   81720908

8. BPCOUOJI   40875732   8._____
 UOHCIPLB   75682014
 GLHUUCBJ   92677843

9. HOIOHJLH   65256361   9._____
 IOJJHHBP   25536640
 OJHBJOPI   53642502

Questions 10-13.

DIRECTIONS: Questions 10 through 13 are to be answered SOLELY on the basis of the information given in the following passage.

The mental attitude of the employee toward safety is exceedingly important in preventing accidents. All efforts designed to keep safety on the employee's mind and to keep accident prevention a live subject in the office will help substantially in a safety program. Although it may seem strange, it is common for people to be careless. Therefore, safety education is a continuous process.

Safety rules should be explained, and the reasons for their rigid enforcement should be given to employees. Telling employees to be careful or giving similar general safety warnings and slogans is probably of little value. Employees should be informed of basic safety fundamentals. This can be done through staff meetings, informal suggestions to employees, movies, and safety instruction cards. Safety instruction cards provide the employees with specific suggestions about safety and serve as a series of timely reminders helping to keep safety on the minds of employees. Pictures, posters, and cartoon sketches on bulletin boards that are located in areas continually used by employees arouse the employees' interest in safety. It is usually good to supplement this type of safety promotion with intensive individual follow-up.

10. The above passage implies that the LEAST effective of the following safety measures is 10._____

  A. rigid enforcement of safety rules
  B. getting employees to think in terms of safety
  C. elimination of unsafe conditions in the office
  D. telling employees to stay alert at all times

11. The reason given by the passage for maintaining ongoing safety education is that 11._____

  A. people are often careless
  B. office tasks are often dangerous
  C. the value of safety slogans increases with repetition
  D. safety rules change frequently

12. Which one of the following safety aids is MOST likely to be preferred by the passage? 12._____
 A

  A. cartoon of a man tripping over a carton and yelling, *Keep aisles clear!*
  B. poster with a large number one and a caption saying, *Safety First*
  C. photograph of a very neatly arranged office
  D. large sign with the word *THINK* in capital letters

13. Of the following, the BEST title for the above passage is   13.____
    A. Basic Safety Fundamentals
    B. Enforcing Safety Among Careless Employees
    C. Attitudes Toward Safety
    D. Making Employees Aware of Safety

Questions 14-21.

DIRECTIONS: Questions 14 through 21 are to be answered SOLELY on the basis of the infor-
              mation and the chart given below.

The following chart shows expenses in five selected categories for a one-year period,
expressed as percentages of these same expenses during the previous year. The chart com-
pares two different offices. In Office T (represented by ▨▨▨▨), a cost reduction program
has been tested for the past year. The other office, Office Q (represented by ▨▨▨), served
as a control, in that no special effort was made' to reduce costs during the past year.

RESULTS OF OFFICE COST REDUCTION PROGRAM

Expenses of Test and Control Groups for 2016
Expressed as Percentages of Same Expenses for 2015

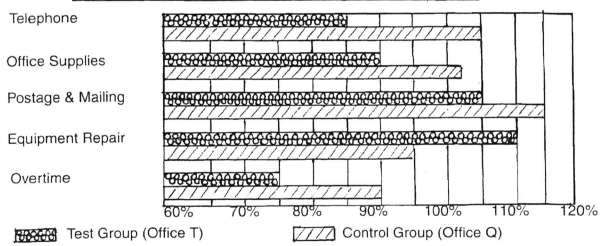

Test Group (Office T)   Control Group (Office Q)

14. In Office T, which category of expense showed the greatest percentage REDUCTION   14.____
    from 2015 to 2016?

    A. Telephone   B. Office Supplies
    C. Postage & Mailing   D. Overtime

15. In which expense category did Office T show the BEST results in percentage terms   15.____
    when compared to Office Q?

    A. Telephone   B. Office Supplies
    C. Postage & Mailing   D. Overtime

16. According to the above chart, the cost reduction program was LEAST effective for the expense category of   16.____

    A. Office Supplies   B. Postage & Mailing
    C. Equipment Repair   D. Overtime

17. Office T's telephone costs went down during 2016 by approximately how many percentage points?   17.____

    A. 15   B. 20   C. 85   D. 105

18. Which of the following changes occurred in expenses for Office Supplies in Office Q in the year 2016 as compared with the year 2015?
They   18.____

    A. increased by more than 100%
    B. remained the same
    C. decreased by a few percentage points
    D. increased by a few percentage points

19. For which of the following expense categories do the results in Office T and the results in Office Q differ MOST NEARLY by 10 percentage points?   19.____

    A. Telephone   B. Postage & Mailing
    C. Equipment Repair   D. Overtime

20. In which expense category did Office Q's costs show the GREATEST percentage increase in 2016?   20.____

    A. Telephone   B. Office Supplies
    C. Postage & Mailing   D. Equipment Repair

21. In Office T, by approximately what percentage did overtime expense change during the past year?
It   21.____

    A. *increased* by 15%   B. *increased* by 75%
    C. *decreased* by 10%   D. *decreased* by 25%

22. In a particular agency, there were 160 accidents in 2007. Of these accidents, 75% were due to unsafe acts and the rest were due to unsafe conditions. In the following year, a special safety program was established. The number of accidents in 2009 due to unsafe acts was reduced to 35% of what it had been in 2007.
How many accidents due to unsafe acts were there in 2009?   22.____

    A. 20   B. 36   C. 42   D. 56

23. At the end of every month, the petty cash fund of Agency A is reimbursed for payments made from the fund during the month. During the month of February, the amounts paid from the fund were entered on receipts as follows: 10 bus fares of 35¢ each and one taxi fare of $3.50.
At the end of the month, the money left in the fund was in the following denominations: 15 one dollar bills, 4 quarters, 10 dimes, and 20 nickels.
If the petty cash fund is reduced by 20% for the following month, how much money will there be available in the petty cash fund for March?   23.____

    A. $11.00   B. $20.00   C. $21.50   D. $25.00

24. The one of the following records which it would be MOST advisable to keep in alphabetical order is a   24._____

   A. continuous listing of phone messages, including time and caller, for your supervisor
   B. listing of individuals currently employed by your agency in a particular title
   C. record of purchases paid for by the petty cash fund
   D. dated record of employees who have borrowed material from the files in your office

25. Assume that you have been asked to copy by hand a column of numbers with two decimal places from one record to another. Each number consists of three, four, and five digits.
In order to copy them quickly and accurately, you should copy   25._____

   A. each number exactly, making sure that the column of digits farthest to the right is in a straight line and all other columns are lined up
   B. the column of digits farthest to the right and then copy the next column of digits moving from right to left
   C. the column of digits farthest to the left and then copy the next column of digits moving from left to right
   D. the digits to the right of each decimal point and then copy the digits to the left of each decimal point

KEY (CORRECT ANSWERS)

1. D		11. A
2. A		12. A
3. D		13. D
4. A		14. D
5. A		15. A
6. C		16. C
7. D		17. A
8. B		18. D
9. C		19. B
10. D		20. C

21. D
22. C
23. B
24. B
25. A

EXAMINATION SECTION
TEST 1

1. A coworker has e-mailed a file containing a spreadsheet for your review. Which of the following programs will open the file?   1._____

    A. Adobe Reader
    B. Microsoft Excel
    C. Microsoft PowerPoint
    D. Adobe Illustrator

2. A report needs to be forwarded immediately to a supervisor in another office. Which of the following is the LEAST effective way of giving the supervisor the report?   2._____

    A. scanning the report and e-mailing the file
    B. faxing it to the supervisor's office
    C. uploading it to the office network and informing the supervisor
    D. waiting for the supervisor to come to your office and giving it to him/her then

3. Suppose your supervisor is on the telephone in his office and an applicant arrives for a scheduled interview with him.   3._____
   Of the following, the BEST procedure to follow ordinarily is to

    A. informally chat with the applicant in your office until your supervisor has finished his phone conversation
    B. escort him directly into your supervisor's office and have him wait for him there
    C. inform your supervisor of the applicant's arrival and try to make the applicant feel comfortable while waiting
    D. have him hang up his coat and tell him to go directly in to see your supervisor

Questions 4-9.

4. The report, along with the accompanying documents, were submitted for review.   4._____

    A. This is an example of acceptable writing.
    B. The words *were submitted* should be changed to *was submitted*.
    C. The word *accompanying* should be spelled *accompaning*.
    D. The comma after the word *report* should be taken out.

5. If others must use your files, be certain that they understand how the system works, but insist that you do all the filing and refiling.   5.____

    A. This is an example of acceptable writing.
    B. There should be a period after the word *works*, and the word *but* should start a new sentence.
    C. The words *filing* and *refiling* should be spelled *fileing* and *refileing*.
    D. There should be a comma after the word *but*.

6. The appeal was not considered because of its late arrival.   6.____

    A. This is an example of acceptable writing.
    B. The word *its* should be changed to *it's*.
    C. The word *its* should be changed to *the*.
    D. The words *late arrival* should be changed to *arrival late*.

7. The letter must be read carefuly to determine under which subject it should be filed.   7.____

    A. This is an example of acceptable writing.
    B. The word *under* should be changed to *at*.
    C. The word *determine* should be spelled *determin*.
    D. The word *carefuly* should be spelled *carefully*.

8. He showed potential as an office manager, but he lacked skill in delegating work.   8.____

    A. This is an example of acceptable writing.
    B. The word *delegating* should be spelled *delagating*.
    C. The word *potential* should be spelled *potencial*.
    D. The words *lie lacked* should be changed to *was lacking*.

9. His supervisor told him that it would be all right to receive personal mail at the office.   9.____

    A. This is an example of acceptable writing.
    B. The words *all right* should be changed to *alright*.
    C. The word *personal* should be spelled *personel*.
    D. The word *mail* should be changed to *letters*.

Questions 10-13.

DIRECTIONS: Questions 10 through 13 are to be answered SOLELY on the basis of the information given in the following passage.

Typed pages can reflect the simplicity of modern art in a machine age. Lightness and evenness can be achieved by proper layout and balance of typed lines and white space. Instead of solid, cramped masses of uneven, crowded typing, there should be a pleasing balance up and down as well as horizontal.

To have real balance, your page must have a center. The eyes see the center of the sheet slightly above the real center. This is the way both you and the reader see it. Try imagining a line down the center of the page that divides the paper in equal halves. On either side of your paper, white space and blocks of typing need to be similar in size and shape. Although left and right margins should be equal, top and bottom margins need not be as exact. It looks better to hold a bottom border wider than a top margin, so that your typing rests upon a cushion of white space. To add interest to the appearance of the page, try making one paragraph between one-half and two-thirds the size of an adjacent paragraph.

Thus, by taking full advantage of your typewriter, the pages that you type will not only be accurate but will also be attractive.

10. It can be inferred from the passage that the BASIC importance of proper balancing on a typed page is that proper balancing

    A. makes a typed page a work of modern art
    B. provides exercise in proper positioning of a typewriter
    C. increases the amount of typed copy on the paper
    D. draws greater attention and interest to the page

10.____

11. A reader will tend to see the center of a typed page

    A. somewhat higher than the true center
    B. somewhat lower than the true center
    C. on either side of the true center
    D. about two-thirds of an inch above the true center

11.____

12. Which of the following suggestions is NOT given by the passage?

    A. Bottom margins may be wider than top borders.
    B. Keep all paragraphs approximately the same size.
    C. Divide your page with an imaginary line down the middle.
    D. Side margins should be equalized.

12.____

13. Of the following, the BEST title for this passage is:

    A. INCREASING THE ACCURACY OF THE TYPED PAGE
    B. DETERMINATION OF MARGINS FOR TYPED COPY
    C. LAYOUT AND BALANCE OF THE TYPED PAGE
    D. HOW TO TAKE FULL ADVANTAGE OF THE TYPEWRITER

13.____

14. In order to type addresses on a large number of envelopes MOST efficiently, you should

    A. insert another envelope into the typewriter before removing each typed envelope
    B. take each typed envelope out of the machine before starting the next envelope
    C. insert several envelopes into the machine at one time, keeping all top and bottom edges even
    D. insert several envelopes into the machine at one time, keeping the top edge of each envelope two inches below the top edge of the one beneath it

14.____

15. A senior typist has completed copying a statistical report from a rough draft.
Of the following, the BEST way to be sure that her typing is correct is for the typist to

    A. fold the rough draft, line it up with the typed copy, compare one-half of the columns with the original, and have a co-worker compare the other half
    B. check each line of the report as it is typed and then have a co-worker check each line again after the entire report is finished

15.____

C. have a co-worker add each column and check the totals on the typed copy with the totals on the original
D. have a co-worker read aloud from the rough draft while the typist checks the typed copy and then have the typist read while the co-worker checks

16. In order to center a heading when typing a report, you should   16.____

A. measure your typing paper with a ruler and begin the heading one-third of the way in from the left margin
B. begin the heading at the point on the typewriter scale which is 50 minus the number of letters in the heading
C. multiply the number of characters in the heading by two and begin the heading that number of spaces in from the left margin
D. begin the heading at the point on the scale which is equal to the center point of your paper minus one-half the number of characters and spaces in the heading

17. Which of the following recommendations concerning the use of copy paper for making   17.____
typewritten copies should NOT be followed?

A. Copy papers should be checked for wrinkles before being used.
B. Legal-size copy paper may be folded if it is too large to fit into a convenient drawer space.
C. When several sheets of paper are being used, they should be fastened with a paper clip at the top after insertion in the typewriter.
D. For making many copies, paper of the same weight and brightness should be used.

18. Assume that a new typist, Norma Garcia, has been assigned to work under your supervi-   18.____
sion and is reporting to work for the first time. You formally introduce Norma to her co-
workers and suggest that a few of the other typists explain the office procedures and typing formats to her. The practice of instructing Norma in her duties in this manner is

A. *good* because she will be made to feel at home
B. *good* because she will learn more about routine office tasks from co-workers than from you
C. *poor* because her co-workers will resent the extra work
D. *poor* because you will not have enough control over her training

19. Suppose that Jean Brown, a typist, is typing a letter following the same format that she   19.____
has always used. However, she notices that the other two typists in her office are also
typing letters, but are using a different format. Jean is concerned that she might not have
been informed of a change in format.
Of the following, the FIRST action that Jean should take is to

A. seek advice from her supervisor as to which format to use
B. ask the other typists whether she should use a new format for typing letters
C. disregard the format that the other typists are using and continue to type in the for-
mat she had been using
D. use the format that the other typists are using, assuming that it is a newly accepted method

20. Suppose that the new office to which you have been assigned has put up Christmas dec- 20.____
    orations, and a Christmas party is being planned by the city agency in which you work.
    However, nothing has been said about Christmas gifts.
    It would be CORRECT for you to assume that

    A. you are expected to give a gift to your supervisor
    B. your supervisor will give you a gift
    C. you are expected to give gifts only to your subordinates
    D. you will neither receive gifts nor will you be expected to give any

---

KEY (CORRECT ANSWERS)

1.	B	11.	A
2.	D	12.	B
3.	C	13.	C
4.	B	14.	A
5.	A	15.	D
6.	A	16.	D
7.	D	17.	B
8.	A	18.	D
9.	A	19.	A
10.	D	20.	D

TEST 2

1. The supervisor you assist is under great pressure to meet certain target dates. He has scheduled an emergency meeting to take place in a few days, and he asks you to send out notices immediately. As you begin to prepare the notices, however, you realize he has scheduled the meeting for a Saturday, which is not a working day. Also, you sense that your supervisor is not in a good mood.
Which of the following is the MOST effective method of handling this situation?

   A. Change the meeting date to the first working day after that Saturday and send out the notices.
   B. Change the meeting date to a working day on which his calendar is clear and send out the notices.
   C. Point out to your supervisor that the date is a Saturday.
   D. Send out the notices as they are since you have received specific instructions.

1.____

Questions 2-7.

2. The typist used an extention cord in order to connect her typewriter to the outlet nearest to her desk.

   A. This is an example of acceptable writing.
   B. A period should be placed after the word *cord,* and the word *in* should have a capital I.
   C. A comma should be placed after the word *typewriter.*
   D. The word *extention* should be spelled *extension.*

2.____

3. He would have went to the conference if he had received an invitation.

   A. This is an example of acceptable writing.
   B. The word *went* should be replaced by the word *gone.*
   C. The word *had* should be replaced by *would have.*
   D. The word *conference* should be spelled *conferance.*

3.____

4. In order to make the report neater, he spent many hours rewriting it.

   A. This is an example of acceptable writing.
   B. The word *more* should be inserted before the word *neater.*
   C. There should be a colon after the word *neater.*
   D. The word *spent* should be changed to *have spent.*

4.____

5. His supervisor told him that he should of read the memorandum more carefully.   5._____

    A. This is an example of acceptable writing.
    B. The word *memorandum* should be spelled *memorandom*.
    C. The word *of* should be replaced by the word *have*.
    D. The word *carefully* should be replaced by the word *careful*.

6. It was decided that two separate reports should be written.   6._____

    A. This is an example of acceptable writing.
    B. A comma should be inserted after the word *decided*.
    C. The word *be* should be replaced by the word *been*.
    D. A colon should be inserted after the word *that*.

7. She don't seem to understand that the work must be done as soon as possible.   7._____

    A. This is an example of acceptable writing.
    B. The word *doesn't* should replace the word *don't*.
    C. The word *why* should replace the word *that*.
    D. The word *as* before the word *soon* should be eliminated.

Questions 8-11.

DIRECTIONS: Questions 8 through 11 are to be answered SOLELY on the basis of the following passage.

There is nothing that will take the place of good sense on the part of the stenographer. You may be perfect in transcribing exactly what the dictator says and your speed may be adequate; but without an understanding of the dictator's intent as well as his words, you are likely to be a mediocre secretary.

A serious error that is made when taking dictation is putting down something that does not make sense. Most people who dictate material would rather be asked to repeat and explain than to receive transcribed material which has errors due to inattention or doubt. Many dictators request that their grammar be corrected by their secretaries; but unless specifically asked to do so, secretaries should not do it without first checking with the dictator. Secretaries should be aware that, in some cases, dictators may use incorrect grammar or slang expressions to create a particular effect.

Some people dictate commas, periods, and paragraphs, while others expect the stenographer to know when, where, and how to punctuate. A well-trained secretary should be able to indicate the proper punctuation by listening to the pauses and tones of the dictator's voice.

A stenographer who has taken dictation from the same person for a period of time should be able to understand him under most conditions. By increasing her tact, alertness, and efficiency, a secretary can become more competent.

8. According to the passage, which of the following statements concerning the dictation of   8._____
punctuation is CORRECT?
A

    A. dictator may use incorrect punctuation to create a desired style

    B.   dictator should indicate all punctuation

    C.   stenographer should know how to punctuate based on the pauses and tones of the dictator

    D.   stenographer should not type any punctuation if it has not been dictated to her

9.   According to the passage, how should secretaries handle grammatical errors in a dicta-   9.____
tion?
Secretaries should

    A.   *not correct* grammatical errors unless the dictator is aware that this is being done

    B.   *correct* grammatical errors by having the dictator repeat the line with proper pauses

    C.   *correct* grammatical errors if they have checked the correctness in a grammar book

    D.   *correct* grammatical errors based on their own good sense

10.   If a stenographer is confused about the method of spacing and indenting of a report   10.____
which has just been dictated to her, she GENERALLY should

    A.   do the best she can

    B.   ask the dictator to explain what she should do

    C.   try to improve her ability to understand dictated material

    D.   accept the fact that her stenographic ability is not adequate

11.   In the last line of the first paragraph, the word *mediocre* means MOST NEARLY   11.____

    A.   superior   B.   disregarded

    C.   respected   D.   second-rate

12.   Assume that is is your responsibility to schedule meetings for your supervisor, who   12.____
believes in starting these meetings strictly on time. He has told you to schedule separate
meetings with Mr. Smith and Ms. Jones, which will last approximately 20 minutes each.
You have told Mr. Smith to arrive at 10:00 A.M. and Ms. Jones at 10:30 A.M. Your supervisor will have an hour of free time at 11:00 A.M. At 10:25 A.M., Mr. Smith arrives and
states that there was a train delay, and he is sorry that he is late. Ms. Jones has not yet
arrived. You do not know who Mr. Smith and Ms. Jones are or what the meetings will be
about.
Of the following, the BEST course of action for you to take is to

    A.   send Mr. Smith in to see your supervisor; and when Ms. Jones arrives, tell her that your supervisor's first meeting will take more time than he expected

    B.   tell Mr. Smith that your supervisor has a meeting at 10:30 A.M. and that you will have to reschedule his meeting for another day

    C.   check with your supervisor to find out if he would prefer to see Mr. Smith immedi-ately or at 11:00 A.M.

    D.   encourage your supervisor to meet with Mr. Smith immediately because Mr. Smith's late arrival was not intentional

13.   Assume that you have been told by your boss not to let anyone disturb him for the rest of   13.____
the afternoon unless absolutely necessary since he has to complete some urgent work.
His supervisor, who is the bureau chief, telephones and asks to speak to him.
The BEST course of action for you to take is to

A. ask the bureau chief if he can leave a message
B. ask your boss if he can take the call
C. tell the bureau chief that your boss is out
D. tell your boss that his instructions will get you into trouble

14. Which one of the following is the MOST advisable procedure for a stenographer to follow   14._____
when a dictator asks her to make extra copies of dictated material?

    A. Note the number of copies required at the beginning of the notes.
    B. Note the number of copies required at the end of the notes.
    C. Make a mental note of the number of copies required to be made.
    D. Make a checkmark beside the notes to serve as a reminder that extra copies are required.

15. Suppose that, as you are taking shorthand notes, the dictator tells you that the sentence   15._____
he has just dictated is to be deleted.
Of the following, the BEST thing for you to do is to

    A. place the correction in the left-hand margin next to the deleted sentence
    B. write the word *delete* over the sentence and place the correction on a separate page for corrections
    C. erase the sentence and use that available space for the correction
    D. draw a line through the sentence and begin the correction on the next available line

16. Assume that your supervisor, who normally dictates at a relatively slow rate, begins dic-   16._____
tating to you very rapidly. You find it very difficult to keep up at this speed. Which one of
the following is the BEST action to take in this situation?

    A. Ask your supervisor to dictate more slowly since you are having difficulty.
    B. Continue to take the dictation at the fast speed and fill in the blanks later.
    C. Interrupt your supervisor with a question about the dictation, hoping that when she begins again it will be slower.
    D. Refuse to take the dictation unless given at the speed indicated in your job description.

17. Assume that you have been asked to put a heading on the second, third, and fourth   17._____
pages of a four-page letter to make sure they can be identified in case they are sepa-
rated from the first page.
Which of the following is it LEAST important to include in such a heading?

    A. Date of the letter
    B. Initials of the typist
    C. Name of the person to whom the letter is addressed
    D. Number of the page

18. Which one of the following is NOT generally accepted when dividing words at the end of   18._____
a line?
Dividing

    A. a hyphenated word at the hyphen
    B. a word immediately after the prefix
    C. a word immediately before the suffix
    D. proper names between syllables

19. In the preparation of a business letter which has two enclosures, the MOST generally   19.____
accepted of the following procedures to follow is to type

    A. *See Attached Items* one line below the last line of the body of the letter
    B. *See Attached Enclosures* to the left of the signature
    C. *Enclosures 2* at the left margin below the signature line
    D. nothing on the letter to indicate enclosures since it will be obvious to the reader
       that there are enclosures in the envelope

20. Standard rules for typing spacing have developed through usage.   20.____
According to these rules, one space is left AFTER

    A. a comma   B. every sentence
    C. a colon   D. an opening parenthesis

KEY (CORRECT ANSWERS)

1.	C	11.	D
2.	D	12.	C
3.	B	13.	B
4.	A	14.	A
5.	C	15.	D
6.	A	16.	A
7.	B	17.	B
8.	C	18.	D
9.	A	19.	C
10.	B	20.	A

EXAMINATION SECTION

TEST 1

DIRECTIONS: Each question or incomplete statement is followed by several suggested answers or completions. Select the one that BEST answers the question or completes the statement. *PRINT THE LETTER OF THE CORRECT ANSWER IN THE SPACE AT THE RIGHT.*

1. As a senior clerk in a city agency, you receive from a member of the public a letter requesting certain information. The information the letter requests is confidential and, according to the rules of the agency, cannot be released. The writer of the letter evidently does not realize that the information is confidential. The one of the following which it is MOST important to include in your answering letter is a(n)
   A. description of the steps the agency takes to safeguard confidential information
   B. suggestion that there might be other sources for this information
   C. explanation of the problems involved in changing the existing rules of the agency
   D. statement that you regret that the information cannot be released

1.____

2. Suppose that you are the assistant to the head of the mail room in a city agency. The bureaus of the agency are scattered in various parts of a large building. A new clerk, without any mail room experience, has been added to the mail room staff. An emergency rises, and you are asked to put the employee to work without giving him any training.
   Of the following mail room tasks, the one which is MOST suitable to give to this clerk is
   A. opening incoming envelopes and attaching the letters to any accompanying enclosures
   B. determining the amount of postage to be affixed to outgoing letters and packages
   C. collecting outgoing mail from the various bureaus of the agency
   D. sorting incoming mail for distribution to the various bureaus of the agency

2.____

3. Assume that you are a senior clerk in charge of a filing system in a large unit and that you are responsible for filing material that the unit supervisor gives you. The supervisor has been unable to find a letter that he was planning to answer. Evidently, the letter was accidentally placed among a number of letters sent to you for filing because it has just been found in the files in the place where it would have been filed eventually.
   Of the following, the BEST recommendation for you to make to the supervisor to avoid such accidental filing in the future is that
   A. he indicate to you the material on which he is working and that, therefore, should not be filed
   B. periodic checks of the files be made to locate material filed accidentally

3.____

C. he mark appropriately each piece of material that he wants filed
D. you be given discretion to decide whether or not a piece of material should be filed

4. Of the following, the MOST important factor in determining whether or not an office filing system is effective is that the

    4.____

    A. information on the records in the files is legible
    B. records in the files are used frequently
    C. information on the records in the files is accurate
    D. records in the files can be located easily

5. As the assistant to the head of a small unit in a city agency, one of your duties is to procure the office supplies need by your unit from the agency supply room. You are permitted to draw supplies every two weeks.
The one of the following which would be the MOST desirable practice for you to follow in obtaining supplies is to

    5.____

    A. obtain a quantity of supplies, sufficient to last for several months, to make certain that enough supplies are always on hand
    B. determine the minimum supply which it is necessary to keep on hand for the various items and obtain an additional quantity as soon as possible after the supply on hand has been reduced to this minimum
    C. review the unit's supplies once a month to determine what items have been exhausted and obtain an additional quantity as soon as possible
    D. order supplies after you run out

6. A typed rough draft of a report should be double-spaced and should have wide margins PRIMARILY in order to

    6.____

    A. estimate the number of pages the report will contain
    B. allow space for making corrections in the report
    C. determine whether the report is well-organized
    D. make the report easy to read

7. A small business uses carbon-copy transaction forms that contain several different colors of carbon paper.
Of the following, the CHIEF reason for the different colors of carbon paper is

    7.____

    A. to help identify the receiver of each copy
    B. easier readability on lighter-colored copies
    C. enhanced aesthetic appeal
    D. to utilize both sides of the carbon paper for typing

8. The one of the following which generally is the CHIEF disadvantage in using office machines in place of human workers in office work is that the machines are

    8.____

    A. slower   B. less accurate
    C. more costly   D. less flexible

9. Employees of a public agency who handle agency funds are sometimes required to be bonded. Of the following, the MOST important reason why such employees should be bonded is to
    A. limit the amount of money the employees will handle in their work
    B. train the employees in the correct methods of safeguarding agency funds
    C. protect the agency from theft of its funds by its employees
    D. determine whether the employees are capable of handling money

9.____

10. Assume that two clerks in a clerical unit suffered back injuries when they attempted to lift a heavy package. Of the following, the MOST important reason why the accident should be investigated is to
    A. prevent accidents of this type from occurring again
    B. find out which of the two clerks was responsible for the accident
    C. determine whether the accident interrupted the work of the unit
    D. demonstrate the need to be careful in lifting heavy packages

10.____

11. Assume that one of your subordinates has been late for work frequently. Under the rules of the agency, you are required to discipline the subordinate. You are reluctant to discipline him because he has been a competent, trustworthy employee. In disciplining him, you should tell him that
    A. you do not believe he should be disciplined, but that the rules of the agency require you to take disciplinary action
    B. his actions violated the rules and that he must be disciplined
    C. his latenesses are not serious, in an effort to minimize any resentment he may feel
    D. the rules sometimes unintentionally penalize the most valuable employees

11.____

12. Performance standards are not self-enforcing. Whether or not these standards are being complied with must usually be determined by either a reporting system or an inspection system. The MOST valid implication of this statement is that
    A. objective measures should be used to evaluate employees
    B. the determination of performance standards does not assure that they are attainable
    C. performance records should be reviewed periodically
    D. failure to meet arbitrarily high performance standards should not be reported

12.____

13. Once the purposes or goals of an organization have been determined, they must be communicated to subordinate levels of supervisory staff.
On the basis of this statement, the MOST accurate of the following statements is that
    A. supervisory personnel should participate in the formulation of the goals of an organization
    B. the structure of an organization should be considered in determining the organization's goals

13.____

C. the goals which have been established for the different levels of an organization should be reviewed regularly
D. information about the goals of an organization should be distributed to supervisory personnel

Questions 14-15.

DIRECTIONS: Questions 14 and 15 are to be answered SOLELY on the basis of the information contained in the following paragraph.

The employees in a unit or division of a government agency may be referred to as a work group. Within a government agency which has existed for some time, the work groups will have evolved traditions of their own. The persons in these work groups acquire these traditions as part of the process of work adjustment within their groups. Usually, a work group in a large organization will contain *old-timers*, *newcomers*, and *in-betweeners*. Like the supervisor of a group, who is not necessarily an old-timer or the oldest member, old-timers usually have great influence. They can recall events unknown to others and are a storehouse of information and advice about current problems in the light of past experience. They pass along the traditions of the group to the others who, in turn, become old-timers themselves. Thus, the traditions of the group which have been honored and revered by long acceptance are continued.

14. According to the above paragraph, the traditions of a work group within a government agency are developed   14.____
    A. at the time the group is established
    B. over a considerable period of time
    C. in order to give recognition to old-timers
    D. for the group before it is established

15. According to the above paragraph, the old-timers within a work group   15.____
    A. are the means by which long accepted practices and customs are perpetuated
    B. would best be able to settle current problems that arise
    C. are honored because of the changes they have made in the traditions
    D. have demonstrated that they have learned to do their work well

Questions 16-17.

DIRECTIONS: Questions 16 and 17 are to be answered SOLELY on the basis of the information contained in the following paragraph.

In public agencies, the success of a person assigned to perform first-line supervisory duties depends in large part upon the personal relations between him and his subordinate employees. The goal of supervising effort is something more than to obtain compliance with procedures established by some central office. The major objective is work accomplishment. In order for this goal to be attained, employees must want to attain it and must exercise initiative in their work. Only if employees are generally satisfied with the type of supervision which exists in an organization will they put forth their best efforts.

16. According to the above paragraph, in order for employees to try to do their work as well as they can, it is essential that   16.____
    A. they participate in determining their working conditions and rates of pay
    B. their supervisors support the employees' viewpoints in meetings with higher management
    C. they are content with the supervisory practices which are being used
    D. their supervisors make the changes in working procedures that the employees request

17. It can be inferred from the above paragraph that the goals of a unit in a public agency will not be reached unless the employees in the unit   17.____
    A. wish to reach them and are given the opportunity to make individual contributions to the work
    B. understand the relationship between the goals of the unit and goals of the agency
    C. have satisfactory personal relationships with employees of other units in the agency
    D. carefully follow the directions issued by higher authorities

Questions 18-20.

DIRECTIONS: Questions 18 through 20 are to be answered SOLELY on the basis of the information contained in the following paragraph.

Discontent of some citizens with the practices and policies of local government leads here and there to creation of those American institutions, the local civic associations. Completely outside of government, manned by a few devoted volunteers, understaff, and with pitifully few dues-paying members, they attempt to arouse widespread public opinion on selected issues by presenting facts and ideas. The findings of these civic associations are widely trusted by press and public, and amidst the records of rebuffs received are found more than enough achievements to justify what little their activities cost. Civic associations can, by use of the initiative, get constructive measures placed on the ballot and the influence of these associations is substantial when brought to bear on a referendum question. Civic associations are politically nonpartisan. Hence, their vitality is drawn from true political independents, who in most communities are a trifling minority. Except in a few large cities, civic associations are seldom affluent enough to maintain an office or to afford even a small paid staff.

18. It can be inferred from the above paragraph that the MAIN reason for the formation of civic associations is to   18.____
    A. provide independent candidates for local public office with an opportunity to be heard
    B. bring about changes in the activities of local government
    C. allow persons who are politically nonpartisan to express themselves on local public issues
    C. permit the small minority of true political independents to supply leadership for nonpartisan causes

19. According to the above paragraph, the statements which civic associations   19.____
    make on issues of general interest are
    A. accepted by large segments of the public
    B. taken at face value only by the few people who are true political
       independents
    C. questioned as to their accuracy by most newspapers
    D. expressed as a result of aroused widespread public opinion

20. On the basis of the information concerning civic associations contained in   20.____
    the above paragraph, it is MOST accurate to conclude that since
    A. they deal with many public issues, the cost of their efforts on each issue
       is small
    B. their attempts to attain their objectives often fail, little money is
       contributed to civic associations
    C. they spend little money in their efforts, they are ineffective when they
       become involved in major issues
    D. their achievements outweigh the small cost of their efforts, civic
       associations are considered worthwhile

21. Assume that, in an office of a city agency, correspondence is filed according   21.____
    to the date received in 12 folders, one for each month of the year. On January
    1, of each year, correspondence dated through December 31 of the preceding
    year is transferred from the active to the inactive files. New folders are then
    inserted in the active files to contain the correspondence to be filed in the next
    year.
    The one of the following which is the CHIEF advantage of this method
    transferring correspondence from active to inactive files is that
    A. the inactive files may lack the capacity to contain all the correspondence
       transferred to them
    B. the folders prepared each year must be labeled the same as the folders in
       preceding years
    C. some of the correspondence from the preceding year may not be in the
       active files on January 1
    D. some of the correspondence transferred to the inactive files may be
       referred to as frequently as some of the correspondence in the active files

22. A clerk who is assigned to inspect office equipment in a large number of   22.____
    offices in a city agency is given a checklist of defects to look for in the
    equipment in each office.
    Of the following, the CHIEF advantage of the checklist is that
    A. the number of defects for which the clerk must look is kept to a minimum
    B. the defects listed on the checklist will not be overlooked
    C. the defects listed on the checklist may suggest to the clerk other defects
       for which he might look
    D. each defect listed on the checklist will be checked only once

23. If 20,000 copies of a form are to be reproduced, the one of the following types   23.____
of duplicating machines that would be the MOST suitable one to use is the
   A. printer   B. photocopy   C. press   D. fax

24. Of the following, the MAIN reason for keeping a perpetual inventory of   24.____
supplies in a storeroom is that such an inventory
   A. provides a continuous record of supplies on hand
   B. eliminates the need for a physical inventory
   C. indicates which supplies are in greatest demand
   D. encourages economy in the use of supplies

25. Assume that you are the head of a unit in a city agency. From time to time,   25.____
your subordinates are assigned to other units to do reception work and other
duties. You receive a note from Mr. Jones, the head of one of these other
units, stating that the work of Miss Smith, one of your subordinates, was
unsatisfactory when she worked for him, and asking you not to assign her to
him again. Although Miss Smith has worked in your unit for a long time, this is
the first time that anyone has complained about her work.
The one of the following actions that you should take FIRST in this situation is
to ask
   A. the heads of the other units for whom Miss Smith has worked whether or
      not her work has been satisfactory
   B. Mr. Jones in what way Miss Smith's work has been unsatisfactory
   C. Miss Smith to explain in what way her work for Mr. Jones was
      unsatisfactory
   D. Mr. Jones which of your subordinates he would prefer to have assigned to
      him

26. Suppose that you are the supervisor of a small unit in a city agency. You   26.____
have given one of your subordinates, Mr. Smith, an assignment which must be
completed by the end of the day. Because he is unfamiliar with the
assignment, Mr. Smith will be unable to complete it on time. Your other
subordinates are too busy to help Mr. Smith, but you have the time to help Mr.
Smith complete the assignment.
Such an action would be
   A. *desirable*, because a supervisor is expected to be familiar with his
      subordinates' work
   B. *undesirable*, because Mr. Smith will come to depend on you to help him
      do his work
   C. *desirable*, because Mr. Smith is likely to appreciate your help and give
      you his cooperation when you need it
   D. *undesirable*, because a supervisor should not perform the same type of
      work as his subordinates do

27. For a supervisor to listen to the personal problems which his subordinates   27.____
bring to him is GENERALLY
   A. *desirable*; it is likely that the supervisor has broader experience in solving
      personal problems than do his subordinates
   B. *undesirable*; the supervisor may be unable to solve such problems

C. *desirable*; the supervisor can better understand his subordinates' behavior on the job
D. *undesirable*; permitting a subordinate to talk about his personal problems may only make them seem worse

28. A generally accepted concept of management is that the authority given to a person should be commensurate with his\   28._____
    A. responsibility   B. ability   C. seniority   D. dependability

29. The one of the following supervisory practices that would be MOST likely to give subordinates in a unit of a public agency a feeling of satisfaction in their work is to   29._____
    A. establish work goals that take a long time to achieve
    B. show the subordinates how their work goals are related to the goals of the agency
    C. set work goals higher than subordinates can achieve
    D. refrain from telling subordinates that they are failing to meet their work goals

30. It has been said that the best supervisor is the one who gives the fewest orders. The one of the following supervisory practices that would be MOST likely to increase the number of orders that a supervisor must give to get out the work is   30._____
    A. set general goals for his subordinates and give them the authority for reaching the goals
    B. train subordinates to make decisions for themselves
    C. establish routines for his subordinates' jobs
    D. introduce frequent changes in the work methods his subordinates are using

31. One of the things that can ruin morale in a work group is the failure to exercise judgment in the assignment of overtime work to your subordinates. Of the following, the MOST desirable supervisory practice in assigning overtime work is to   31._____
    A. rotate overtime on a uniform basis among all your subordinates
    B. assign overtime to those who are *moonlighting* after regular work hours
    C. rotate overtime as much as possible among employees willing to work additional hours
    D. assign overtime to those employees who take frequent long weekend vacations

32. The consistent delegation of authority by you to experienced and reliable subordinates in your work group is generally considered   32._____
    A. *undesirable*, because your authority in the group may be threatened by an unscrupulous subordinate
    B. *undesirable*, because it demonstrates that you cannot handle your own workload

C. *desirable*, because it shows that you believe that you have been accepted by your subordinates
D. *desirable*, because the development of subordinates creates opportunities for assuming broader responsibilities yourself

33. The MOST effective way for you to deal with a false rumor circulating among your subordinates is to
    A. have a trusted subordinate start a counter-rumor
    B. recommend disciplinary action against the rumor mongers
    C. point out to your subordinates that rumors degrade both listener and initiator
    D. furnish your subordinates with sufficient authentic information

33.____

34. Two of your subordinates tell you about a mistake they made in a report that has already been sent to top management.
    Which of the following questions is MOST likely to elicit the most valuable information from your subordinates?
    A. Who is responsible?
    B. How can we explain this to top management?
    C. How did it happen?
    D. Why weren't you more careful?

34.____

35. Assume that you are responsible for implementing major changes in work flow patterns and personnel assignments in the unit of which you are in charge.
    The one of the following actions which is MOST likely to secure the willing cooperation of those persons who will have to change their assignments is
    A. having the top administrators of the agency urge their cooperation at a group meeting
    B. issuing very detailed and carefully planned instructions to the affected employees regarding the changes
    C. integrating employee participation into the planning of the changes
    D. reminding the affected employees that career advancement depends upon compliance with organizational objectives

35.____

36. Of the following, the BEST reason for using face-to-face communication instead of written communication is that face-to-face communication
    A. allows for immediate feedback
    B. is more credible
    C. enables greater use of detail and illustration
    D. is more polite

36.____

37. Of the following, the MOST likely disadvantage of giving detailed instructions when assigning a task to a subordinate is that such instructions may
    A. conflict with the subordinate's ideas of how the tasks should be done
    B. reduce standardization of work performance
    C. cause confusion in the mind of the subordinate
    D. inhibit the development of new procedures by the subordinate

37.____

38. Assume that you are a supervisor of a unit consisting of a number of subordinates and that one subordinate, whose work is otherwise acceptable, keeps on making errors in one particular task assigned to him in rotation. This task consists of routine duties which all your subordinates should be able to perform.
    Of the following, the BEST way for you to handle this situation is to
    A. do the task yourself when the erring employee is scheduled to perform it and assign this employee other duties
    B. reorganize work assignments so that the task in question is no longer performed in rotation but assigned full-time to your most capable subordinate
    C. find out why this subordinate keeps on making the errors in question and see that he learns how to do the task properly
    D. threaten to fire the subordinate if he does not stop making these errors

    38.____

39. In the past, Mr. Whary, one of your subordinates, had been generally withdrawn and suspicious of others, but he had produced acceptable work. However, Mr. Whary has lately started to get into arguments with his fellow workers during which he displays intense rage. Friction between this subordinate and the others in your unit is mounting and the unit's work is suffering.
    Of the following, which would be the BEST way for you to handle this situation?
    A. Rearrange work schedules and assignments so as to give Mr. Whary no cause for complaints.
    B. Instruct the other workers to avoid Mr. Whary and not to respond to any abuse.
    C. Hold a unit meeting and appear for harmony and submergence of individual differences in the interest of work.
    D. Maintain a record of incidents and explore with Mr. Whary the possibility of seeking professional help.

    39.____

40. You are responsible for seeing to it that your unit is functioning properly in the accomplishment of its budgeted goals.
    Which of the following will provide the LEAST information on how well you are accomplishing such goals?
    A. Measurement of employee performance
    B. Identification of alternative goals
    C. Detection of employee errors
    D. Preparation of unit reports

    40.____

Questions 41-45.

DIRECTIONS: Each of Questions 41 through 45 consists of a statement which contains one word that is incorrectly used because it is not in keeping with the meaning that the quotation is evidently intended to convey. Determine which word is incorrectly used. Then, select from among the words lettered A, B, C, D, or E the word which, when substituted for the incorrectly used word, would BEST help to convey the meaning of the statement. *PRINT THE LETTER OF THE CORRECT ANSWER IN THE SPACE AT THE RIGHT.*

41.   Supervisors should be trained to display patterns of performance that are signs   41.____
of trouble and to prepare for that trouble well in advance of the time when it is
necessary to make a disciplinary decision.
    A. required   B. action   C. recognize
    D. provide   E. enforce

42.   When supervisors and subordinates trust each other, employee grievances   42.____
rarely occur, and when they do appear, remedies are seldom found.
    A. suspect   B. easily   C. while
    D. increase   E. spread

43.   A supervisor must justify his trust in people with a certain shrewdness that   43.____
places him on guard against those not worthy of complete confidence.
    A. kindness   B. respect   C. balance
    D. show   E. understanding

44.   Given a clear knowledge of what is expected of him, the subordinate   44.____
requires in addition the definite assurance that he will have the independence
of his superiors so long as his actions are consistent with established policies
and are taken within the limits of his responsibility.
    A. satisfactory   B. duties   C. known
    D. support   E. authorized

45.   A public agency should maintain close contact with its public because, in a   45.____
democracy, public administration preserves its essential nature if it is not
constantly related to the requirements of the people to whom it is dedicated.
    A. loses   B. needs   C. respect
    D. responsive   E. strengthen

Questions 46-50.

DIRECTIONS: In each of Questions 46 through 50, determine the relationship which the first word in capital letters has to the second word in capital letters. The third word which is underlined has the same relationship to one of the four choices lettered A, B, C, or D. Select the one of the choices to which the third word (underlined) has this relationship. *PRINT THE LETTER OF THE CORRECT ANSWER IN THE SPACE AT THE RIGHT.*

SAMPLE: SCALE is to WEIGHT as thermometer is to
A. weather   B. temperature   C. pounds   D. spring

The relationship which SCALE has to WEIGHT is that a scale is used to measure weight. A thermometer is used to measure temperature. The relationship of the scale to weight is the same as the relationship of thermometer to temperature. Therefore, the correct answer is B.

46.   CONGRESS is o SENATOR as convention is to   46._____
A. election   B. chairman   C. delegate   D. nominee

47.   DIVIDEND is to INVESTOR as wage is to   47._____
A. employee   B. salary   C. consumer   D. price

48.   TERMINATE is to COMMENCE as adjourn is to   48._____
A. enact   B. convene   C. conclude   D. veto

49.   SANITATION is to HEALTH as education is to   49._____
A. school   B. hygiene   C. knowledge   D. teacher

50.   ADMINISTRATOR is to POLICY as clerk is to   50._____
A. subordinate   B. organization C. coordination   D. procedure

KEY (CORRECT ANSWERS)

1.	D	11.	B	21.	D	31.	C	41.	C
2.	A	12.	C	22.	B	32.	D	42.	B
3.	C	13.	D	23.	C	33.	D	43.	C
4.	D	14.	B	24.	A	34.	C	44.	D
5.	B	15.	A	25.	B	35.	C	45.	A
6.	B	16.	C	26.	C	36.	A	46.	C
7.	A	17.	A	27.	C	37.	D	47.	A
8.	D	18.	B	28.	A	38.	C	48.	B
9.	C	19.	A	29.	B	39.	D	49.	C
10.	A	20.	D	30.	D	40.	B	50.	D

TEST 2

DIRECTIONS: Each question or incomplete statement is followed by several suggested answers or completions. Select the one that BEST answers the question or completes the statement. *PRINT THE LETTER OF THE CORRECT ANSWER IN THE SPACE AT THE RIGHT.*

Questions 1-20.

DIRECTIONS: Each of Questions 1 through 20 consists of a word in capitals followed by four suggested meanings of the word. For each question, select the letter preceding the word which means MOST NEARLY the same as the word in capitals.

1. DISSENT
   A. detain
   C. disagree
   B. make an accusation
   D. call back

   1.____

2. PASSIVE
   A. inactive
   B. impartial
   C. gloomy
   D. former

   2.____

3. CHRONIC
   A. painful
   B. hopeless
   C. complex
   D. lingering

   3.____

4. INCUR
   A. wait for
   C. bring upon oneself
   B. happen again
   D. prevent from happening

   4.____

5. MANIFEST
   A. likely
   B. evident
   C. accidental
   D. convenient

   5.____

6. DISSIPATE
   A. absorb
   B. disturb
   C. expect
   D. squander

   6.____

7. INSIGHT
   A. mistake
   C. confidence
   B. understanding
   D. investigation

   7.____

8. SURMOUNT
   A. overcome
   B. come down
   C. undermine
   D. go together

   8.____

9. ASTUTE
   A. shrewd
   B. fair
   C. sensitive
   D. cruel

   9.____

10. INHIBIT
    A. replace
    B. illustrate
    C. restrain
    D. include

    10.____

11. PERENNIAL   11.____
    A. superficial   B. lasting for years
    C. pleasing   D. requiring little attention

12. CONSOLIDATE   12.____
    A. correct   B. review   C. control   D. unite

13. ACCRUE   13.____
    A. accumulate   B. report   C. delay   D. pay

14. DIFFUSE   14.____
    A. distinct   B. spread out   C. twisted   D. clinging to

15. MOMENTOUS   15.____
    A. well-timed   B. late in arriving
    C. important   D. temporary

16. INNOCUOUS   16.____
    A. inadequate   B. cautious   C. harmless   D. protected

17. PROLIFIC   17.____
    A. expressive   B. prompt   C. skillful   D. productive

18. SUPPLANT   18.____
    A. take the place of   B. give an advantage to
    C. settle finally   D. support strongly

19. INFRINGE   19.____
    A. approach   B. insist   C. copy   D. trespass

20. CONDONE   20.____
    A. connect closely   B. pardon
    C. follow up   D. anticipate

Questions 21-34.

DIRECTIONS: Each of Questions 21 through 34 consists of a sentence may be classified appropriately under one of the following four categories:
    A. Incorrect because of faulty grammar\
    B. Incorrect because of faulty punctuation
    C. Incorrect because of faulty spelling
    D. Correct
Examine each sentence carefully. Then, in the corresponding space at the right, indicate the letter preceding the category which is the BEST of the four suggested above. Each incorrect sentence contains only one type of error. Consider a sentence correct if it contains no errors, although there may be other correct ways of writing the sentence.

21. Of the two employees, the one in our office is the most efficient.   21._____

22. No one can apply or even understand, the new rules and regulations.   22._____

23. A large amount of supplies were stored in the empty office.   23._____

24. If an employee is occassionally asked to work overtime, he should do so   24._____
    willingly.

25. It is true that the new procedures are difficult to use but, we are certain   25._____
    that you will learn them quickly.

26. The office manager said that he did not know who could be given a large   26._____
    allotment under the new plan.

27. It was at the supervisor's request that the clerk agreed to postpone his   27._____
    vacation.

28. We do not believe that it is necessary for both he and the clerk to attend   28._____
    the conference.

29. All employees, who display perseverance, will be given adequate   29._____
    recognition.

30. He regrets that some of us employees are dissatisfied with our new   30._____
    assignments.

31. "Do you think that the raise was merited," asked the supervisor?   31._____

32. The new manual of procedure is a valuable supplament to our rules and   32._____

33. The typist admitted that she had attempted to pursuade the other   33._____
    employees to assist her in her work.

34. The supervisor asked that all amendments to the regulations be handled   34._____
    by you and I.

Questions 35-42.

DIRECTIONS: Questions 35 through 42 are to be answered SOLELY on the basis of the
              information and directions below:

Assume that you are a senior clerk in a city agency. Your supervisor has asked you to
classify each of the accidents that happened to employees in the agency into the following five
categories:

A. An accident that occurred in the period from January through June, between 9 A.M. and 12 Noon, that was the result of carelessness on the part of the injured employee, that caused the employee to lose less than seven working hours, that happened to an employee who was 40 years of age or over, and who was employed in the agency for less than three years.

B. An accident that occurred in the period from July through December, after 1 P.M., that was the result of unsafe conditions, that caused the injured employee to lose less than seven working hours, that happened to an employee who was 40 years of age or over, and who was employed in the agency for three years or more.

C. An accident that occurred in the period from January through June, after 1 P.M., that was the result of carelessness on the part of the injured employee, that caused the injured employee who was less than 40 years old, and who was employed in the agency for three years or more.

D. An accident that occurred in the period from July through December, between 9 A.M. and 12 Noon, that was the result of unsafe conditions, that caused the injured employee to lose seven or more working hours, that happened to an employee who was less than 40 years old, and who was employed in the agency for less than three years.

E. Accidents that cannot be classified in any of the foregoing groups.

NOTE: In classifying these accidents, an employee's age and length of service are computed as of the date of accident. In all cases, it is to be assumed that each employee has been employed continuously in city service, and that each employee works seven hours a day, from 9 A.M. to 5 P.M., with lunch from 12 Noon to 1 P.M. In each question, consider only the information which will assist you in classifying the accident. Any information which is of no assistance in classifying an accident should not be considered.

SAMPLE: Mr. Jones, a veteran of the Middle East conflict, began working for the agency on January 2014. On August 15, 2016, at 11 A.M., he injured his left hand on an unsafe office machine. At the time of the accident, Mr. Jones was 39 years old and earned $24,000 a year.

The correct answer to this sample is D, since the accident, a result of unsafe conditions, occurred between 9 A.M. and 12 Noon in the period from July through December, happened to an employee less than 40 years old who was employed in the agency for less than three years as of the date of the accident, and resulted in the loss of more than seven working hours. Such facts Mr. Jones' veteran's status and his salary were not considered since they were of no assistance in classifying the accident into any of the five categories.

35. The unsafe condition of the stairs in the building caused Miss Perkins to have an accident on October 14, 2013 at 4 P.M. When she returned to work the following day at 1 P.M., Miss Perkins said that the accident was the first one that had occurred to her in her ten years of employment with the agency. She was born on April 27, 1972.   35.____

36. On the day after she completed her six-month probationary period of employment with the agency, Miss Green, who had been considered a careful worker b her supervisor, injured her left foot in an accident caused by her own carelessness. She went home immediately after the accident, which occurred at 10 A.M., March 19, 2014, but returned to work at the regular time on the following morning. Miss Green was born July 2, 1973 in New York City.

36.____

37. The unsafe condition of a copy machine caused Mr. Martin to injure himself in an accident on September 8, 2016 at 2 P.M. As a result of the accident, he was unable to work the remainder of the day, but returned to his office ready for work on the following morning. Mr. Martin, who has been working for the agency since 2013, was born in St. Louis on February 1, 1978.

37.____

38. Mr. Smith was hospitalized for two weeks because of a back injury which resulted from an accident on the morning of November 16, 2016. Investigation of the accident revealed that it was caused by the unsafe condition of the floor on which Mr. Smith had been walking. Mr. Smith, who is an accountant, has been an employee of the agency since March 1, 2014 and was born in Ohio on June 10, 1978.

38.____

39. Mr. Allen cut his right hand because he was careless in operating a press machine. Mr. Allen, who was 39 years old when the accident took place, has been employed by the agency since August 17, 2012. The accident, which occurred on January 26, 2016 at 2 P.M., caused Mr. Allen to be absent from work for the rest of the day. He was able to return to work the next morning.

39.____

40. Mr. Rand, who is a college graduate, was born on December 2, 1977, and has been working for the agency since January 7, 2012. On Monday, April 25, 2015, at 2 P.M., his carelessness in operating a copy machine caused him to have an accident and to be sent home from work immediately. Fortunately, he was able to return to work at his regular time on the following Wednesday.

40.____

41. Because he was careless in running down a flight of stairs, Mr. Brown fell, bruising his right hand. Although the accident occurred shortly after he arrived for work on the morning of May 22, 2016, he was unable to resume work until 3 P.M. that day. Mr. Brown was born on August 15, 1965 and began working for the agency on September 12, 2013 as a clerk, at a salary of $11,000 per annum.

41.____

42. On December 5, 2015, four weeks after he had begun working for the agency, the unsafe condition of an automatic stapling machine caused Mr. Thomas to injure himself in an accident. Mr. Thomas, who was born on May 19, 1985, lost three working days because of the accident, which occurred at 11:45 A.M.

42.____

Questions 43-50.

DIRECTIONS: Questions 43 through 50 are based on the table shown below, which relates to the Licenses and Inspections Division in a public agency for the months of May and June. The Division has an office in each of the five counties.

	COUNTY I		COUNTY II		COUNTY III		COUNTY IV		COUNTY V	
	May	June	May	June	May	June	May	June	May	June
Number of Clerks in Office Assigned to Issue Applications for Licenses	3	4	6	8	6	8	3	5	3	4
Number of Licenses Issued	950	1010	1620	1940	1705	2025	895	1250	685	975
Amount Collected in License Fees	$4240	$521	$7760	$9450	$8370	$9880	$3930	$6550	$3060	$4820
Number of Inspectors	4	5	6	7	7	8	4	5	2	4
Number of Inspections Made	420	450	630	710	690	740	400	580	320	440
Number of Violations Found as a Result of Inspections	211	153	352	378	320	385	256	304	105	247

43. Of the following statements, the one which is NOT accurate on the basis of an inspection of the information contained in the above table is that, for each office, the increase from May to June in the number of
    A. inspectors was accompanied by an increase in the number of inspections made
    B. licenses issued was accompanied by an increase in the amount collected in license fees
    C. inspections made was accompanied by an increase in the number of violations found
    D. licenses issued was accompanied by an increase in the number of clerks assigned to issue applications for licenses

44. The TOTAL number of licenses issued by all five offices in the Division in May was
    A. 4,800　　　B. 5,855　　　C. 6,865　　　D. 7,200

45. The total number of inspectors in all five county offices in June exceeded the number in May by MOST NEARLY
    A. 21%　　　B. 26%　　　C. 55%　　　D. 70%

46. In the month of June, the number of violations found per inspection made was the HIGHEST in County
    A. II　　　B. III　　　C. IV　　　D. V

47. In the month of May, the average number of inspections made by an inspector in the Bronx was the same as the average number of inspections made by an inspector in County
    A. II　　　B. III　　　C. IV　　　D. V

48. Assume that in June, all of the inspectors in the Division spent 7 hours a day   48.____
making inspections on each of the 21 working days in the month. Then, the
average amount of time that an inspector in the County III office spent on an
inspection that month was MOST NEARLY
    A. 2 hours   B. 1 hour and 35 minutes
    C. 1 hour and 3 minute   D. 38 minutes

49. If an average fine of $10 was imposed for a violation found by the Division,   49.____
what was the TOTAL amount in fines imposed for all the violations found by the
Division in May?
    A. $12,440   B. $13,350   C. $14,670   D. $26,700

50. Assume that the amount collected in license fees by the entire Division in   50.____
May was 80 percent of the amount collected by the entire Division in April.
How much was collected by the entire Division in April?
    A. $21,888   B. $32,832   C. $34,200   D. $41,040

KEY (CORRECT ANSWERS)

1.	C	11.	B	21.	A	31.	B	41.	A
2.	A	12.	D	22.	B	32.	C	42.	D
3.	D	13.	A	23.	A	33.	C	43.	C
4.	C	14.	B	24.	C	34.	A	44.	B
5.	B	15.	C	25.	B	35.	B	45.	B
6.	D	16.	C	26.	D	36.	A	46.	D
7.	B	17.	D	27.	D	37.	E	47.	A
8.	A	18.	A	28.	A	38.	D	48.	B
9.	A	19.	D	29.	B	39.	E	49.	A
10.	C	20.	B	30.	D	40.	C	50.	C

EXAMINATION SECTION
TEST 1

DIRECTIONS: Each question or incomplete statement is followed by several suggested answers or completions. Select the one that BEST answers the question or completes the statement. *PRINT THE LETTER OF THE CORRECT ANSWER IN THE SPACE AT THE RIGHT.*

1. The MOST important reason for a supervisor to encourage his staff to make suggestions   1._____
   for improving the work of the unit is that such suggestions may

   A. indicate who is the most efficient employee in the unit
   B. increase the productivity of the unit
   C. raise the morale of the employees who make the suggestions
   D. reduce the amount of supervision necessary to perform the work of the unit

2. The PRIMARY purpose of a probationary period for a new employee is to   2._____

   A. thoroughly train the new employee in his job duties
   B. permit the new employee to become adjusted to his duties
   C. determine the fitness of the new employee for the job
   D. acquaint the new employee fully with the objectives of his agency

3. A unit supervisor finds that he is spending too much time on routine tasks, and not   3._____
   enough time on coordinating the work of his employees.
   It would be MOST advisable for this supervisor to

   A. delegate the task of work coordination to a capable subordinate
   B. eliminate some of the routine tasks that the unit is required to perform
   C. assign some of the routine tasks to his subordinates
   D. postpone the performance of routine tasks until he has achieved proper coordina-
       tion of his employees' work

4. Of the following, the MOST important reason for having an office manual in looseleaf   4._____
   form rather than in permanent binding is that the looseleaf form

   A. facilitates the addition of new material and the removal of obsolete material
   B. permits several people to use different sections of the manual at the same time
   C. is less expensive to prepare than permanent binding
   D. is more durable than permanent binding

5. In his first discussion with an employee newly appointed to the title of Clerk in an agency,   5._____
   the LEAST important of the following topics for a supervisor of a clerical unit to include is
   the

   A. duties the subordinate is expected to perform on the job
   B. functions of the unit
   C. methods of determining standards of clerical performance
   D. nature and duration of the training the subordinate will receive on the job

6. Assume that you have been assigned to organize the files so that all the records now located in the various units in your bureau will be centrally located in a separate files unit. In setting up this system of centrally located files, you should be concerned LEAST with making certain that

    A. the material stored in the files has been checked for accuracy of content
    B. the filing system will be flexible enough to allow for possible future expansion
    C. material stored in the files can be located readily when needed
    D. the filing system will be readily understood by employees assigned to maintaining the files

6.____

7. A supervisor of a unit in a city department has just been told by a subordinate, Mr. Jones, that another employee, Mr. Smith, deliberately disobeyed an important rule of the department by taking home some confidential departmental material.
Of the following courses of action, it would be MOST advisable for the supervisor first to

    A. discuss the matter privately with both Mr. Jones and Mr. Smith at the same time
    B. call a meeting of the entire unit and discuss the matter generally without mentioning any employee by name
    C. arrange to supervise Mr. Smith's activities more closely
    D. discuss the matter privately with Mr. Smith

7.____

8. A clerk who has the choice of sending a business letter either by certified mail or by registered mail should realize that

    A. it is less expensive to send letters by certified mail than by registered mail
    B. it is safer to send letters by certified mail than by registered mail
    C. letters sent by certified mail reach their destinations faster than those sent by registered mail
    D. the person to whom a certified letter is sent is not asked to acknowledge receipt of the letter

8.____

9. If the management of a public agency wishes to retain the elasticity of youth among employees who have been with the agency for a long time, it must furnish variety and novelty of work.
To carry out the above recommendation, the BEST course of action for an agency to take is to

    A. encourage older employees to retire at the minimum retirement age
    B. vary its employees' assignments from time to time
    C. assign the routine tasks to newer and younger employees
    D. provide its employees with varied recreational activities

9.____

10. The one of the following actions which would be MOST efficient and economical for a supervisor to take to minimize the effect of seasonal fluctuations in the work load of his unit is to

    A. increase his permanent staff until it is large enough to handle the work of the busy season
    B. request the purchase of time and labor saving equipment to be used primarily during the busy season

10.____

C. lower, temporarily, the standards for quality of work performance during peak loads
D. schedule for the slow season work that it is not essential to perform during the busy season

11. A clerk in an agency should realize that each letter he sends out in response to a letter of inquiry from the public represents an expenditure of time and money by his agency. The one of the following which is the MOST valid implication of this statement is that such a clerk should

    11.____

    A. use the telephone to answer letters of inquiry directly and promptly
    B. answer mail inquiries with lengthy letters to eliminate the need for further correspondence
    C. prevent the accumulation of a large number of similar inquiries by answering each of these letters promptly
    D. use simple, concise language in answer to letters of inquiry

12. The forms and methods of discipline used in public agencies are as varied as the offenses which prompt disciplinary action, and range in severity from a frown of disapproval to dismissal from the service and even to prosecution in the courts.
On the basis of this sentence, the MOST accurate of the following statements is that

    12.____

    A. the severity of disciplinary measures varies directly with the seriousness of the offenses
    B. dismissal from the service is the most severe action that can be taken by a public agency
    C. public agencies use a variety of disciplinary measures to cope with offenses
    D. public agencies sometimes administer excessive punishments

13. A well-planned training program can assist new employees to acquire the information they need to work effectively. Of the following, the information that a newly-appointed clerk would need LEAST in order to perform his work effectively is knowledge of the

    13.____

    A. acceptable ways of taking and recording telephone messages
    B. techniques of evaluating the effectiveness of office forms used in the agency
    C. methods of filing papers used in his bureau
    D. proper manner of handling visitors to the agency

14. A supervisor of a unit who is not specific when making assignments creates a dangerous source of friction, misunderstanding, and inefficiency.
The MOST valid implication of this statement is that

    14.____

    A. supervisors are usually unaware that they are creating sources of friction
    B. it is often difficult to remove sources of friction and misunderstanding
    C. a competent supervisor attempts to find a solution to each problem facing him
    D. employees will perform more efficiently if their duties are defined clearly

15. The employees' interest in the subject matter of a training course must be fully aroused if they are to derive the maximum benefits from the training.
Of the following, the LEAST effective method of arousing such interest is to

    15.____

    A. state to the employees that the subject matter of the training course will be of interest to mature, responsible workers
    B. point out to the employees that the training course may help them to win promotion

    C.   explain to the employees how the training course will help them to perform their work better

    D.   relate the training course to the employees' interests and previous experiences

16. The control of clerical work in a public agency appears impossible if the clerical work is regarded merely as a series of duties unrelated to the functions of the agency. However, this control becomes feasible when it is realized that clerical work links and coordinates the functions of the agency.
On the basis of this statement, the MOST accurate of the following statements is that the   16._____

    A.   complexity of clerical work may not be fully understood by those assigned to control it

    B.   clerical work can be readily controlled if it is coordinated by other work of the agency

    C.   number of clerical tasks may be reduced by regarding coordination as the function of clerical work

    D.   purposes of clerical work must be understood to make possible its proper control

17. Assume that as supervisor of a unit you are to prepare a vacation schedule for the employees in your unit.
Of the following, the factor which is LEAST important for you to consider in setting up this schedule is   17._____

    A.   the vacation preferences of each employee in the unit

    B.   the anticipated work load in the unit during the vacation period

    C.   how well each employee has performed his work

    D.   how essential a specific employee's services will be during the vacation period

18. In order to promote efficiency and economy in an agency, it is advisable for the management to systematize and standardize procedures and relationships insofar as this can be done; however, excessive routinizing which does not permit individual contributions or achievements should be avoided.
On the basis of this statement, it is MOST accurate to state that   18._____

    A.   systematized procedures should be designed mainly to encourage individual achievements

    B.   standardized procedures should allow for individual accomplishments

    C.   systematization of procedures may not be possible in organizations which have a large variety of functions

    D.   individual employees of an organization must fully accept standardized procedures if the procedures are to be effective

19. Trained employees work most efficiently and with a minimum expenditure of time and energy. Suitable equipment and definite, well-developed procedures are effective only when employees know how to use the equipment and procedures. This statement means MOST NEARLY that   19._____

    A.   employees can be trained most efficiently when suitable equipment and definite procedures are used

    B.   training of employees is a costly but worthwhile investment

C. suitable equipment and definite procedures are of greatest value when employees have been properly trained to use them
D. the cost of suitable equipment and definite procedures is negligible when the saving in time and energy that they bring is considered

20. Assume that your supervisor has asked you to present to him comprehensive, periodic reports on the progress that your unit is making in meeting its work goals.
For you to give your superior oral reports rather than written ones is

    20.____

A. *desirable*; it will be easier for him to transmit your oral report to his superiors
B. *undesirable*; the oral reports will provide no permanent record to which he may refer
C. *undesirable;* there will be less opportunity for you to discuss the oral reports with him than the written ones
D. *desirable;* the oral reports will require little time and effort to prepare

21. Assume that an employee under your supervision complains to you that your evaluation of his work is too low.
The MOST appropriate action for you to take FIRST is to

    21.____

A. explain how you arrived at the evaluation of his work
B. encourage him to improve the quality of his work by pointing out specifically how he can do so
C. suggest that he appeal to an impartial higher authority if he disagrees with your evaluation
D. point out to him specific instances in which his work has been unsatisfactory

22. The nature of the experience and education that are made a prerequisite to employment determines in large degree the training job to be done after employment begins.
On the basis of this statement, it is MOST accurate to state that

    22.____

A. the more comprehensive the experience and education required for employment the more extensive the training that is usually given after appointment
B. the training that is given to employees depends upon the experience and education required of them before appointment
C. employees who possess the experience and education required for employment should need little additional training after appointment
D. the nature of the work that employees are expected to perform determines the training that they will need

23. Assume that you are preparing a report evaluating the work of a clerk who was transferred to your unit from another unit in the agency about a year ago.
Of the following, the method that would probably be MOST helpful to you in making this evaluation is to

    23.____

A. consult the evaluations this employee received from his former supervisors
B. observe this employee at his work for a week shortly before you prepare the report
C. examine the employee's production records and compare them with the standards set for the position
D. obtain tactfully from his fellow employees their frank opinions of his work

24. Of the following, the CHIEF value of a flow-of-work chart to the management of an orga-   24.___
    nization is its usefulness in

    A.   locating the causes of delay in carrying out an operation
    B.   training new employees in the performance of their duties
    C.   determining the effectiveness of the employees in the organization
    D.   determining the accuracy of its organization chart

25. Assume that a procedure for handling certain office forms has just been extensively   25.___
    revised. As supervisor of a small unit, you are to instruct your subordinates in the use of
    the new procedure, which is rather complicated.
    Of the following, it would be LEAST helpful to your subordinates for you to

    A.   compare the revised procedure with the one it has replaced
    B.   state that you believe the revised procedure to be better than the one it has
         replaced
    C.   tell them that they will probably find it difficult to learn the new procedure
    D.   give only a general outline of the revised procedure at first and then follow with
         more detailed instructions

26. A supervisor may make assignments to his subordinates in the form of a command, a   26.___
    request, or a call for volunteers. It is LEAST desirable for a supervisor to make an assign-
    ment in the form of a command when

    A.   a serious emergency has risen
    B.   an employee objects to carrying out an assignment
    C.   the assignment must be completed immediately
    D.   the assignment is an unpleasant one

27. For an office supervisor to confer periodically with his subordinates in order to anticipate   27.___
    job problems which are likely to arise is desirable MAINLY because

    A.   there will be fewer problems for which hasty decisions will have to be made
    B.   some problems which are anticipated may not arise
    C.   his subordinates will learn to refer the problems arising in the unit to him
    D.   constant anticipation of future problems tends to raise additional problems

28. A methods improvement program might be called a war against habit.   28.___
    The MOST accurate implication of this statement is that

    A.   routine handling of routine office assignments should be discouraged
    B.   standardization of office procedures may encourage employees to form inefficient
         work habits
    C.   employees tend to continue the use of existing procedures, even when such proce-
         dures are inefficient
    D.   procedures should be changed constantly to prevent them from becoming habits

29. An office supervisor may give either a written or an oral order to his subordinates when   29.___
    making an assignment.
    Of the following, it would be MOST appropriate for a supervisor to issue an order in
    writing when

    A.   a large number of two-page reports must be stapled together before the end of the
         day
    B.   the assignment is to be completed within two hours after it is issued to his subordi-
         nates

C. his subordinates have completed an identical assignment the day before
D. several entries must be made on a form at varying intervals of time by different clerks

30. A supervisor should always remember that the instruction or training of new employees is most effective if it is given when and where it is needed.
On the basis of this statement, it is MOST appropriate to conclude that

    30.____

    A. the new employee should be trained to handle any aspect of his work at the time he starts his job
    B. the new employee should be given the training essential to get him started and additional training when he requires it
    C. an employee who has received excessive training will be just as ineffective as one who has received inadequate training
    D. a new employee is trained most effectively by his own supervisor

31. Some employees see an agency training program as a threat. Of the following, the MOST likely reason for such an employee attitude toward training is that the employees involved feel that

    31.____

    A. some trainers are incompetent
    B. training rarely solves real work-a-day problems
    C. training may attempt to change comfortable behavior patterns
    D. training sessions are boring

32. Of the following, the CHIEF characteristic which distinguishes a good supervisor from a poor supervisor is the good supervisor's

    32.____

    A. ability to favorably impress others
    B. unwillingness to accept monotony or routine
    C. ability to deal constructively with problem situations
    D. strong drive to overcome opposition

33. Of the following, the MAIN disadvantage of on-the-job training is that, generally,

    33.____

    A. special equipment may be needed
    B. production may be slowed down
    C. the instructor must maintain an individual relationship with the trainee
    D. the on-the-job instructor must be better qualified than the classroom instructor

34. All of the following are correct methods for a supervisor to use in connection with employee discipline EXCEPT:

    34.____

    A. Trying not to be too lenient or too harsh
    B. Informing employees of the rules and the penalties for violations of the rules
    C. Imposing discipline immediately after the violation is discovered
    D. Making sure, when you apply discipline, that the employee understands that you do not want to do it

35. Of the following, the MAIN reason for a supervisor to establish standard procedures for his unit is to

    35.____

    A. increase the motivation of his subordinates
    B. make it easier for the subordinates to submit to authority

    C.   reduce the number of times that his subordinates have to consult him
    D.   reduce the number of mistakes that his subordinates will make

36. When delegating responsibility for an assignment to a subordinate, it is MOST important that you   36.___

    A.   retain all authority necessary to complete the assignment
    B.   make yourself generally available for consultation with the subordinate
    C.   inform your superiors that you are no longer responsible for the assignment
    D.   decrease the number of subordinates whom you have to supervise

37. You, as a unit head, have been asked to submit budget estimates of staff, equipment, and supplies in terms of programs for your unit for the coming fiscal year.
In addition to their use in planning, such unit budget estimates can be BEST used to   37.___

    A.   reveal excessive costs in operations
    B.   justify increases in the debt limit
    C.   analyze employee salary adjustments
    D.   predict the success of future programs

38. Because higher status is important to many employees, they will often make an effort to achieve it as an end in itself.
Of the following, the BEST course of action for the supervisor to take on the basis of the preceding statement is to   38.___

    A.   attach higher status to that behavior of subordinates which is directed toward reaching the goals of the organization
    B.   avoid showing sympathy toward subordinates' wishes for increased wages, improved working conditions, or other benefits
    C.   foster interpersonal competitiveness among subordinates so that personal friendliness is replaced by the desire to protect individual status
    D.   reprimand subordinates whenever their work is in some way unsatisfactory in order to adjust their status accordingly

39. Assume that a large office in a certain organization operates long hours and is thus on two shifts with a slight overlap. Those employees, including supervisors, who are most productive are given their choice of shifts. The earlier shift is considered preferable by most employees.
As a result of this method of assignment, which of the following is MOST likely to result?   39.___

    A.   Most non-supervisory employees will be assigned to the late shift; most supervisors will be assigned to the early shift.
    B.   Most supervisors will be assigned to the late shift; most non-supervisory employees will be assigned to the early shift.
    C.   The early shift will be more productive than the late shift.
    D.   The late shift will be more productive than the early shift.

40. Assume that a supervisor of a unit in which the employees are of average friendliness tells a newly hired employee on her first day that her co-workers are very friendly. The other employees hear his remarks to the new employee. Which of the following is the MOST likely result of this action of the supervisor? The   40.___

A.   newly hired employee will tend to feel less friendly than if the supervisor had said nothing
B.   newly hired employee will tend to believe that her co-workers are very friendly
C.   other employees will tend to feel less friendly toward one another
D.   other employees will tend to see the newly hired employee as insincerely friendly

41. A recent study of employee absenteeism showed that, although unscheduled absence for part of a week is relatively high for young employees, unscheduled absence for a full week is low. However, although full-week unscheduled absence is least frequent for the youngest employees, the frequency of such absence increases as the age of employees increases.
Which of the following statements is the MOST logical explanation for the greater full-week absenteeism among older employees?

A.   Older employees are more likely to be males.
B.   Older employees are more likely to have more relatively serious illnesses.
C.   Younger employees are more likely to take longer vacations.
D.   Younger employees are more likely to be newly hired.

42. An employee can be motivated to fulfill his needs as he sees them. He is not motivated by what others think he ought to have, but what he himself wants.
Which of the following statements follows MOST logically from the foregoing viewpoint?

A.   A person's different traits may be separately classified, but they are all part of one system comprising a whole person.
B.   Every job, however simple, entitles the person who does it to proper respect and recognition of his unique aspirations and abilities.
C.   No matter what equipment and facilities an organization has, they cannot be put to use except by people who have been motivated.
D.   To an observer, a person's needs may be unrealistic, but they are still controlling.

43. Assume that you are a supervisor of a unit which is about to start work on an urgent job. One of your subordinates starts to talk to you about the urgent job but seems not to be saying what is really on his mind.
What is the BEST thing for you to say under these circumstances?

A.   I'm not sure I understand. Can you explain that?
B.   Please come to the point. We haven't got all day.
C.   What is it? Can't you see I'm busy?
D.   Haven't you got work to do? What do you want?

44. Assume that you have recently been assigned to a new subordinate. You have explained to this subordinate how to fill out certain forms which will constitute the major portion of her job. After the first day, you find that she has filled out the forms correctly but has not completed as many as most other workers normally complete in a day.
Of the following, the MOST appropriate action for you to take is to

A.   tell the subordinate how many forms she is expected to complete
B.   instruct the subordinate in the correct method of filling out the forms
C.   monitor the subordinate's production to see if she improves
D.   reassign the job of filling out the forms to a more experienced worker in the unit

45. One of the problems commonly met by the supervisor is the *touchy* employee who imag-   45.___
ines slights when none is intended.
Of the following, the BEST way to deal with such an employee is to

    A. ignore him until he sees the error of his behavior
    B. frequently reassure him of his value as a person
    C. advise him that oversensitive people rarely get promoted
    D. issue written instructions to him to avoid misinterpretation

46. The understanding supervisor should recognize that a certain amount of anxiety is com-   46.___
mon to all newly hired employees.
If you are a supervisor of a unit and a newly-hired employee has been assigned to you,
you can usually assume that the LEAST likely worry that the new employee has is
worry about

    A. the job and the standards required in the job
    B. his acceptance by the other people in your unit
    C. the difficulty of advancing to top positions in the agency
    D. your fairness in evaluating his work

47. In assigning work to subordinates, it is often desirable for you to tell them the overall or   47.___
ultimate objective of the assignment.
Of the following, the BEST reason for telling them the objective is that it will

    A. assure them that you know what you are doing
    B. eliminate most of the possible complaints about the assignment
    C. give them confidence in their ability to do the assignment
    D. help them to make decisions consistent with the objective

48. Assume that the regular 8-hour working day of a laborer is from 8 A.M. to 5 P.M., with an   48.___
hour off for lunch. He earns a regular hourly rate of pay for these 8 hours and is paid at
the rate of time-and-a-half for each hour worked after his regular working day.
If, on a certain day, he works from 8 A.M. to 6 P.M., with an hour off for lunch, and
earns $99.76, his regular hourly rate of pay is

    A. $8.50   B. $9.00   C. $10.50   D. $11.50

49. Two clerical units, X and Y, each having a different number of clerks, are assigned to file   49.___
registration cards. It takes Unit X, which contains 8 clerks, 21 days to file the same number of cards that Unit Y can file, in 28 days. It is also a fact that Unit X can file 174,528
cards in 72 days.
Assuming that all the clerks in both units work at the same rate of speed, the number
of cards which can be filed by Unit Y in 144 days, if 4 more clerks are added to the staff
of Unit Y, is MOST NEARLY

    A. 349,000   B. 436,000   C. 523,000   D. 669,000

50. Each side of a square room which is being used as an office measures 66 feet. The floor of the room is divided by six traffic aisles, each aisle being six feet wide. Three of the aisles run parallel to the east and west sides of the room and the other three run parallel to the north and south sides of the room, so that the remaining floor space is divided into 16 equal sections.

    If all of the floor space which is not being used for traffic aisles is occupied by desk and chair sets, and each set takes up 24 square feet of floor space, the number of desk and chair sets in the room is

    A. 80   B. 64   C. 36   D. 96

    50.____

KEY (CORRECT ANSWERS)

1.	B	11.	D	21.	A	31.	C	41.	B
2.	C	12.	C	22.	B	32.	C	42.	D
3.	C	13.	B	23.	C	33.	B	43.	A
4.	A	14.	D	24.	A	34.	D	44.	C
5.	C	15.	A	25.	C	35.	C	45.	B
6.	A	16.	B	26.	D	36.	B	46.	C
7.	D	17.	C	27.	A	37.	A	47.	D
8.	A	18.	B	28.	C	38.	A	48.	C
9.	B	19.	C	29.	D	39.	C	49.	B
10.	D	20.	B	30.	B	40.	B	50.	D

TEST 2

DIRECTIONS: Each question or incomplete statement is followed by several suggested answers or completions. Select the one that BEST answers the question or completes the statement. *PRINT THE LETTER OF THE CORRECT ANSWER IN THE SPACE AT THE RIGHT.*

Questions 1-6.

DIRECTIONS: Each of Questions 1 through 6 consists of statements which contains one word that is incorrectly used because it is not in keeping with the meaning that the statement is evidently intended to convey. For each of these questions, you are to select the incorrectly used word and substitute for it one of the words lettered A, B, C, D, or E, which helps BEST to convey the meaning of the quotation. In the space at the right, write the letter preceding the word which should be substituted for the incorrectly used word.

1. The determination of the value of the employees in an organization is fundamental not only as a guide to the administration of salary schedules, promotion, demotion, and transfer, but also as a means of keeping the working force on its toes and of checking the originality of selection methods.   1.____

    A. effectiveness   B. initiation   C. increasing
    D. system   E. none of these

2. No training course can operate to full advantage without job descriptions which indicate training requirements so that those parts of the job requiring the most training can be carefully analyzed before the training course is completed.   2.____

    A. improved   B. started   C. least
    D. meet   E. predict

3. The criticism that supervisors are discriminatory in their treatment of subordinates is to some extent untrue, for the subjective nature of many supervisory decisions makes it probable that many employees who have not progressed will attribute their lack of success to supervisory favoritism.   3.____

    A. knowledge   B. unavoidable   C. detrimental
    D. deny   E. indifferent

4. Some demands of employees will, if satisfied, result in a decrease in production. Some supervisors largely ignore such demands on the part of their subordinates, and instead, concentrate on the direction and production of work; others yield to such requests and thereby emphasize the production goals and objectives set by higher levels of authority.   4.____

    A. responsibility   B. increase   C. neglect
    D. value   E. morale

5. It is generally accepted that when a supervisor is at least as well informed about the work of his unit as are his subordinates, he will fail to win their approval, which is essential to him if he is to supervise the unit effectively.   5.____

    A. unimportant   B. preferable   C. unless
    D. attention   E. poorly

6. The laws of almost every state permit certain classes of persons to vote despite their absence from home at election time. Sometimes this privilege is given only to members of the armed forces of the United States, though more commonly it is extended to all voters whose occupations make absence preventable.

6.____

    A. prohibition   B. sanction   C. intangible
    D. avoidable   E. necessary

Questions 7-25.

DIRECTIONS: Each of Questions 7 through 25 consists of a word in capitals followed by four suggested meanings of the word. Print in the space at the right the number preceding the word which means MOST NEARLY the same as the word in capitals.

7. ALLEVIATE

7.____

    A. soothe   B. make difficult
    C. introduce gradually   D. complicate

8. OSTENSIBLE

8.____

    A. intelligent   B. successful
    C. necessary   D. apparent

9. REDUNDANT

9.____

    A. excessive   B. sufficient
    C. logical   D. unpopular

10. TANTAMOUNT

10.____

    A. superior   B. opposed
    C. equivalent   D. disturbing

11. EXPUNGE

11.____

    A. leap over   B. erase
    C. exploit   D. concede fully

12. VESTIGE

12.____

    A. ancestor   B. basis   C. choice   D. remnant

13. CONTENTION

13.____

    A. modification   B. controversy
    C. cooperation   D. sight

14. PROSCRIBE

14.____

    A. recommend   B. avoid   C. provide   D. prohibit

15. URBANE

15.____

    A. polite   B. adjacent to a city
    C. modern   D. common

16. INADVERTENT   16._____

    A. unknown   B. public
    C. deliberate   D. unintentional

17. EVINCE   17._____

    A. enlarge   B. conceal   C. display   D. evade

18. SIMULATE   18._____

    A. attempt   B. imitate   C. elude   D. arouse

19. PRECLUDE   19._____

    A. prevent   B. contribute generously
    C. simplify   D. prepare gradually

20. REMISS   20._____

    A. careless   B. absent   C. guilty   D. thorough

21. CONTRIVE   21._____

    A. contract   B. restrict   C. scheme   D. contribute

22. MALIGN   22._____

    A. mislead deliberately   B. slander
    C. flatter excessively   D. disturb

23. CONTINGENT   23._____

    A. loose   B. intentional
    C. dependent   D. forceful

24. SPORADIC   24._____

    A. quick   B. alert   C. destroyed   D. scattered

25. COALESCE   25._____

    A. unite   B. reveal   C. abate   D. freeze

Questions 26-33.

DIRECTIONS: Each of Questions 26 through 33 consists of three sentences lettered A, B, and C. In each of these questions, one of the sentences may contain an error in grammar, sentence structure, or punctuation, or all three sentences may be correct. If one of the sentences in a question contains an error in grammar, sentence structure, or punctuation, write in the space at the right, the letter preceding the sentence which contains the error. If all three sentences are correct, write the letter D.

26.   A. Mr. Smith appears to be less competent than I in performing these duties.   26._____
        B. The supervisor spoke to the employee, who had made the error, but did not reprimand him.
        C. When he found the book lying on the table, he immediately notified the owner.

27.   A.   Being locked in the desk, we were certain that the papers would not be taken.   27.____
         B.   It wasn't I who dictated the telegram; I believe it was Eleanor.
         C.   You should interview whoever comes to the office today.

28.   A.   The clerk was instructed to set the machine on the table before summoning the   28.____
            manager.
         B.   He said that he was not familiar with those kind of activities.
         C.   A box of pencils, in addition to erasers and blotters, was included in the shipment
            of supplies.

29.   A.   The supervisor remarked, "Assigning an employee to the proper type of work is not   29.____
            always easy."
         B.   The employer found that each of the applicants were qualified to perform the
            duties of the position.
         C.   Any competent student is permitted to take this course if he obtains the consent
            of the instructor.

30.   A.   The prize was awarded to the employee whom the judges believed to be most   30.____
            deserving.
         B.   Since the instructor believes this book is the better of the two, he is recommend-
            ing it for use in the school.
         C.   It was obvious to the employees that the completion of the task by the scheduled
            date would require their working overtime.

31.   A.   These reports have been typed by employees who were trained by a capable   31.____
            supervisor.
         B.   This employee is as old, if not older, than any other employee in the department.
         C.   Running rapidly down the street, the manager soon reached the office.

32.   A.   It is believed, that if these terms are accepted, the building can be constructed at a   32.____
            reasonable cost.
         B.   The typists are seated in the large office; the stenographers, in the small office.
         C.   Either the operators or the machines are at fault.

33.   A.   Mr. Jones, who is the head of the agency, will come today to discuss the plans for   33.____
            the new training program.
         B.   The reason the report is not finished is that the supply of paper is exhausted.
         C.   It is now obvious that neither of the two employees is able to handle this type of
            assignment.

Questions 34-40.

DIRECTIONS: Each of Questions 34 through 40 consists of four words. In each question, one
                 of the words may be spelled incorrectly or all four words may be spelled cor-
                 rectly. If one of the words in a question is spelled incorrectly, print in the space
                 at the right the letter preceding the word which is spelled incorrectly. If all four
                 words are spelled correctly, print the letter E.

34. A. guarantee   B. committment   34.____
     C. mitigate   D. publicly

35. A. prerogative   B. apprise   35.____
    C. extrordinary   D. continual

36. A. arrogant   B. handicapped   36.____
    C. judicious   D. perennial

37. A. permissable   B. deceive   37.____
    C. innumerable   D. retrieve

38. A. notable   B. allegiance   38.____
    C. reimburse   D. illegal

39. A. interceed   B. benefited   39.____
    C. analogous   D. altogether

40. A. seizure   B. irrelevant   40.____
    C. inordinate   D. dissapproved

Questions 41-50.

DIRECTIONS: Questions 41 through 50 are based on the Production Record table shown on the following page for the Information Unit in Agency X for the work week ended Friday, December 6. The table shows, for each employee, the quantity of each type of work performed and the percentage of the work week spent in performing each type of work.

NOTE: Assume that each employee works 7 hours a day and 5 days a week, making a total of 35 hours for the work week.

PRODUCTION RECORD - INFORMATION UNIT IN AGENCY X
(For the work week ended Friday, December 6)

Number of

	Papers Filed	Sheets Proofread	Visitors Received	Envelopes Addressed
Miss Agar	3120	33	178	752
Mr. Brun	1565	59	252	724
Miss Case	2142	62	214	426
Mr. Dale	4259	29	144	1132
Miss Earl	2054	58	212	878
Mr. Farr	1610	69	245	621
Miss Glen	2390	57	230	790
Mr. Hope	3425	32	176	805
Miss Iver	3736	56	148	650
Mr. Joad	3212	55	181	495

Percentage of Work Week Spent On

	Filing Papers	Proof-reading	Receiving Visitors	Addressing Envelopes	Performing Miscellaneous Work
Miss Agar	30%	9%	34%	11%	16%
Mr . Brun	13%	15%	52%	10%	10%
Miss Case	23%	18%	38%	6%	15%
Mr. Dale	50%	7%	17%	16%	10%
Miss Earl	24%	14%	37%	14%	11%
Mr. Farr	16%	19%	48%	8%	9%
Miss Glen	27%	12%	42%	12%	7%
Mr . Hope	38%	8%	32%	13%	9%
Miss Iver	43%	13%	24%	9%	11%
Mr. Joad	33%	11%	36%	7%	13%

41. For the week, the average amount of time which the employees spent in proofreading was MOST NEARLY _____ hours. 41._____

    A. 3.1   B. 3.6   C. 4.4   D. 5.1

42. The average number of visitors received daily by an employee was MOST NEARLY 42._____

    A. 40   B. 57   C. 198   D. 395

43. Of the following employees, the one who addressed envelopes at the FASTEST rate was 43._____

    A. Miss Agar   B. Mr. Brun
    C. Miss Case   D. Mr. Dale

44. Mr. Farr's rate of filing papers was MOST NEARLY _____ pages per minute. 44._____

    A. 2   B. 1.7   C. 5   D. 12

45. The average number of hours that Mr. Brun spent daily on receiving visitors exceeded the average number of hours that Miss Iver spent daily on the same type of work by MOST NEARLY _____ hours. 45._____

    A. 2   B. 3   C. 4   D. 5

46. Miss Earl worked at a faster rate than Miss Glen in 46._____

    A. filing papers   B. proofreading sheets
    C. receiving visitors   D. addressing envelopes

47. Mr. Joad's rate of filing papers _____ Miss Iver's rate of filing papers by approximately 47._____
    _____%.

    A. was less than; 10   B. exceeded; 33
    C. C. was less than; 16   D. exceeded; 12

48. Assume that in the following week, Miss Case is instructed to increase the percentage of her time spent in filing papers to 35%.
If she continued to file papers at the same rate as she did for the week ended December 6, the number of additional papers that she filed the following week was MOST NEARLY

    A. 3260   B. 5400   C. 250   D. 1120

48.____

49. Assume that in the following week, Mr. Hope increased his weekly total of envelopes addressed to 1092.
If he continued to spend the same amount of time on this assignment as he did for the week ended December 6, the increase in his rate of addressing envelopes the following week was MOST NEARLY _____ envelopes per hour.

    A. 15   B. 65   C. 155   D. 240

49.____

50. Assume that in the following week, Miss Agar and Mr. Dale spent 3 and 9 hours less, respectively, on filing papers than they had spent for the week ended December 6, without changing their rates of work.
The total number of papers filed during the following week by both Miss Agar and Mr. Dale was MOST NEARLY

    A. 4235   B. 4295   C. 4315   D. 4370

50.____

KEY (CORRECT ANSWERS)

1. A	11. B	21. C	31. B	41. C
2. B	12. D	22. B	32. A	42. A
3. B	13. B	23. C	33. D	43. B
4. C	14. D	24. D	34. B	44. C
5. C	15. A	25. A	35. C	45. A
6. E	16. D	26. B	36. E	46. C
7. A	17. C	27. A	37. A	47. D
8. D	18. B	28. B	38. E	48. D
9. A	19. A	29. B	39. A	49. B
10. C	20. A	30. D	40. D	50. B

PUBLIC CONTACT

INTRODUCTION

These questions test for the ability to interact with other people, to gather and present information, and to provide assistance, advice, and effective customer service in a courteous and professional manner. Questions will cover such topics as understanding and responding to people with diverse needs, perspectives, personalities, and levels of familiarity with agency operations, as well as acting in a way that both serves the public and reflects well on your agency.

Test Task: You will be presented with situations in which you must apply knowledge of how best to interact with other people.

1.   A person approaches you expressing anger about a recent action by your department. Which one of the following should be your FIRST response to this person?

    A. Interrupt to say you cannot discuss the situation until he calms down.
    B. Say that you are sorry that he has been negatively affected by your department's action.
    C. Listen and express understanding that he has been upset by your department's action.
    D. Give him an explanation of the reasons for your department's action.

1.____

KEY (CORRECT ANSWERS)

1.   The correct answer is C.

Choice A is not correct. It would be inappropriate to interrupt. In addition, saying that you cannot discuss the situation until the person calms down will likely aggravate him further.

Choice B is not correct. Apologizing for your department's action implies that the action was improper.

Choice C is the correct answer. By listening and expressing understanding that your department's action has upset him, you demonstrate that you have heard and understand his feelings and point of view.

Choice D is not correct. While an explanation of the reasons for the action may be appropriate at a later time, at this moment the person is angry and would not be receptive to such an explanation.

EXAMINATION SECTION
TEST 1

DIRECTIONS: Each question or incomplete statement is followed by several suggested answers or completions. Select the one that BEST answers the question or completes the statement. *PRINT THE LETTER OF THE CORRECT ANSWER IN THE SPACE AT THE RIGHT.*

1. In public agencies, communications should be based PRIMARILY on a   1.____

    A. two-way flow from the top down and from the bottom up, most of which should be given in writing to avoid ambiguity
    B. multidirection flow among all levels and with outside persons
    C. rapid, internal one-way flow from the top down
    D. two-way flow of information, most of which should be given orally for purposes of clarity

2. In some organizations, changes in policy or procedures are often communicated by word   2.____
    of mouth from supervisors to employees with no prior discussion or exchange of viewpoints with employees.
    This procedure often produces employee dissatisfaction CHIEFLY because

    A. information is mostly unusable since a considerable amount of time is required to transmit information
    B. lower-level supervisors tend to be excessively concerned with minor details
    C. management has failed to seek employees' advice before making changes
    D. valuable staff time is lost between decision-making and the implementation of decisions

3. For good letter writing, you should try to visualize the person to whom you are writing,   3.____
    especially if you know him.
    Of the following rules, it is LEAST helpful in such visualization to think of

    A. the person's likes and dislikes, his concerns, and his needs
    B. what you would be likely to say if speaking in person
    C. what you would expect to be asked if speaking in person
    D. your official position in order to be certain that your words are proper

4. One approach to good informal letter writing is to make letters sound conversational.   4.____
    All of the following practices will usually help to do this EXCEPT:

    A. If possible, use a style which is similar to the style used when speaking
    B. Substitute phrases for single words (e.g., *at the present time* for *now*)
    C. Use contractions of words (e.g., *you're* for *you are*)
    D. Use ordinary vocabulary when possible

5. All of the following rules will aid in producing clarity in report-writing EXCEPT: 5.____

    A. Give specific details or examples, if possible
    B. Keep related words close together in each sentence
    C. Present information in sequential order
    D. Put several thoughts or ideas in each paragraph

6. The one of the following statements about public relations which is MOST accurate is that   6.____

    A. in the long run, appearance gains better results than performance
    B. objectivity is decreased if outside public relations consultants are employed
    C. public relations is the responsibility of every employee
    D. public relations should be based on a formal publicity program

7. The form of communication which is usually considered to be MOST personally directed to the intended recipient is the   7.____

    A. brochure   B. film   C. letter   D. radio

8. In general, a document that presents an organization's views or opinions on a particular topic is MOST accurately known as a   8.____

    A. tear sheet   B. position paper
    C. flyer   D. journal

9. Assume that you have been asked to speak before an organization of persons who oppose a newly announced program in which you are involved. You feel tense about talking to this group.
Which of the following rules generally would be MOST useful in gaining rapport when speaking before the audience?   9.____

    A. Impress them with your experience
    B. Stress all areas of disagreement
    C. Talk to the group as to one person
    D. Use formal grammar and language

10. An organization must have an effective public relations program since, at its best, public relations is a bridge to change.
All of the following statements about communication and human behavior have validity EXCEPT: 10.____

    A. People are more likely to talk about controversial matters with like-minded people than with those holding other views
    B. The earlier an experience, the more powerful its effect since it influences how later experiences will be interpreted
    C. In periods of social tension, official sources gain increased believability
    D. Those who are already interested in a topic are the ones who are most open to receive new communications about it

11. An employee should be encouraged to talk easily and frankly when he is dealing with his supervisor.
In order to encourage such free communication, it would be MOST appropriate for a supervisor to behave in a(n)   11.____

    A. sincere manner; assure the employee that you will deal with him honestly and openly
    B. official manner; you are a supervisor and must always act formally with subordinates

C. investigative manner; you must probe and question to get to a basis of trust
D. unemotional manner; the employee's emotions and background should play no part in your dealings with him

12. Research findings show that an increase in free communication within an agency GEN-ERALLY results in which one of the following?   12.____

    A. Improved morale and productivity
    B. Increased promotional opportunities
    C. An increase in authority
    D. A spirit of honesty

13. Assume that you are a supervisor and your superiors have given you a new-type procedure to be followed.   13.____
    Before passing this information on to your subordinates, the one of the following actions that you should take FIRST is to

    A. ask your superiors to send out a memorandum to the entire staff
    B. clarify the procedure in your own mind
    C. set up a training course to provide instruction on the new procedure
    D. write a memorandum to your subordinates

14. Communication is necessary for an organization to be effective.   14.____
    The one of the following which is LEAST important for most communication systems is that

    A. messages are sent quickly and directly to the person who needs them to operate
    B. information should be conveyed understandably and accurately
    C. the method used to transmit information should be kept secret so that security can be maintained
    D. senders of messages must know how their messages are received and acted upon

15. Which one of the following is the CHIEF advantage of listening willingly to subordinates and encouraging them to talk freely and honestly?   15.____
    It

    A. reveals to supervisors the degree to which ideas that are passed down are accepted by subordinates
    B. reduces the participation of subordinates in the operation of the department
    C. encourages subordinates to try for promotion
    D. enables supervisors to learn more readily what the *grapevine* is saying

16. A supervisor may be informed through either oral or written reports.   16.____
    Which one of the following is an ADVANTAGE of using oral reports?

    A. There is no need for a formal record of the report.
    B. An exact duplicate of the report is not easily transmitted to others.
    C. A good oral report requires little time for preparation.
    D. An oral report involves two-way communication between a subordinate and his supervisor.

17. Of the following, the MOST important reason why supervisors should communicate effectively with the public is to   17.____

    A. improve the public's understanding of information that is important for them to know
    B. establish a friendly relationship
    C. obtain information about the kinds of people who come to the agency
    D. convince the public that services are adequate

18. Supervisors should generally NOT use phrases like *too hard*, *too easy*, and *a lot* PRINCI-PALLY because such phrases   18.____

    A. may be offensive to some minority groups
    B. are too informal
    C. mean different things to different people
    D. are difficult to remember

19. The ability to communicate clearly and concisely is an important element in effective leadership.   19.____
Which of the following statements about oral and written communication is GENER-ALLY true?

    A. Oral communication is more time-consuming.
    B. Written communication is more likely to be misinterpreted.
    C. Oral communication is useful only in emergencies.
    D. Written communication is useful mainly when giving information to fewer than twenty people.

20. Rumors can often have harmful and disruptive effects on an organization.   20.____
Which one of the following is the BEST way to prevent rumors from becoming a problem?

    A. Refuse to act on rumors, thereby making them less believable.
    B. Increase the amount of information passed along by the *grapevine*.
    C. Distribute as much factual information as possible.
    D. Provide training in report writing.

21. Suppose that a subordinate asks you about a rumor he has heard. The rumor deals with a subject which your superiors consider *confidential*.   21.____
Which of the following BEST describes how you should answer the subordinate?
Tell

    A. the subordinate that you don't make the rules and that he should speak to higher ranking officials
    B. the subordinate that you will ask your superior for information
    C. him only that you cannot comment on the matter
    D. him the rumor is not true

22. Supervisors often find it difficult to *get their message across* when instructing newly appointed employees in their various duties.   22.____
The MAIN reason for this is generally that the

A. duties of the employees have increased
B. supervisor is often so expert in his area that he fails to see it from the learner's point of view
C. supervisor adapts his instruction to the slowest learner in the group
D. new employees are younger, less concerned with job security and more interested in fringe benefits

23. Assume that you are discussing a job problem with an employee under your supervision. During the discussion, you see that the man's eyes are turning away from you and that he is not paying attention.
In order to get the man's attention, you should FIRST

    A. ask him to look you in the eye
    B. talk to him about sports
    C. tell him he is being very rude
    D. change your tone of voice

23.____

24. As a supervisor, you may find it necessary to conduct meetings with your subordinates. Of the following, which would be MOST helpful in assuring that a meeting accomplishes the purpose for which it was called?

    A. Give notice of the conclusions you would like to reach at the start of the meeting.
    B. Delay the start of the meeting until everyone is present.
    C. Write down points to be discussed in proper sequence.
    D. Make sure everyone is clear on whatever conclusions have been reached and on what must be done after the meeting.

24.____

25. Every supervisor will occasionally be called upon to deliver a reprimand to a subordinate. If done properly, this can greatly help an employee improve his performance.
Which one of the following is NOT a good practice to follow when giving a reprimand?

    A. Maintain your composure and temper.
    B. Reprimand a subordinate in the presence of other employees so they can learn the same lesson.
    C. Try to understand why the employee was not able to perform satisfactorily.
    D. Let your knowledge of the man involved determine the exact nature of the reprimand.

25.____

KEY (CORRECT ANSWERS)

1.	C		11.	A
2.	B		12.	A
3.	D		13.	B
4.	B		14.	C
5.	D		15.	A
6.	C		16.	D
7.	C		17.	A
8.	B		18.	C
9.	C		19.	B
10.	C		20.	C

21.	B
22.	B
23.	D
24.	D
25.	B

———

TEST 2

DIRECTIONS: Each question or incomplete statement is followed by several suggested answers or completions. Select the one that BEST answers the question or completes the statement. *PRINT THE LETTER OF THE CORRECT ANSWER IN THE SPACE AT THE RIGHT.*

1. Usually one thinks of communication as a single step, essentially that of transmitting an idea.
   Actually, however, this is only part of a total process, the FIRST step of which should be

   A. the prompt dissemination of the idea to those who may be affected by it
   B. motivating those affected to take the required action
   C. clarifying the idea in one's own mind
   D. deciding to whom the idea is to be communicated

   1.____

2. Research studies on patterns of informal communication have concluded that most individuals in a group tend to be passive recipients of news, while a few make it their business to spread it around in an organization.
   With this conclusion in mind, it would be MOST correct for the supervisor to attempt to identify these few individuals and

   A. give them the complete facts on important matters in advance of others
   B. inform the other subordinates of the identify of these few individuals so that their influence may be minimized
   C. keep them straight on the facts on important matters
   D. warn them to cease passing along any information to others

   2.____

3. The one of the following which is the PRINCIPAL advantage of making an oral report is that it

   A. affords an immediate opportunity for two-way communication between the subordinate and superior
   B. is an easy method for the superior to use in transmitting information to others of equal rank
   C. saves the time of all concerned
   D. permits more precise pinpointing of praise or blame by means of follow-up questions by the superior

   3.____

4. An agency may sometimes undertake a public relations program of a defensive nature. With reference to the use of defensive public relations, it would be MOST correct to state that it

   A. is bound to be ineffective since defensive statements, even though supported by factual data, can never hope to even partly overcome the effects of prior unfavorable attacks
   B. proves that the agency has failed to establish good relationships with newspapers, radio stations, or other means of publicity
   C. shows that the upper echelons of the agency have failed to develop sound public relations procedures and techniques
   D. is sometimes required to aid morale by protecting the agency from unjustified criticism and misunderstanding of policies or procedures

   4.____

5. Of the following factors which contribute to possible undesirable public attitudes towards an agency, the one which is MOST susceptible to being changed by the efforts of the individual employee in an organization is that

    A. enforcement of unpopular regulations has offended many individuals
    B. the organization itself has an unsatisfactory reputation
    C. the public is not interested in agency matters
    D. there are many errors in judgment committed by individual subordinates

5.___

6. It is not enough for an agency's services to be of a high quality; attention must also be given to the acceptability of these services to the general public.
This statement is GENERALLY

    A. *false;* a superior quality of service automatically wins public support
    B. *true;* the agency cannot generally progress beyond the understanding and support of the public
    C. *false;* the acceptance by the public of agency services determines their quality
    D. *true;* the agency is generally unable to engage in any effective enforcement activity without public support

6.___

7. Sustained agency participation in a program sponsored by a community organization is MOST justified when

    A. the achievement of agency objectives in some area depends partly on the activity of this organization
    B. the community organization is attempting to widen the base of participation in all community affairs
    C. the agency is uncertain as to what the community wants
    D. there is an obvious lack of good leadership in a newly formed community organization

7.___

8. Of the following, the LEAST likely way in which a records system may serve a supervisor is in

    A. developing a sympathetic and cooperative public attitude toward the agency
    B. improving the quality of supervision by permitting a check on the accomplishment of subordinates
    C. permit a precise prediction of the exact incidences in specific categories for the following year
    D. helping to take the guesswork out of the distribution of the agency

8.___

9. Assuming that the *grapevine* in any organization is virtually indestructible, the one of the following which it is MOST important for management to understand is:

    A. What is being spread by means of the *grapevine* and the reason for spreading it
    B. What is being spread by means of the *grapevine* and how it is being spread
    C. Who is involved in spreading the information that is on the *grapevine*
    D. Why those who are involved in spreading the information are doing so

9.___

10. When the supervisor writes a report concerning an investigation to which he has been assigned, it should be LEAST intended to provide   10.____

    A. a permanent official record of relevant information gathered
    B. a summary of case findings limited to facts which tend to indicate the guilt of a suspect
    C. a statement of the facts on which higher authorities may base a corrective or disciplinary action
    D. other investigators with information so that they may continue with other phases of the investigation

11. In survey work, questionnaires rather than interviews are sometimes used.
The one of the following which is a DISADVANTAGE of the questionnaire method as compared with the interview is the   11.____

    A. difficulty of accurately interpreting the results
    B. problem of maintaining anonymity of the participant
    C. fact that it is relatively uneconomical
    D. requirement of special training for the distribution of questionnaires

12. In his contacts with the public, an employee should attempt to create a good climate of support for his agency. This statement is GENERALLY   12.____

    A. *false;* such attempts are clearly beyond the scope of his responsibility
    B. *true;* employees of an agency who come in contact with the public have the opportunity to affect public relations
    C. *false;* such activity should be restricted to supervisors trained in public relations techniques
    D. *true;* the future expansion of the agency depends to a great extent on continued public support of the agency

13. The repeated use by a supervisor of a call for volunteers to get a job done is objectionable MAINLY because it   13.____

    A. may create a feeling of animosity between the volunteers and the non-volunteers
    B. may indicate that the supervisor is avoiding responsibility for making assignments which will be most productive
    C. is an indication that the supervisor is not familiar with the individual capabilities of his men
    D. is unfair to men who, for valid reasons, do not, or cannot volunteer

14. Of the following statements concerning subordinates' expressions to a supervisor of their opinions and feelings concerning work situations, the one which is MOST correct is that   14.____

    A. by listening and responding to such expressions the supervisor encourages the development of complaints
    B. the lack of such expressions should indicate to the supervisor that there is a high level of job satisfaction
    C. the more the supervisor listens to and responds to such expressions, the more he demonstrates lack of supervisory ability
    D. by listening and responding to such expressions, the supervisor will enable many subordinates to understand and solve their own problems on the job

15. In attempting to motivate employees, rewards are considered preferable to punishment PRIMARILY because   15.____

    A. punishment seldom has any effect on human behavior
    B. punishment usually results in decreased production
    C. supervisors find it difficult to punish
    D. rewards are more likely to result in willing cooperation

16. In an attempt to combat the low morale in his organization, a high-level supervisor publicized an *open-door* policy to allow employees who wished to do so to come to him with their complaints.
   Which of the following is LEAST likely to account for the fact that no employee came in with a complaint?   16.____

    A. Employees are generally reluctant to go over the heads of their immediate supervisors.
    B. The employees did not feel that management would help them.
    C. The low morale was not due to complaints associated with the job.
    D. The employees felt that they had more to lose than to gain.

17. It is MOST desirable to use written instructions rather than oral instructions for a particular job when   17.____

    A. a mistake on the job will not be serious
    B. the job can be completed in a short time
    C. there is no need to explain the job minutely
    D. the job involves many details

18. If you receive a telephone call regarding a matter which your office does not handle, you should FIRST   18.____

    A. give the caller the telephone number of the proper office so that he can dial again
    B. offer to transfer the caller to the proper office
    C. suggest that the caller re-dial since he probably dialed incorrectly
    D. tell the caller he has reached the wrong office and then hang up

19. When you answer the telephone, the MOST important reason for identifying yourself and your organization is to   19.____

    A. give the caller time to collect his or her thoughts
    B. impress the caller with your courtesy
    C. inform the caller that he or she has reached the right number
    D. set a business-like tone at the beginning of the conversation

20. As soon as you pick up the phone, a very angry caller begins immediately to complain about city agencies and *red tape*. He says that he has been shifted to two or three different offices. It turns out that he is seeking information which is not immediately available to you. You believe you know, however, where it can be found. Which of the following actions is the BEST one for you to take?   20.____

    A. To eliminate all confusion, suggest that the caller write the agency stating explicitly what he wants.
    B. Apologize by telling the caller how busy city agencies now are, but also tell him directly that you do not have the information he needs.

C. Ask for the caller's telephone number and assure him you will call back after you have checked further.
D. Give the caller the name and telephone number of the person who might be able to help, but explain that you are not positive he will get results.

21. Which of the following approaches usually provides the BEST communication in the objectives and values of a new program which is to be introduced?

    A. A general written description of the program by the program manager for review by those who share responsibility
    B. An effective verbal presentation by the program manager to those affected
    C. Development of the plan and operational approach in carrying out the program by the program manager assisted by his key subordinates
    D. Development of the plan by the program manager's supervisor

21.____

22. What is the BEST approach for introducing change?
A

    A. combination of written and also verbal communication to all personnel affected by the change
    B. general bulletin to all personnel
    C. meeting pointing out all the values of the new approach
    D. written directive to key personnel

22.____

23. Of the following, committees are BEST used for

    A. advising the head of the organization
    B. improving functional work
    C. making executive decisions
    D. making specific planning decisions

23.____

24. An effective discussion leader is one who

    A. announces the problem and his preconceived solution at the start of the discussion
    B. guides and directs the discussion according to pre-arranged outline
    C. interrupts or corrects confused participants to save time
    D. permits anyone to say anything at anytime

24.____

25. The human relations movement in management theory is basically concerned with

    A. counteracting employee unrest
    B. eliminating the *time and motion* man
    C. interrelationships among individuals in organizations
    D. the psychology of the worker

25.____

KEY (CORRECT ANSWERS)

1.	C	11.	A
2.	C	12.	B
3.	A	13.	B
4.	D	14.	D
5.	D	15.	D
6.	B	16.	C
7.	A	17.	D
8.	C	18.	B
9.	A	19.	C
10.	B	20.	C

21.	C
22.	A
23.	A
24.	B
25.	C

———

READING COMPREHENSION
UNDERSTANDING AND INTERPRETING WRITTEN MATERIAL
EXAMINATION SECTION
TEST 1

DIRECTIONS: Each question or incomplete statement is followed by several suggested answers or completions. Select the one that BEST answers the question or completes the statement. *PRINT THE LETTER OF THE CORRECT ANSWER IN THE SPACE AT THE RIGHT.*

Questions 1-6.

DIRECTIONS: Questions 1 through 6 are to be answered SOLELY on the basis of the information contained in the following passage.

Duplicating is the process of making a number of identical copies of letters, documents, etc from an original. Some duplicating processes make copies directly from the original document. Other duplicating processes require the preparation of a special master, and copies are then made from the master. Four of the most common duplicating processes are stencil, fluid, offset, and xerox.

In the stencil process, the typewriter is used to cut the words into a master called a stencil. Drawings, charts, or graphs can be cut into the stencil using a stylus. As many as 3,500 good-quality copies can be reproduced from one stencil. Various grades of finished paper from inexpensive mimeograph to expensive bond can be used.

The fluid process is a good method of copying from 50 to 125 good-quality copies from a master, which is prepared with a special dye. The master is placed on the duplicator, and special paper with a hard finish is moistened and then passed through the duplicator. Some of the dye on the master is dissolved, creating an impression on the paper. The impression becomes lighter as more copies are made; and once the dye on the master is used up, a new master must be made.

The offset process is the most adaptable office duplicating process because this process can be used for making a few copies or many copies. Masters can be made on paper or plastic for a few hundred copies, or on metal plates for as many as 75,000 copies. By using a special technique called photo-offset, charts, photographs, illustrations, or graphs can be reproduced on the master plate. The offset process is capable of producing large quantities of fine, top-quality copies on all types of finished paper.

The xerox process reproduces an exact duplicate from an original. It is the fastest duplicating method because the original material is placed directly on the duplicator, eliminating the need to make a special master. Any kind of paper can be used. The xerox process is the most expensive duplicating process; however, it is the best method of reproducing small quantities of good-quality copies of reports, letters, official documents, memos, or contracts.

1. Of the following, the MOST efficient method of reproducing 5,000 copies of a graph is   1.___

    A. stencil   B. fluid
    C. offset   D. Xerox

2. The offset process is the MOST adaptable office duplicating process because   2.___

    A. it is the quickest duplicating method
    B. it is the least expensive duplicating method
    C. it can produce a small number or large number of copies
    D. a softer master can be used over and over again

3. Which one of the following duplicating processes uses moistened paper?   3.___

    A. Stencil   B. Fluid
    C. Offset   D. Xerox

4. The fluid process would be the BEST process to use for reproducing   4.___

    A. five copies of a school transcript
    B. fifty copies of a memo
    C. five hundred copies of a form letter
    D. five thousand copies of a chart

5. Which one of the following duplicating processes does NOT require a special master?   5.___

    A. Fluid   B. Xerox
    C. Offset   D. Stencil

6. Xerox is NOT used for all duplicating jobs because   6.___

    A. it produces poor-quality copies
    B. the process is too expensive
    C. preparing the master is too time-consuming
    D. it cannot produce written reports

Questions 7-10.

DIRECTIONS: Questions 7 through 10 are to be answered SOLELY on the basis of the infor-
              mation contained in the following passage.

City government is committed to providing a safe and healthy work environment for all
city employees. An effective agency safety program reduces accidents by educating employees about the types of careless acts which can cause accidents. Even in an office, accidents
can happen. If each employee is aware of possible safety hazards, the number of accidents
on the job can be reduced.

Careless use of office equipment can cause accidents and injuries. For example, file cabinet drawers which are filled with papers can be so heavy that the entire cabinet could tip over
from the weight of one open drawer.

The bottom drawers of desks and file cabinets should never be left open since employees could easily trip over open drawers and injure themselves.

When reaching for objects on a high shelf, an employee should use a strong, sturdy object such as a step stool to stand on. Makeshift platforms made out of books, papers, or boxes can easily collapse. Even chairs can slide out from under foot, causing serious injury.

Even at an employee's desk, safety hazards can occur. Frayed or cut wires should be repaired or replaced immediately. Typewriters which are not firmly anchored to the desk or table could fall, causing injury.

Smoking is one of the major causes of fires in the office. A lighted match or improperly extinguished cigarette thrown into a wastebasket filled with paper could cause a major fire with possible loss of life. Where smoking is permitted, ashtrays should be used. Smoking is particularly dangerous in offices where flammable chemicals are used.

7. The goal of an effective safety program is to 7.____

    A.   reduce office accidents
    B.   stop employees from smoking on the job
    C.   encourage employees to continue their education
    D.   eliminate high shelves in offices

8. Desks and file cabinets can become safety hazards when 8.____

    A.   their drawers are left open
    B.   they are used as wastebaskets
    C.   they are makeshift
    D.   they are not anchored securely to the floor

9. Smoking is especially hazardous when it occurs 9.____

    A.   near exposed wires
    B.   in a crowded office
    C.   in an area where flammable chemicals are used
    D.   where books and papers are stored

10. Accidents are likely to occur when 10.____

    A.   employees' desks are cluttered with books and papers
    B.   employees are not aware of safety hazards
    C.   employees close desk drawers
    D.   step stools are used to reach high objects

Questions 11-18.

DIRECTIONS: Questions 11 through 18 are to be answered SOLELY on the basis of the information contained in the following passage.

The telephone directory is made up of two books. The first book consists of the introductory section and the alphabetical listing of names section. The second book is the classified directory (also known as the yellow pages). Many people who are familiar with one book do not realize how useful the other can be. The efficient office worker should become familiar with both books in order to make the best use of this important source of information.

The introductory section gives general instructions for finding numbers in the alphabetical listing and classified directory. This section also explains how to use the telephone company's many services, including the operator and information services, gives examples of charges for local and long distance calls, and lists area codes for the entire country. In addition, this section provides a useful postal zip code map.

The alphabetical listing of names section lists the names, addresses, and telephone numbers of subscribers in an area. Guide names, or *telltales*, are on the top corner of each page. These guide names indicate the first and last name to be found on that page. *Telltales* help locate any particular name quickly. A cross-reference spelling is also given to help locate names which are spelled several different ways. City, state, and federal government agencies are listed under the major government heading. For example, an agency of the federal government would be listed under *United States Government*.

The classified directory, or yellow pages, is a separate book. In this section are advertising services, public transportation line maps, shopping guides, and listings of businesses arranged by the type of product or services they offer. This book is most useful when looking for the name or phone number of a business when all that is known is the type of product offered and the address, or when trying to locate a particular type of business in an area. Businesses listed in the classified directory can usually be found in the alphabetical listing of names section. When the name of the business is known, you will find the address or phone number more quickly in the alphabetical listing of names section.

11. The introductory section provides

    A. shopping guides   B. government listings
    C. business listings   D. information services

11.____

12. Advertising services would be found in the

    A. introductory section
    B. alphabetical listing of names section
    C. classified directory
    D. information services

12.____

13. According to the information in the above passage for locating government agencies, the Information Office of the Department of Consumer Affairs of New York City government would be alphabetically listed FIRST under

    A. *I* for Information Offices
    B. *D* for Department of Consumer Affairs
    C. *N* for New York City
    D. *G* for government

13.____

14. When the name of a business is known, the QUICKEST way to find the phone number is to look in the

    A. classified directory
    B. introductory section
    C. alphabetical listing of names section
    D. advertising service section

14.____

15. The QUICKEST way to find the phone number of a business when the type of service a 15._____
business offers and its address is known is to look in the

    A. classified directory
    B. alphabetical listing of names section
    C. introductory section
    D. information service

16. What is a *telltale*? 16._____
A(n)

    A. alphabetical listing   B. guide name
    C. map   D. cross-reference listing

17. The BEST way to find a postal zip code is to look in the 17._____

    A. classified directory
    B. introductory section
    C. alphabetical listing of names section
    D. government heading

18. To help find names which have several different spellings, the telephone directory pro- 18._____
vides

    A. cross-reference spelling
    B. *tell tales*
    C. spelling guides
    D. advertising services

Questions 19-24.

DIRECTIONS: Questions 19 through 24 are to be answered on the basis of the information
contained in the following instructions on

SWEEPING

    All sweeping must be done with damp sawdust, which is used to prevent the raising of dust when sweeping platforms and mezzanines. Soak sawdust thoroughly in a bucket of water for two to three hours before use. Drain before use so that no stains are left on concrete from excess water. In order to keep sawdust moist while being used, spread for an area of 120 feet in advance of actual sweeping. Never sweep sawdust over drains. To assure good footing, do not spread it on stairways or on damp or wet floor areas.

19. Dampened sawdust should be used when 19._____

    A. scrapping   B. dusting
    C. sweeping   D. mopping

20. Of the following procedures, which is the CORRECT order to be followed when sweeping 20._____
with sawdust?

    A. Soak, drain, and spread   B. Spread, drain, and soak
    C. Spread, soak, and drain   D. Drain, spread, and soak

21. Of the following, it is MOST correct to soak the sawdust in a bucket of water for _____ hour(s).   21.____

    A. a half-hour to an   B. one to two
    C. two to three   D. three to four

22. The water should be drained from the bucket of sawdust so that excess water does NOT   22.____

    A. cause passengers to lose their footing
    B. stain the concrete
    C. flood the tracks
    D. slow down the sweeping

23. Sawdust is dampened in order to   23.____

    A. assure good footing on stairways
    B. prevent the raising of dust when sweeping
    C. prevent the staining of concrete
    D. cool off platforms

24. The dampened sawdust may be spread on   24.____

    A. wet floors   B. drains
    C. stairways   D. mezzanines

Questions 25-27.

DIRECTIONS: Questions 25 through 27 are to be answered on the basis of the information contained in the following paragraph.

Whether a main lobby or upper corridor requires scrubbing or mopping and whether it should be done nightly or less frequently depends on the nature of the floor surface and the amount of traffic. In a building with heavy traffic, it may be desirable every night to scrub the main lobby and to mop the upper floor corridors. In such cases, it may also be found desirable to scrub the upper floors once a week. If traffic is light, it may be only necessary to mop the main lobby every other night and to mop the upper floor corridors once a week. If there is any traffic or usage at all, it will be necessary to at least sweep the corridors nightly.

25. According to the above paragraph, in a building with light traffic, the upper floor corridors should be   25.____

    A. swept every other night
    B. mopped every night
    C. swept nightly
    D. mopped every other night

26. According to the above paragraph, the number of times a floor is cleaned depends   26.____

    A. mainly on the type of floor surface
    B. mainly on the type of traffic
    C. only on the amount of traffic
    D. on both the floor surface and amount of traffic

27. According to the above paragraph, it may be DESIRABLE to have a heavily used main lobby swept   27.____

    A. daily and scrubbed weekly
    B. daily and mopped weekly
    C. and mopped weekly
    D. and scrubbed daily

Questions 28-30.

DIRECTIONS: Questions 28 through 30 are to be answered SOLELY on the basis of the information contained in the passage below.

SENIOR CITIZEN AND HANDICAPPED PASSENGER REDUCED FARE PROGRAM

Upon display of his or her Medicare Card, Senior Citizen Reduced Fare Card, or Handicapped Photo I.D. Card to the Railroad Clerk on duty, and upon purchase of a token or evidence of having a token, a passenger will be issued a free return trip ticket. The passenger will then be directed to deposit full fare in a turnstile and enter the controlled area. Return trip tickets are valid 24 hours a day, 7 days a week, for the day of purchase and the following two (2) calendar days.

Each return trip ticket will be stamped with the station name and the date only at the time of issuing to a properly identified senior citizen or handicapped passenger. Overstamping of tickets is not allowed. Return trip tickets issued from 2300 hours will be stamped with the date of the following day.

On the return trip, the Railroad Clerk on duty will direct the passenger to enter the controlled area via the exit gate upon the passenger turning in the return trip ticket and displaying his/her Medicare Card, Senior Citizen Reduced Fare Card, or Handicapped Photo I.D. Card.

28. A Railroad Clerk issued a free return ticket to a senior citizen who displayed a birth certificate and a token. The Railroad Clerk's action was   28.____

    A. *proper* because the Railroad Clerk had proof of the senior citizen's age
    B. *improper* because the senior citizen did not display a Medicare Card, Senior Citizen Reduced Fare Card, or Handicapped Photo I.D. Card
    C. *proper* because it is inconvenient for many senior citizens to obtain a Medicare Card, Senior Citizen Reduced Fare Card, or Handicapped Photo I.D. Card
    D. *improper* because the senior citizen did not buy a token from the Railroad Clerk

29. The return trip ticket issued to a senior citizen is valid for ONLY   29.____

    A. 24 hours
    B. the day of purchase
    C. two days
    D. the day of purchase and the following two calendar days

30. A Railroad Clerk denied entry to the controlled area via the exit gate to an 18 year-old   30.___
handicapped passenger who turned in a correctly stamped return trip ticket, but did not
display any type of identification card. The Railroad Clerk's action was

    A. *proper* because the passenger should have displayed his Handicapped Photo I.D.
Card

    B. *improper* because the passenger turned in a correctly stamped return trip ticket

    C. *proper* because the passenger should have displayed either his Handicapped
Photo I.D. Card or Social Security Card

    D. *improper* because it should have been obvious to the Railroad Clerk that the pas-
senger was handicapped

KEY (CORRECT ANSWERS)

1.	C	16.	B
2.	C	17.	B
3.	B	18.	A
4.	B	19.	C
5.	B	20.	A
6.	A	21.	C
7.	A	22.	B
8.	A	23.	B
9.	C	24.	D
10.	B	25.	C
11.	D	26.	D
12.	C	27.	D
13.	C	28.	B
14.	C	29.	D
15.	A	30.	A

TEST 2

DIRECTIONS: Each question or incomplete statement is followed by several suggested answers or completions. Select the one that BEST answers the question or completes the statement. *PRINT THE LETTER OF THE CORRECT ANSWER IN THE SPACE AT THE RIGHT.*

Questions 1-2.

DIRECTIONS: Questions 1 and 2 are to be answered on the basis of the information given in the following passage.

The Commissioner of Investigation shall have general responsibility for the investigation and elimination of corrupt or other criminal activity, conflicts of interest, unethical conduct, misconduct, and incompetence by city agencies, by city officers and employees, and by persons regulated by, doing business with, or receiving funds directly or indirectly from the city, with respect to their dealings with the city. All agency heads shall be responsible for establishing, subject to review for completeness and inter-agency consistency by the Commissioner of Investigation, written standards of conduct for the officials and employees of their respective agencies, and fair and efficient disciplinary systems to maintain those standards of conduct. All agencies shall have an Inspector General who shall report directly to the respective agency head and to the Commissioner of Investigation and be responsible for maintaining standards of conduct as may be established in such agency under this Order. Inspectors General shall be responsible for the investigation and elimination of corrupt or other criminal activity, conflicts of interest, unethical conduct, misconduct, and incompetence within their respective agencies. Except to the extent otherwise provided by law, the employment or continued employment of all existing and prospective Inspectors General and members of their staffs shall be subject to complete background investigations and approval by the Department of Investigation.

1. According to the above passage, establishing written standards of conduct for each   1.____
   agency is the responsibility of the

   A. agency head
   B. Commissioner of Investigation
   C. Department of Investigation
   D. Inspector General

2. According to the above passage, maintaining standards of conduct within each agency is   2.____
   the responsibility of the

   A. agency head
   B. Commissioner of Investigation
   C. Department of Investigation
   D. Inspector General

Questions 3-6.

DIRECTIONS: Questions 3 through 6 are to be answered on the basis of the following information.

Assume that Warehouse X uses the following procedures for receiving stock. When a delivery is received, the stock handler who receives the delivery should immediately unpack and check the delivery. This check is to ensure that the quantity and kinds of stock items delivered match those on the purchase order which had been sent to the vendor. After the delivery is checked, a receiving report is prepared by the same stock handler. This receiving report should include the name of the shipper, the purchase order number, the description of the item, and the actual count or weight of the item. The receiving report, along with the packing slip, should then be checked by the stores clerk against the purchase order to make sure that the quantity received is correct. This is necessary before credit can be obtained from the vendor for any items that are missing or damaged. After the checking is completed, the stock items can be moved to the stockroom.

3. According to the procedures described above, the stock person who receives the delivery should   3.____

   A. place the unopened delivery in a secure area for checking at a later date
   B. notify the stores clerk that the delivery has arrived and is ready for checking
   C. unpack the delivery and check the quantity and types of stock items against the purchase order
   D. closely examine the outside of the delivery containers for dents and damages

4. According to the procedures described above, credit can be obtained from the vendor   4.____

   A. *before* the stock handler checks the delivery of stock items
   B. *after* the stock handler checks the delivery of stock items
   C. *before* the stores clerk checks the receiving report against the purchase order
   D. *after* the stores clerk checks the receiving report against the purchase order

5. According to the procedures described above, all of the following information should be included when filling out a receiving report EXCEPT the   5.____

   A. purchase order number
   B. name of the shipper
   C. count or weight of the item
   D. unit cost per item

6. According to the procedures described above, after the stores clerk has checked the receiving report against the purchase order, the NEXT step is to   6.____

   A. move the stock items to the stockroom
   B. return the stock items received to the vendor
   C. give the stock items to the stock handler for final checking
   D. file the packing slip for inventory purposes

Questions 7-9.

DIRECTIONS: Questions 7 through 9 are to be answered on the basis of the information given in the following passage.

A filing system for requisition forms used in a warehouse will be of maximum benefit only if it provides ready access to information needed and is not too complex. How effective the system will be depends largely on how well the filing system is organized. A well-organized system usually results in a smooth-running operation.

When setting up a system for filing requisition forms, one effective method would be to first make an alphabetical listing of all the authorized requisitioning agencies. Then file folders should be prepared for each of these agencies and arranged alphabetically in file cabinets. Following this, each agency should be assigned a series of numbers corresponding to those on the blank requisition forms with which they will be supplied. When an agency then submits a requisition and it is filled, the form should be filed in numerical order in the designated agency folder. By using this system, any individual requisition form which is missing from its folder can be easily detected. Regardless of the filing system used, simplicity is essential if the filing system is to be successful.

7. According to the above passage, a filing system is MOST likely to be successful if it is   7._____

    A. alphabetical   B. uncomplicated
    C. numerical   D. reliable

8. According to the above passage, the reason numbers are assigned to each agency is to   8._____

    A. simplify stock issuing procedures
    B. keep a count of all incoming requisition forms
    C. be able to know when a form is missing from its folder
    D. eliminate the need for an alphabetical filing system

9. According to the above passage, which one of the following is an ACCURATE statement   9._____
regarding the establishment of a well-organized filing system?

    A. Requisitioned stock items will be issued at a faster rate.
    B. Stock items will be stored in storage areas alphabetically arranged.
    C. Information concerning ordered stock items will be easily obtainable.
    D. Maximum productivity can be expected from each employee.

Questions 10-13.

DIRECTIONS: Questions 10 through 13 are to be answered SOLELY on the basis of the information in the following paragraph.

On Tuesday, October 21, Protection Agent Williams, on duty at the Jamaica Depot, observed a man jump over the fence and into the parking lot at 2:12 P.M. and run to a car that was parked with the engine running. The man, who limped slightly, opened the car door, jumped into the car, and sped out of the yard. The car was a 1991 gray Buick Electra, license plate 563-JYN, with parking decal No. 6043. The man was white, about 6 feet tall, about 175 pounds, in his mid-20's, with a scar on his left cheek. He wore a blue sportcoat, tan slacks, a white shirt open at the neck with no tie, and brown loafers.

10. What was the color of the car?   10._____

    A. White   B. Blue
    C. Two-tone brown and tan   D. Gray

11. What were the distinguishing personal features of the man who jumped over the fence? 11.___

    A. A scar on the left cheek
    B. Pockmarks on his face
    C. A cast on his left wrist
    D. Bushy eyebrows

12. What was the number on the car's parking decal? 12.___

    A. 1991   B. 673-JYN
    C. 6043   D. 175

13. On what day of the week did the incident occur? 13.___

    A. Monday   B. Tuesday
    C. Wednesday   D. Sunday

14. *It is a violation of rules for a Protection Agent to carry a firearm while on Transit Authority*   14.___
property. The possession of such a weapon, whether carried on the person, in a personal vehicle, or stored in a locker, can result in charges being filed against the Agent.
According to the above information, the carrying of a firearm

    A. on Authority property by any employee is prohibited
    B. anywhere by an Agent is prohibited under all circumstances
    C. on Authority property by an Agent is prohibited under all circumstances
    D. anywhere by an Authority employee may be reason for charges being filed against that employee

15. *News reporters may enter Authority property if they have the written authorization of a*   15.___
Public Affairs Department official. The Agent on duty must get permission from the Property Protection Control Desk before admitting to the property a news person who has no such written authorization.
If a reporter tells a Protection Agent that she has received permission from the Authority President to enter the property, what is the FIRST thing the Agent should do?

    A. Call the Authority police.
    B. Admit the reporter immediately.
    C. Call the Authority President's office.
    D. Call the Property Protection Control Desk.

Questions 16-20.

DIRECTIONS: Questions 16 through 20 are to be answered SOLELY on the basis of the information in the paragraphs below.

FIRES AND EXTINGUISHERS

There are four classes of fires.

Trash fires, paper fires, cloth fires, wood fires, etc. are classified as Class A fires. Water or a water-base solution should be used to extinguish Class A fires. They also can be extinguished by covering the combustibles with a multi-purpose dry chemical.

Burning liquids, gasoline, oil, paint, tar, etc. are considered Class B fires. Such fires can be extinguished by smothering or blanketing them. Extinguishers used for Class B fires are Halon, CO_2, or multi-purpose dry chemical. Water tends to spread such fires and should not be used.

Fires in electrical equipment and switchboards are classified as Class C fires. When live electrical equipment is involved, a non-conducting extinguishing agent like CO_2, a multi-purpose dry chemical, or Halon should always be used. Soda-acid or other water-type extinguishers should not be used.

Class D fires consist of burning metals in finely-divided forms like chips, turnings, and shavings. Specially-designed extinguishing agents that provide a smothering blanket or coating should be used to extinguish Class D fires. Multipurpose dry-powder extinguishants are such agents.

16. The ONLY type of extinguishing agent that can be used on any type of fire is

16._____

    A. a multi-purpose, dry-chemical extinguishing agent
    B. soda-acid
    C. water
    D. carbon dioxide

17. A fire in litter swept from a subway car in a yard is MOST likely to be a Class _____ fire.

17._____

    A. A   B. B
    C. C   D. D

18. Fire coming from the underbody of a subway car is MOST likely to be a Class _____ fire.

18._____

    A. A   B. B
    C. C   D. D

19. Which of the following extinguishing agents should NOT be used in fighting a Class C fire involving live electrical equipment?

19._____

    A. Halon
    B. Carbon dioxide
    C. A multi-purpose dry chemical
    D. Soda-acid

20. Water is NOT recommended for use on Class B fires because water

20._____

    A. would cool the fire   B. evaporates too quickly
    C. might spread the fire   D. would smother the fire

Questions 21-24.

DIRECTIONS: Questions 21 through 24 are to be answered SOLELY on the basis of the information in the paragraph below.

Protection Agent Brown, working the midnight to 8:00 A.M. tour at the Flushing Bus
Depot, discovered a fire at 2:17 A.M. in Bus No. 4651, which was parked in the southeast portion of the depot yard. He turned in an alarm to the Fire Department from Box 3297 on the
nearby street at 2:18 A.M. At 2:20 A.M., he called the Property Protection Control Desk and
reported the fire and his action to Line Supervisor Wilson. Line Supervisor Wilson instructed
Agent Brown to lock his booth and go to the fire alarm box to direct the fire companies. The
first arriving companies were Engine 307 and Ladder 154. Brown directed them to the burning bus. Two minutes later, at 2:23 A.M. Battalion Chief Welsh arrived from Battalion 14. The
fire had made little headway. It was extinguished in about two minutes. Brown then wrote a
fire report for submittal to Line Supervisor Wilson.

21.   What was the FIRST thing Protection Agent Brown did after observing the fire?   21.____
He

A.   called Battalion Chief Welsh
B.   called the Fire Dispatcher
C.   transmitted an alarm from a nearby alarm box
D.   called 911

22.   In what part of the yard was the burning bus?   22.____

A.   Northeast section   B.   Southwest end
C.   Northwest part   D.   Southeast portion

23.   What time did Agent Brown call Line Supervisor Wilson?   23.____

A.   2:18 PM   B.   2:20 AM
C.   2:29 AM   D.   2:36 AM

24.   Which of the following CORRECTLY describes the sequence of Agent Brown's actions?   24.____
He

A.   saw the fire, turned in an alarm, called the Property Protection Control Desk,
directed the fire companies to the fire, and wrote a report
B.   called the Property Protection Control Desk, directed the fire apparatus, directed
Chief Welsh, and wrote a report
C.   called Line Supervisor Wilson, turned in an alarm, waited by the burning bus, and
directed the fire companies
D.   called Line Supervisor Wilson, directed the firefighters, waited for instructions from
Line Supervisor Wilson, and wrote a report

Questions 25-26.

DIRECTIONS: Questions 25 and 26 are to be answered SOLELY on the basis of the following
paragraph and rule.

Protection Agents may admit to Transit Authority headquarters only persons with Transit
Authority passes, persons with job appointment letters, and persons who have permission to
enter from Transit Authority officials.

During his tour in the Authority's headquarters lobby, Protection Agent Williams admitted to the building 326 persons with Authority passes and 41 persons with job appointment letters. He telephoned authorized officials for permission to admit 14 others, 13 of whom were granted permission and entered and one of whom was denied permission. He also turned away two persons who wanted to enter to sell to employees merchandise for their personal use, and one person who appeared inebriated.

25. How many persons did Agent Williams admit to the building?　　25.____

    A.　326　　　　　　　　　　B.　367
    C.　380　　　　　　　　　　D.　382

26. To how many persons did Agent Williams refuse admittance?　　26.____

    A.　4　　　　　　　　　　　B.　13
    C.　14　　　　　　　　　　D.　41

Questions 27-30.

DIRECTIONS:　Questions 27 through 30 are to be answered on the basis of the information contained in the following instructions on LOST PROPERTY.

LOST PROPERTY

All inquiries for information regarding lost property will be referred to the Lost Property Office. Any Station Department employee finding a lost article, of any description, will immediately hand it over to the railroad clerk in the nearest 24-hour booth of the station where the article is found. The clerk must give the employee a receipt for the article. Should a passenger hand over a lost article to a cleaner, the cleaner will offer to escort the passenger to the nearest 24-hour booth in order that a receipt may be given by the railroad clerk there. If the passenger declines, the cleaner will accept the lost article without giving a receipt and proceed as described above. Each employee who receives lost property will be held responsible for it unless he produces a receipt for it from another employee. Should any lost property disappear, the last employee who signed for it will be held strictly accountable.

27. If a cleaner turns in a lost article to a railroad clerk in the nearest 24-hour booth, he　　27.____
should make sure that he

    A.　gets a receipt for the article
    B.　notifies his supervisor about the lost article
    C.　finds out the name of the owner of the article
    D.　writes a report on the incident

28. If a lost article disappears after a cleaner has properly turned it in to the railroad clerk in　　28.____
the nearest 24-hour booth, the one who will be held accountable is the

    A.　person who found the lost article
    B.　cleaner who turned in the article
    C.　supervisor in charge of the station
    D.　last employee to sign a receipt for the article

29. A passenger finds a lost article and gives it to a cleaner. The cleaner gives the passenger a receipt. The cleaner's action was   29.___

    A. *proper* because the passenger was relieved of any responsibility for the lost article
    B. *improper* because the cleaner should have offered to escort the passenger to the nearest 24-hour booth
    C. *proper* because the cleaner is required to give the passenger a receipt
    D. *improper* because the cleaner should have sent the passenger to the Lost Property Office

30. A cleaner finds a five dollar bill on a crowded station platform. Three passengers who see him pick it up rush up and claim the money. The first passenger said he had just taken a roll of bills out of his pocket and must have dropped it. The second said he had just given two five dollar bills to his wife, and she had dropped one of them. The third said he had a hole in his pocket and the bill fell out of it. The cleaner should   30.___

    A. give the five dollar bill to the second passenger because he had his wife as a witness
    B. give the five dollar bill to the third passenger because he had a hole in his pocket
    C. keep the five dollar bill
    D. bring the five dollar bill to the railroad clerk in the nearest 24-hour booth

---

KEY (CORRECT ANSWERS)

1.	A		16.	A
2.	D		17.	A
3.	C		18.	C
4.	D		19.	D
5.	D		20.	C
6.	A		21.	C
7.	B		22.	D
8.	C		23.	B
9.	C		24.	A
10.	D		25.	C
11.	A		26.	A
12.	C		27.	A
13.	B		28.	D
14.	C		29.	B
15.	D		30.	D

RECORD KEEPING
EXAMINATION SECTION
TEST 1

DIRECTIONS: Each question or incomplete statement is followed by several suggested answers or completions. Select the one that BEST answers the question or completes the statement. *PRINT THE LETTER OF THE CORRECT ANSWER IN THE SPACE AT THE RIGHT.*

Questions 1-7.

DIRECTIONS: In answering Questions 1 through 7, use the following master list. For each question, determine where the name would fit on the master list. Each answer choice indicates right before or after the name in the answer choice.

Aaron, Jane
Armstead, Brendan
Bailey, Charles
Dent, Ricardo
Grant, Mark
Mars, Justin
Methieu, Justine
Parker, Cathy
Sampson, Suzy
Thomas, Heather

1. Schmidt, William   1.____
    A. Right before Cathy Parker   B. Right after Heather Thomas
    C. Right after Suzy Sampson   D. Right before Ricardo Dent

2. Asanti, Kendall   2.____
    A. Right before Jane Aaron   B. Right after Charles Bailey
    C. Right before Justine Methieu   D. Right after Brendan Armstead

3. O'Brien, Daniel   3.____
    A. Right after Justine Methieu   B. Right before Jane Aaron
    C. Right after Mark Grant   D. Right before Suzy Sampson

4. Marrow, Alison   4.____
    A. Right before Cathy Parker   B. Right before Justin Mars
    C. Right after Mark Grant   D. Right after Heather Thomas

5. Grantt, Marissa   5.____
    A. Right before Mark Grant   B. Right after Mark Grant
    C. Right after Justin Mars   D. Right before Suzy Sampson

6. Thompson, Heath   6._____
    A. Right after Justin Mars   B. Right before Suzy Sampson
    C. Right after Heather Thomas   D. Right before Cathy Parker

DIRECTIONS: Before answering Question 7, add in all of the names from Questions 1 through 6. Then fit the name in alphabetical order based on the new list.

7. Francisco, Mildred   7._____
    A. Right before Mark Grant   B. Right after Marissa Grantt
    C. Right before Alison Marrow   D. Right after Kendall Asanti

Questions 8-10.

DIRECTIONS: In answering Questions 8 through 10, compare each pair of names and addresses. Indicate whether they are the same or different in any way.

8. William H. Pratt, J.D.   William H. Pratt, J.D.   8._____
   Attourney at Law   Attorney at Law
    A. No differences   B. 1 difference
    C. 2 differences   D. 3 differences

9. 1303 Theater Drive,; Apt. 3-B   1330 Theatre Drive,; Apt. 3-B   9._____
    A. No differences   B. 1 difference
    C. 2 differences   D. 3 differences

10. Petersdorff, Briana and Mary   Petersdorff, Briana and Mary   10._____
    A. No differences   B. 1 difference
    C. 2 differences   D. 3 differences

11. Which of the following words, if any, are misspelled?   11._____
    A. Affordable   B. Circumstansial
    C. Legalese   D. None of the above

Questions 12-13.

DIRECTIONS: Questions 12 and 13 are to be answered on the basis of the following table.

Standardized Test Results for High School Students in District #1230

	English	Math	Science	Reading
High School 1	21	22	15	18
High School 2	12	16	13	15
High School 3	16	181	21	17
High School 4	19	14	15	16

The scores for each high school in the district were averaged out and listed for each subject tested. Scores of 0-10 are significantly below College Readiness Standards. 11-15 are below College Readiness, 16-20 meet College Readiness, and 21-25 are above College Readiness.

12. If the high schools need to meet or exceed in at least half the categories   12.____
    in order to NOT be considered "at risk," which schools are considered "at risk"?
    A. High School 2   B. High School 3
    C. High School 4   D. Both A and C

13. What percentage of subjects did the district as a whole meet or exceed   13.____
    College Readiness standards?
    A. 25%   B. 50%   C. 75%   D. 100%

Questions 14-15.

DIRECTIONS: Questions 14 and 15 are to be answered on the basis of the following
              information.

You have seven employees working as a part of your team: Austin, Emily, Jeremy,
Christina, Martin, Harriet, and Steve. You have just sent an e-mail informing them that
there will be a mandatory training session next week. To ensure that work still gets done,
you are offering the training twice during the week: once on Tuesday and also on
Thursday. This way half the employees will still be working while the other half attend the
training. The only other issue is that Jeremy doesn't work on Tuesdays and Harriet
doesn't work on Thursdays due to compressed work schedules.

14. Which of the following is a possible attendance roster for the first training   14.____
    session?
    A. Emily, Jeremy, Steve   B. Steve, Christina, Harriet
    C. Harriet, Jeremy, Austin   D. Steve, Martin, Jeremy

15. If Harriet, Christina, and Steve attend the training session on Tuesday, which   15.____
    of the following is a possible roster for Thursday's training session?
    A. Jeremy, Emily, and Austin   B. Emily, Martin, and Harriet
    C. Austin, Christina, and Emily   D. Jeremy, Emily, and Steve

Questions 16-20.

DIRECTIONS: In answering Questions 16 through 20, you will be given a word and will need
              to choose the answer choice that is MOST similar or different to the word.

16. Which word means the SAME as *annual*?   16.____
    A. Monthly   B. Usually   C. Yearly   D. Constantly

17. Which word means the SAME as *effort*?   17.____
    A. Energy   B. Equate   C. Cherish   D. Commence

18. Which word means the OPPOSITE of *forlorn*?   18.____
    A. Neglected   B. Lethargy   C. Optimistic   D. Astonished

19. Which word means the SAME as *risk*?   19.____
    A. Admire   B. Hazard   C. Limit   D. Hesitant

20. Which word means the OPPOSITE of *translucent*?   20.____
    A. Opaque   B. Transparent   C. Luminous   D. Introverted

21. Last year, Jamie's annual salary was $50,000. Her boss called her today   21.____
to inform her that she would receive a 20% raise for the upcoming year. How
much more money will Jamie receive next year?
    A. $60,000   B. $10,000   C. $1,000   D. $51,000

22. You and a co-worker work for a temp hiring agency as part of their office   22.____
staff. You both are given 6 days off per month. How many days off are you
and your co-worker given in a year?
    A. 24   B. 72   C. 144   D. 48

23. If Margot makes $34,000 per year and she works 40 hours per week for   23.____
all 52 weeks, what is her hourly rate?
    A. $16.34/hour   B. $17.00/hour   C. $15.54/hour   D. $13.23/hour

24. How many dimes are there in $175.00?   24.____
    A. 175   B. 1,750   C. 3,500   D. 17,500

25. If Janey is three times as old as Emily, and Emily is 3, how old is Janey?   25.____
    A. 6   B. 9   C. 12   D. 15

KEY (CORRECT ANSWERS)

1.	C		11.	B
2.	D		12.	A
3.	A		13.	D
4.	B		14.	B
5.	B		15.	A
6.	C		16.	C
7.	A		17.	A
8.	B		18.	C
9.	C		19.	B
10.	A		20.	A

21.	B
22.	C
23.	A
24.	B
25.	B

TEST 2

DIRECTIONS: Each question or incomplete statement is followed by several suggested answers or completions. Select the one that BEST answers the question or completes the statement. *PRINT THE LETTER OF THE CORRECT ANSWER IN THE SPACE AT THE RIGHT.*

Questions 1-6.

DIRECTIONS: Questions 1 through 6 are to be answered on the basis of the following information.

item	name of item to be ordered
quantity	minimum number that can be ordered
beginning amount	amount in stock at start of month
amount received	amount receiving during month
ending amount	amount in stock at end of month
amount used	amount used during month
amount to order	will need at least as much of each item as used in the previous month
unit price	cost of each unit of an item
total price	total price for the order

Item	Quantity	Beginning	Received	Ending	Amount Used	Amount to Order	Unit Price	Total Price
Pens	10	22	10	8	24	20	$0.11	$2.20
Spiral notebooks	8	30	13	12			$0.25	
Binder clips	2 boxes	3 boxes	1 box	1 box			$1.79	
Sticky notes	3 packs	12 packs	4 packs	2 packs			$14.29	
Dry erase markers	1 pack (dozen)	34 markers	8 markers	40 markers			$16.49	
Ink cartridges (printer)	1 cartridge	3 cartridges	1 cartridge	2 cartridges			$79.99	
Folders	10 folders	25 folders	15 folders	10 folders			$1.08	

1. How many packs of sticky notes were used during the month?   1.____
   A. 16   B. 10   C. 12   D. 14

2. How many folders need to be ordered for next month?   2.____
   A. 15   B. 20   C. 30   D. 40

3. What is the total price of notebooks that you will need to order?   3.____
   A. $6.00   B. $0.25   C. $4.50   D. $2.75

4. Which of the following will you spend the second most money on?   4.____
   A. Ink cartridges   B. Dry erase markers
   C. Sticky notes   D. Binder clips

5. How many packs of dry erase markers should you order?   5.____
   A. 1   B. 8   C. 12   D. 0

6. What will be the total price of the file folders you order?
6.____
    A. $20.16   B. $2.16   C. $1.08   D. $4.32

Questions 7-11.

DIRECTIONS: Questions 7 through 11 are to be answered on the basis of the following table.

Number of Car Accidents, By Location and Cause, for 2014						
	Location 1		Location 2		Location 3	
Cause	Number	Percent	Number	Percent	Number	Percent
Severe Weather	10		25		30	
Excessive Speeding	20	40	5		10	
Impaired Driving	15		15	25	8	
Miscellaneous	5		15		2	4
TOTALS	50	100	60	100	50	100

7. Which of the following is the third highest cause of accidents for all three locations?
7.____
    A. Severe Weather   B. Impaired Driving
    C. Miscellaneous   D. Excessive Speeding

8. The average number of Severe Weather accidents per week at Location 3 for the year (52 weeks) was MOST NEARLY
8.____
    A. 0.57   B. 30   C. 1   D. 1.25

9. Which location had the LARGEST percentage of accidents caused by Impaired Driving?
9.____
    A. 1   B. 2   C. 3   D. Both A and B

10. If one-third of the accidents at all three locations resulted in at least one fatality, what is the LEAST amount of deaths caused by accidents last year?
10.____
    A. 60   B. 106   C. 66   D. 53

11. What is the percentage of accidents caused by miscellaneous means from all three locations in 2014?
11.____
    A. 5%   B. 10%   C. 13%   D. 25%

12. How many pairs of the following groups of letters are exactly alike?
12.____
    ACDOBJ   ACDBOJ
    HEWBWR   HEWRWB
    DEERVS   DEERVS
    BRFQSX   BRFQSX
    WEYRVB   WEYRVB
    SPQRZA   SQRPZA

    A. 2   B. 3   C. 4   D. 5

Questions 13-19.

DIRECTIONS: Questions 13 through 19 are to be answered on the basis of the following information.

In 2012, the most current information on the American population was finished. The population was compiled by 200 people from each of the 50 states. The territory of Puerto Rico, a sovereign of the United States, had 25 people assigned to compile data. In February of 2010, each state began collecting information. In Puerto Rico, data collection finished by January 31st, 2011, while the United States finished on June 30, 2012. Each volunteer gathered data on the population of each state or sovereign. When the information was compiled, each volunteer had to send their information to the nation's capital, Washington, D.C. Each worker worked 20 hours per month and put together 10 reports per month. After the data was compiled in total, 50 people reviewed the data and worked from January 2012 to December 2012.

13. How many reports were generated from February 2010 to April 2010 in Illinois and Ohio?   13._____
    A. 3,000   B. 6,000   C. 12,000   D. 15,000

14. How many workers in total were collecting data in January 2012?   14._____
    A. 200   B. 25   C. 225   D. 0

15. How many reports were put together in May 2012?   15._____
    A. 2,000   B. 50,000   C. 100,000   D. 100,250

16. How many hours did the Puerto Rican volunteers work in the fall (September-November)?   16._____
    A. 60   B. 500   C. 1,500   D. 0

17. How many workers were there in February 2011?   17._____
    A. 25   B. 200   C. 225   D. 250

18. What was the total amount of hours worked in July 2010?   18._____
    A. 500   B. 4,000   C. 4,500   D. 5,000

19. How many reviewers worked in January 2013?   19._____
    A. 75   B. 50   C. 0   D. 25

20. John has to file 10 documents per shelf. How many documents would it take for John to fill 40 shelves?   20._____
    A. 40   B. 400   C. 4,500   D. 5,000

21. Jill wants to travel from New York City to Los Angeles by bike, which is approximately 2,772 miles. How many miles per day would Jill need to average if she wanted to complete the trip in 4 weeks?   21._____
    A. 100   B. 89   C. 99   D. 94

22. If there are 24 CPU's and only 7 monitors, how many more monitors do you need to have the same amount of monitors as CPU's?

    A. Not enough information   B. 17

    C. 31   D. 0

22._____

23. If Gerry works 5 days a week and 8 hours each day, and John works 3 days a week and 10 hours each day, how many more hours per year will Gerry work than John?

    A. They work the same amount of hours.

    B. 450

    C. 520

    D. 832

23._____

24. Jimmy gets transferred to a new office. The new office has 25 employees, but only 16 are there due to a blizzard. How many coworkers was Jimmy able to meet on his first day?

    A. 16   B. 25   C. 9   D. 7

24._____

25. If you do a fundraiser for charities in your area and raise $500 total, how much would you give to each charity if you were donating equal amounts to 3 of them?

    A. $250.00   B. $167.77   C. $50.00   D. $111.11

25._____

KEY (CORRECT ANSWERS)

1.	D		11.	C
2.	B		12.	B
3.	A		13.	C
4.	C		14.	A
5.	D		15.	A
6.	B		16.	C
7.	D		17.	B
8.	A		18.	C
9.	A		19.	C
10.	D		20.	B

21.	C
22.	B
23.	C
24.	A
25.	B

TEST 3

DIRECTIONS: Each question or incomplete statement is followed by several suggested answers or completions. Select the one that BEST answers the question or completes the statement. *PRINT THE LETTER OF THE CORRECT ANSWER IN THE SPACE AT THE RIGHT.*

Questions 1-3.

DIRECTIONS: In answering Questions 1 through 3, choose the correctly spelled word.

1. A. allusion   B. alusion   C. allusien   D. allution   1.____

2. A. altitude   B. alltitude   C. atlitude   D. altlitude   2.____

3. A. althogh   B. allthough   C. althrough   D. although   3.____

Questions 4-9.

DIRECTIONS: In answering Questions 4 through 9, choose the answer that BEST completes the analogy.

4. Odometer is to mileage as compass is to   4.____
    A. speed   B. needle   C. hiking   D. direction

5. Marathon is to race as hibernation is to   5.____
    A. winter   B. dream   C. sleep   D. bear

6. Cup is to coffee as bowl is to   6.____
    A. dish   B. spoon   C. food   D. soup

7. Flow is to river as stagnant is to   7.____
    A. pool   B. rain   C. stream   D. canal

8. paw is to cat as hoof is to   8.____
    A. lamb   B. horse   C. lion   D. elephant

9. Architect is to building as sculptor is to   9.____
    A. museum   B. chisel   C. stone   D. statue

Questions 10-14.

DIRECTIONS: Questions 10 through 14 are to be answered on the basis of the following graph.

Population of Carroll City Broken Down by Age and Gender (in Thousands)			
Age	Female	Male	Total
Under 15	60	60	120
15-23		22	
24-33		20	44
34-43	13	18	31
44-53	20		67
64 and Over	65	65	130
TOTAL	230	232	462

10. How many people in the city are between the ages of 15-23?   10.____
    A. 70   B. 46,000   C. 70,000   D. 225,000

11. Approximately what percentage of the total population of the city was   11.____
    female aged 24-33?
    A. 10%   B. 5%   C. 15%   D. 25%

12. If 33% of the males have a job and 55% of females don't have a job,   12.____
    which of the following statements is TRUE?
    A. Males have approximately 2,600 more jobs than females.
    B. Females have approximately 49,000 more jobs than males.
    C. Females have approximately 26,000 more jobs than males.
    D. None of the above statements are true.

13. How many females between the ages of 15-23 live in Carroll City?   13.____
    A. 67,000   B. 24,000   C. 48,000   D. 91,000

14. Assume all males 44-53 living in Carroll city are employed. If two-thirds   14.____
    of males age 44-53 work jobs outside of Carroll City, how many work within city
    limits?
    A. 31,333
    B. 15,667
    C. 47,000
    D. Cannot answer the question with the information provided

Questions 15-16.

DIRECTIONS: Questions 15 and 16 are labeled as shown. Alphabetize them for filing. Choose the answer that correctly shows the order.

15. (1) AED
    (2) OOS
    (3) FOA
    (4) DOM
    (5) COB

    A. 2-5-4-3-2   B. 1-4-5-2-3   C. 1-5-4-2-3   D. 1-5-4-3-2

15.____

16. Alphabetize the names of the people. Last names are given last.
    (1) Lindsey Jamestown
    (2) Jane Alberta
    (3) Ally Jamestown
    (4) Allison Johnston
    (5) Lyle Moreno

    A. 2-1-3-4-5   B. 3-4-2-1-5   C. 2-3-1-4-5   D. 4-3-2-1-5

16.____

17. Which of the following words is misspelled?
    A. disgust   B. whisper
    C. vocale   D. none of the above

17.____

Questions 18-21.

DIRECTIONS: Questions 18 through 21 are to be answered on the basis of the following list of employees.

Robertson, Aaron
Bacon, Gina
Jerimiah, Trace
Gillette, Stanley
Jacks, Sharon

18. Which employee name would come in third in alphabetized list?
    A. Robertson, Aaron   B. Jerimiah, Trace
    C. Gillette, Stanley   D. Jacks, Sharon

18.____

19. Which employee's first name starts with the letter in the alphabet that is five letters after the first letter of their last name?
    A. Jerimiah, Trace   B. Bacon, Gina
    C. Jacks, Sharon   D. Gillette, Stanley

19.____

20. How many employees have last names that are exactly five letters long?
    A. 1   B. 2   C. 3   D. 4

20.____

21. How many of the employees have either a first or last name that starts with the letter "G"?
    A. 1   B. 2   C. 4   D. 5   21.____

Questions 22-25.

DIRECTIONS: Questions 22 through 25 are to be answered on the basis of the following chart.

Bicycle Sales (Model #34JA32)							
Country	May	June	July	August	September	October	Total
Germany	34	47	45	54	56	60	296
Britain	40	44	36	47	47	46	260
Ireland	37	32	32	32	34	33	200
Portugal	14	14	14	16	17	14	89
Italy	29	29	28	31	29	31	177
Belgium	22	24	24	26	25	23	144
Total	176	198	179	206	208	207	1166

22. What percentage of the overall total was sold to the German importer?   22.____
    A. 25.3%   B. 22%   C. 24.1%   D. 23%

23. What percentage of the overall total was sold in September?   23.____
    A. 24.1%   B. 25.6%   C. 17.9%   D. 24.6%

24. What is the average number of units per month imported into Belgium over the first four months shown?   24.____
    A. 26   B. 20   C. 24   D. 31

25. If you look at the three smallest importers, what is their total import percentage?   25.____
    A. 35.1%   B. 37.1%   C. 40%   D. 28%

KEY (CORRECT ANSWERS)

1.	A		11.	B
2.	A		12.	C
3.	D		13.	C
4.	D		14.	B
5.	C		15.	D
6.	D		16.	C
7.	A		17.	D
8.	B		18.	D
9.	D		19.	B
10.	C		20.	B

21.	B
22.	A
23.	C
24.	C
25.	A

TEST 4

DIRECTIONS: Each question or incomplete statement is followed by several suggested answers or completions. Select the one that BEST answers the question or completes the statement. *PRINT THE LETTER OF THE CORRECT ANSWER IN THE SPACE AT THE RIGHT.*

Questions 1-6.

DIRECTIONS: In answering Questions 1 through 6, choose the sentence that represents the BEST example of English grammar.

1.   A.   Joey and me want to go on a vacation next week.   1._____
     B.   Gary told Jim he would need to take some time off.
     C.   If turning six years old, Jim's uncle would teach Spanish to him.
     D.   Fax a copy of your resume to Ms. Perez and me.

2.   A.   Jerry stood in line for almost two hours.   2._____
     B.   The reaction to my engagement was less exciting than I thought it would be.
     C.   Carlos and me have done great work on this project.
     D.   Two parts of the speech needs to be revised before tomorrow.

3.   A.   Arriving home, the alarm was tripped.   3._____
     B.   Jonny is regarded as a stand up guy, a responsible parent, and he doesn't give up until a task is finished.
     C.   Each employee must submit a drug test each month.
     D.   One of the documents was incinerated in the explosion.

4.   A.   As soon as my parents get home, I told them I finished all of my chores.   4._____
     B.   I asked my teacher to send me my missing work, check my absences, and how did I do on my test.
     C.   Matt attempted to keep it concealed from Jenny and me.
     D.   If Mary or him cannot get work done on time, I will have to split them up.

5.   A.   Driving to work, the traffic report warned him of an accident on Highway 47.   5._____
     B.   Jimmy has performed well this season.
     C.   Since finishing her degree, several job offers have been given to Cam.
     D.   Our boss is creating unstable conditions for we employees.

6.   A.   The thief was described as a tall man with a wiry mustache weighing approximately 150 pounds.   6._____
     B.   She gave Patrick and I some more time to finish our work.
     C.   One of the books that he ordered was damaged in shipping.
     D.   While talking on the rotary phone, the car Jim was driving skidded off the road.

Questions 7-9.

DIRECTIONS: Questions 7 through 9 are to be answered on the basis of the following graph.

Ice Lake Frozen Flight (2002-2013)		
Year	Number of Participants	Temperature (Fahrenheit)
2002	22	4°
2003	50	33°
2004	69	18°
2005	104	22°
2006	108	24°
2007	288	33°
2008	173	9°
2009	598	39°
2010	698	26°
2011	696	30°
2012	777	28°
2013	578	32°

7. Which two year span had the LARGEST difference between temperatures?   7.____
    A. 2002 and 2003   B. 2011 and 2012
    C. 2008 and 2009   D. 2003 and 2004

8. How many total people participated in the years after the temperature   8.____
reached at least 29°?
    A. 2,295   B. 1,717   C. 2,210   D. 4,543

9. In 2007, the event saw 288 participants, while in 2008 that number   9.____
dropped to 173. Which of the following reasons BEST explains the drop in
participants?
    A. The event had not been going on that long and people didn't know about
       it.
    B. The lake water wasn't cold enough to have people jump in.
    C. The temperature was too cold for many people who would have normally
       participated.
    D. None of the above reasons explain the drop in participants.

10. In the following list of numbers, how many times does 4 come just after 2   10.____
when 2 comes just after an odd number?
23652476538986324885724863924 24
    A. 2   B. 3   C. 4   D. 5

11. Which choice below lists the letter that is as far after B as S is after N in   11.____
the alphabet?
    A. G   B. H   C. I   D. J

Questions 12-15.

DIRECTIONS: Questions 12 through 15 are to be answered on the basis of the following directory and list of changes.

Directory		
Name	Emp. Type	Position
Julie Taylor	Warehouse	Packer
James King	Office	Administrative Assistant
John Williams	Office	Salesperson
Ray Moore	Warehouse	Maintenance
Kathleen Byrne	Warehouse	Supervisor
Amy Jones	Office	Salesperson
Paul Jonas	Office	Salesperson
Lisa Wong	Warehouse	Loader
Eugene Lee	Office	Accountant
Bruce Lavine	Office	Manager
Adam Gates	Warehouse	Packer
Will Suter	Warehouse	Packer
Gary Lorper	Office	Accountant
Jon Adams	Office	Salesperson
Susannah Harper	Office	Salesperson

Directory Updates:
- Employee e-mail address will adhere to the following guidelines: lastnamefirstname@apexindustries.com (ex. Susannah Harper is harpersusannah@apexindustries.com). Currently, employees in the warehouse share one e-mail, distribution@apexindustries.com.
- The "Loader" position was now be referred to as "Specialist I"
- Adam Gates has accepted a Supervisor position within the Warehouse and is no longer a Packer. All warehouses employees report to the two Supervisors and all office employees report to the Manager.

12. Amy Jones tried to send an e-mail to Adam Gates, but it wouldn't send. Which of the following offers the BEST explanation?
    A. Amy put Adam's first name first and then his last name.
    B. Adam doesn't check his e-mail, so he wouldn't know if he received the e-mail or not.
    C. Adam does not have his own e-mail.
    D. Office employees are not allowed to send e-mails to each other.

12.____

13. How many Packers currently work for Apex Industries?
    A. 2   B. 3   C. 4   D. 5

13.____

14. What position does Lisa Wong currently hold?
    A. Specialist I   B. Secretary
    C. Administrative Assistant   D. Loader

14.____

15. If an employee wanted to contact the office manager, which of the   15.____
    following e-mails should the e-mail be sent to?
    A. officemanager@apexindustries.com
    B. brucelavine@apexindustries.com
    C. lavinebruce@apexindustries.com
    D. distribution@apexindustries.com

Questions 16-19.

DIRECTIONS: In answering Questions 16 through 19, compare the three names, numbers or
              addresses.

16. Smiley Yarnell   Smiley Yarnel   Smily Yarnell   16.____
    A. All three are exactly alike.
    B. The first and second are exactly alike.
    C. The second and third are exactly alike.
    D. All three are different.

17. 1583 Theater Drive   1583 Theater Drive   1583 Theatre Drive   17.____
    A. All three are exactly alike.
    B. The first and second are exactly alike.
    C. The second and third are exactly alike.
    D. All three are different.

18. 3341893212   3341893212   3341893212   18.____
    A. All three are exactly alike.
    B. The first and second are exactly alike.
    C. The second and third are exactly alike.
    D. All three are different.

19. Douglass Watkins   Douglas Watkins   Douglass Watkins   19.____
    A. All three are exactly alike.
    B. The first and third are exactly alike.
    C. The second and third are exactly alike.
    D. All three are different.

Questions 20-24.

DIRECTIONS: In answering Questions 20 through 24, you will be presented with a word.
              Choose the synonym that BEST represents the word in question.

20. Flexible   20.____
    A. delicate   B. inflammable   C. strong   D. pliable

21. Alternative   21.____
    A. choice   B. moderate   C. lazy   D. value

22. Corroborate   22.____
    A. examine   B. explain   C. verify   D. explain

23. Respiration   23.____
    A. recovery   B. breathing   C. sweating   D. selfish

24. Negligent   24.____
    A. lazy   B. moderate   C. hopeless   D. lax

25. Plumber is to Wrench as Painter is to   25.____
    A. pipe   B. shop   C. hammer   D. brush

KEY (CORRECT ANSWERS)

1.	D		11.	A
2.	A		12.	C
3.	D		13.	A
4.	C		14.	A
5.	B		15.	C
6.	C		16.	D
7.	C		17.	B
8.	B		18.	A
9.	C		19.	B
10.	C		20.	D

21.	A
22.	C
23.	B
24.	D
25.	D

CLERICAL ABILITIES

EXAMINATION SECTION
TEST 1

DIRECTIONS: Each question or incomplete statement is followed by several suggested answers or completions. Select the one that BEST answers the question or completes the statement. *PRINT THE LETTER OF THE CORRECT ANSWER IN THE SPACE AT THE RIGHT.*

Questions 1-4.

DIRECTIONS: Questions 1 through 4 are to be answered on the basis of the information given below.

The most commonly used filing system and the one that is easiest to learn is alphabetical filing. This involves putting records in an A to Z order, according to the letters of the alphabet. The name of a person is filed by using the following order: first, the surname or last name; second, the first name; third, the middle name or middle initial. For example, *Henry C. Young* is filed under *Y* and thereafter under *Young, Henry C.* The name of a company is filed in the same way. For example, *Long Cabinet Co.* is filed under *L,* while *John T. Long Cabinet Co.* is filed under *L* and thereafter under *Long., John T. Cabinet Co.*

1. The one of the following which lists the names of persons in the CORRECT alphabetical order is:

    A. Mary Carrie, Helen Carrol, James Carson, John Carter
    B. James Carson, Mary Carrie, John Carter, Helen Carrol
    C. Helen Carrol, James Carson, John Carter, Mary Carrie
    D. John Carter, Helen Carrol, Mary Carrie, James Carson

1.____

2. The one of the following which lists the names of persons in the CORRECT alphabetical order is:

    A. Jones, John C.; Jones, John A.; Jones, John P.; Jones, John K.
    B. Jones, John P.; Jones, John K.; Jones, John C.; Jones, John A.
    C. Jones, John A.; Jones, John C.; Jones, John K.; Jones, John P.
    D. Jones, John K.; Jones, John C.; Jones, John A.; Jones, John P.

2.____

3. The one of the following which lists the names of the companies in the CORRECT alphabetical order is:

    A. Blane Co., Blake Co., Block Co., Blear Co.
    B. Blake Co., Blane Co., Blear Co., Block Co.
    C. Block Co., Blear Co., Blane Co., Blake Co.
    D. Blear Co., Blake Co., Blane Co., Block Co.

3.____

4. You are to return to the file an index card on *Barry C. Wayne Materials and Supplies Co.* Of the following, the CORRECT alphabetical group that you should return the index card to is

    A. A to G   B. H to M   C. N to S   D. T to Z

4.____

Questions 5-10.

DIRECTIONS: In each of Questions 5 through 10, the names of four people are given. For each question, choose as your answer the one of the four names given which should be filed FIRST according to the usual system of alphabetical filing of names, as described in the following paragraph.

   In filing names, you must start with the last name. Names are filed in order of the first letter of the last name, then the second letter, etc. Therefore, BAILY would be filed before BROWN, which would be filed before COLT. A name with fewer letters of the same type comes first; i.e., Smith before Smithe. If the last names are the same, the names are filed alphabetically by the first name. If the first name is an initial, a name with an initial would come before a first name that starts with the same letter as the initial. Therefore, I. BROWN would come before IRA BROWN. Finally, if both last name and first name are the same, the name would be filed alphabetically by the middle name, once again an initial coming before a middle name which starts with the same letter as the initial. If there is no middle name at all, the name would come before those with middle initials or names.

   Sample Question: A.   Lester Daniels
                      B.   William Dancer
                      C.   Nathan Danzig
                      D.   Dan Lester

   The last names beginning with D are filed before the last name beginning with L. Since DANIELS, DANCER, and DANZIG all begin with the same three letters, you must look at the fourth letter of the last name to determine which name should be filed first. C comes before I or Z in the alphabet, so DANCER is filed before DANIELS or DANZIG. Therefore, the answer to the above sample question is B.

5.   A.   Scott Biala   5.____
     B.   Mary Byala
     C.   Martin Baylor
     D.   Francis Bauer

6.   A.   Howard J. Black   6.____
     B.   Howard Black
     C.   J. Howard Black
     D.   John H. Black

7.   A.   Theodora Garth Kingston   7.____
     B.   Theadore Barth Kingston
     C.   Thomas Kingston
     D.   Thomas T. Kingston

8.   A.   Paulette Mary Huerta   8.____
     B.   Paul M. Huerta
     C.   Paulette L. Huerta
     D.   Peter A. Huerta

9. A. Martha Hunt Morgan
    B. Martin Hunt Morgan
    C. Mary H. Morgan
    D. Martine H. Morgan

9.____

10. A. James T. Meerschaum
    B. James M. Mershum
    C. James F. Mearshaum
    D. James N. Meshum

10.____

Questions 11-14.

DIRECTIONS: Questions 11 through 14 are to be answered SOLELY on the basis of the following information.

You are required to file various documents in file drawers which are labeled according to
the following pattern:

DOCUMENTS

MEMOS		LETTERS	
File	Subject	File	Subject
84PM1 - (A-L)		84PC1 - (A-L)	
84PM2 - (M-Z)		84PC2 - (M-Z)	

REPORTS		INQUIRIES	
File	Subject	File	Subject
84PR1 - (A-L)		84PQ1 - (A-L)	
84PR2 - (M-Z)		84PQ2 - (M-Z)	

11. A letter dealing with a burglary should be filed in the drawer labeled

11.____

    A. 84PM1   B. 84PC1   C. 84PR1   D. 84PQ2

12. A report on Statistics should be found in the drawer labeled

12.____

    A. 84PM1   B. 84PC2   C. 84PR2   D. 84PQ2

13. An inquiry is received about parade permit procedures. It should be filed in the drawer
labeled

13.____

    A. 84PM2   B. 84PC1   C. 84PR1   D. 84PQ2

14. A police officer has a question about a robbery report you filed.
You should pull this file from the drawer labeled

14.____

    A. 84PM1   B. 84PM2   C. 84PR1   D. 84PR2

Questions 15-22.

DIRECTIONS: Each of Questions 15 through 22 consists of four or six numbered names. For
each question, choose the option (A, B, C, or D) which indicates the order in
which the names should be filed in accordance with the following filing instructions:
- File alphabetically according to last name, then first name, then middle initial.
- File according to each successive letter within a name.

- When comparing two names in which, the letters in the longer name are identical to the corresponding letters in the shorter name, the shorter name is filed first.
- When the last names are the same, initials are always filed before names beginning with the same letter.

15.   I. Ralph Robinson   15.__
        II. Alfred Ross
       III. Luis Robles
       IV. James Roberts

The CORRECT filing sequence for the above names should be

A. IV, II, I, III   B. I, IV, III, II
C. III, IV, I, II   D. IV, I, III, II

16.   I. Irwin Goodwin   16.__
        II. Inez Gonzalez
       III. Irene Goodman
       IV. Ira S. Goodwin
        V. Ruth I. Goldstein
      VI. M.B. Goodman

The CORRECT filing sequence for the above names should be

A. V, II, I, IV, III, VI   B. V, II, VI, III, IV, I
C. V, II, III, VI, IV, I   D. V, II, III, VI, I, IV

17.   I. George Allan   17.__
        II. Gregory Allen
       III. Gary Allen
       IV. George Allen

The CORRECT filing sequence for the above names should be

A. IV, III, I, II   B. I, IV, II, III
C. III, IV, I, II   D. I, III, IV, II

18.   I. Simon Kauffman   18.__
        II. Leo Kaufman
       III. Robert Kaufmann
       IV. Paul Kauffmann

The CORRECT filing sequence for the above names should be

A. I, IV, II, III   B. II, IV, III, I
C. III, II, IV, I   D. I, II, III, IV

19.   I. Roberta Williams   19.__
        II. Robin Wilson
       III. Roberta Wilson
       IV. Robin Williams

The CORRECT filing sequence for the above names should be

A. III, II, IV, I   B. I, IV, III, II
C. I, II, III, IV   D. III, I, II, IV

20.
    I. Lawrence Shultz
    II. Albert Schultz
    III. Theodore Schwartz
    IV. Thomas Schwarz
    V. Alvin Schultz
    VI. Leonard Shultz

The CORRECT filing sequence for the above names should be

A. II, V, III, IV, I, VI   B. IV, III, V, I, II, VI
C. II, V, I, VI, III, IV   D. I, VI, II, V, III, IV

20.____

21.
    I. McArdle
    II. Mayer
    III. Maletz
    IV. McNiff
    V. Meyer
    VI. MacMahon

The CORRECT filing sequence for the above names should be

A. I, IV, VI, III, II, V   B. II, I, IV, VI, III, V
C. VI, III, II, I, IV, V   D. VI, III, II, V, I, IV

21.____

22.
    I. Jack E. Johnson
    II. R.H. Jackson
    III. Bertha Jackson
    IV. J.T. Johnson
    V. Ann Johns
    VI. John Jacobs

The CORRECT filing sequence for the above names should be

A. II, III, VI, V, IV, I   B. III, II, VI, V, IV, I
C. VI, II, III, I, V, IV   D. III, II, VI, IV, V, I

22.____

Questions 23-30.

DIRECTIONS: The code table below shows 10 letters with matching numbers. For each question, there are three sets of letters. Each set of letters is followed by a set of numbers which may or may not match their correct letter according to the code table. For each question, check all three sets of letters and numbers and mark your answer:
    A. if no pairs are correctly matched
    B. if only one pair is correctly matched
    C. if only two pairs are correctly matched
    D. if all three pairs are correctly matched

CODE TABLE

T	M	V	D	S	P	R	G	B	H
1	2	3	4	5	6	7	8	9	0

Sample Question: TMVDSP - 123456
    RGBHTM - 789011
    DSPRGB - 256789

In the sample question above, the first set of numbers correctly matches its set of letters. But the second and third pairs contain mistakes. In the second pair, M is incorrectly matched with number 1. According to the code table, letter M should be correctly matched with number 2. In the third pair, the letter D is incorrectly matched with number 2. According to the code table, letter D should be correctly matched with number 4. Since only one of the pairs is correctly matched, the answer to this sample question is B.

23. RSBMRM 759262
    GDSRVH 845730
    VDBRTM 349713   23.____

24. TGVSDR 183247
    SMHRDP 520647
    TRMHSR 172057   24.____

25. DSPRGM 456782
    MVDBHT 234902
    HPMDBT 062491   25.____

26. BVPTRD 936184
    GDPHMB 807029
    GMRHMV 827032   26.____

27. MGVRSH 283750
    TRDMBS 174295
    SPRMGV 567283   27.____

28. SGBSDM 489542
    MGHPTM 290612
    MPBMHT 269301   28.____

29. TDPBHM 146902
    VPBMRS 369275
    GDMBHM 842902   29.____

30. MVPTBV 236194
    PDRTMB 647128
    BGTMSM 981232   30.____

KEY (CORRECT ANSWERS)

1.	A	11.	B	21.	C
2.	C	12.	C	22.	B
3.	B	13.	D	23.	B
4.	D	14.	D	24.	B
5.	D	15.	D	25.	C
6.	B	16.	C	26.	A
7.	B	17.	D	27.	D
8.	B	18.	A	28.	A
9.	A	19.	B	29.	D
10.	C	20.	A	30.	A

TEST 2

DIRECTIONS: Each question or incomplete statement is followed by several suggested answers or completions. Select the one that BEST answers the question or completes the statement. *PRINT THE LETTER OF THE CORRECT ANSWER IN THE SPACE AT THE RIGHT.*

Questions 1-10.

DIRECTIONS: Questions 1 through 10 each consists of two columns, each containing four lines of names, numbers and/or addresses. For each question, compare the lines in Column I with the lines in Column II to see if they match exactly, and mark your answer A, B, C, or D, according to the following instructions:
A. all four lines match exactly
B. only three lines match exactly
C. only two lines match exactly
D. only one line matches exactly

COLUMN I	COLUMN II	
1.		1.____
I. Earl Hodgson	Earl Hodgson	
II. 1409870	1408970	
III. Shore Ave.	Schore Ave.	
IV. Macon Rd.	Macon Rd.	
2.		2.____
I. 9671485	9671485	
II. 470 Astor Court	470 Astor Court	
III. Halprin, Phillip	Halperin, Phillip	
IV. Frank D. Poliseo	Frank D. Poliseo	
3.		3.____
I. Tandem Associates	Tandom Associates	
II. 144-17 Northern Blvd.	144-17 Northern Blvd.	
III. Alberta Forchi	Albert Forchi	
IV. Kings Park, NY 10751	Kings Point, NY 10751	
4.		4.____
I. Bertha C. McCormack	Bertha C. McCormack	
II. Clayton, MO.	Clayton, MO.	
III. 976-4242	976-4242	
IV. New City, NY 10951	New City, NY 10951	
5.		5.____
I. George C. Morill	George C. Morrill	
II. Columbia, SC 29201	Columbia, SD 29201	
III. Louis Ingham	Louis Ingham	
IV. 3406 Forest Ave.	3406 Forest Ave.	
6.		6.____
I. 506 S. Elliott Pl.	506 S. Elliott Pl.	
II. Herbert Hall	Hurbert Hall	
III. 4712 Rockaway Pkway	4712 Rockaway Pkway	
IV. 169 E. 7 St.	169 E. 7 St.	

	COLUMN I	COLUMN II	

7.
    I.   345 Park Ave.   345 Park Pl.   7.____
    II. Colman Oven Corp.   Coleman Oven Corp.
    III. Robert Conte   Robert Conti
    IV. 6179846   6179846

8.
    I.   Grigori Schierber   Grigori Schierber   8.____
    II. Des Moines, Iowa   Des Moines, Iowa
    III. Gouverneur Hospital   Gouverneur Hospital
    IV. 91-35 Cresskill Pl.   91-35 Cresskill Pl.

9.
    I.   Jeffery Janssen   Jeffrey Janssen   9.____
    II. 8041071   8041071
    III. 40 Rockefeller Plaza   40 Rockafeller Plaza
    IV. 407 6 St.   406 7 St.

10.
    I.   5971996   5871996   10.____
    II. 3113 Knickerbocker Ave. 3113 Knickerbocker Ave.
    III. 8434 Boston Post Rd. 8424 Boston Post Rd.
    IV. Penn Station   Penn Station

Questions 11-14.

DIRECTIONS: Questions 11 through 14 are to be answered by looking at the four groups of names and addresses listed below (I, II, III, and IV) and then finding out the number of groups that have their corresponding numbered lines exactly the same.

GROUP I
Line 1. Richmond General Hospital
Line 2. Geriatric Clinic
Line 3. 3975 Paerdegat St.
Line 4   Loudonville, New York 11538

GROUP II
Richman General Hospital
Geriatric Clinic
3975 Peardegat St.
Londonville, New York 11538

GROUP III
Line 1. Richmond General Hospital
Line 2. Geriatric Clinic
Line 3. 3795 Paerdegat St.
Line 4. Loudonville, New York 11358

GROUP IV
Richmend General Hospital
Geriatric Clinic
3975 Paerdegat St.
Loudonville, New York 11538

11. In how many groups is line one exactly the same?   11.____

    A. Two   B. Three   C. Four   D. None

12. In how many groups is line two exactly the same?   12.____

    A. Two   B. Three   C. Four   D. None

13. In how many groups is line three exactly the same?   13.____

    A. Two   B. Three   C. Four   D. None

14. In how many groups is line four exactly the same?   14.___

   A. Two   B. Three   C. Four   D. None

Questions 15-18.

DIRECTIONS: Each of Questions 15 through 18 has two lists of names and addresses. Each list contains three sets of names and addresses. Check each of the three sets in the list on the right to see if they are the same as the corresponding set in the list on the left. Mark your answers:
- A. if none of the sets in the right list are the same as those in the left list
- B. if only one of the sets in the right list is the same as those in the left list
- C. if only two of the sets in the right list are the same as those in the left list
- D. if all three sets in the right list are the same as those in the left list

15.
Mary T. Berlinger 2351 Hampton St. Monsey, N.Y. 20117	Mary T. Berlinger 2351 Hampton St. Monsey, N.Y. 20117	15.___
Eduardo Benes 473 Kingston Avenue Central Islip, N.Y. 11734	Eduardo Benes 473 Kingston Avenue Central Islip, N.Y. 11734	
Alan Carrington Fuchs 17 Gnarled Hollow Road Los Angeles, CA 91635	Alan Carrington Fuchs 17 Gnarled Hollow Road Los Angeles, CA 91685	

16.
David John Jacobson 178 35 St. Apt. 4C New York, N.Y. 00927	David John Jacobson 178 53 St. Apt. 4C New York, N.Y. 00927	16.___
Ann-Marie Calonella 7243 South Ridge Blvd. Bakersfield, CA 96714	Ann-Marie Calonella 7243 South Ridge Blvd. Bakersfield, CA 96714	
Pauline M. Thompson 872 Linden Ave. Houston, Texas 70321	Pauline M. Thomson 872 Linden Ave. Houston, Texas 70321	

17.
Chester LeRoy Masterton 152 Lacy Rd. Kankakee, Ill. 54532	Chester LeRoy Masterson 152 Lacy Rd. Kankakee, Ill. 54532	17.___
William Maloney S. LaCrosse Pla. Wausau, Wisconsin 52146	William Maloney S. LaCross Pla. Wausau, Wisconsin 52146	
Cynthia V. Barnes 16 Pines Rd. Greenpoint, Miss. 20376	Cynthia V. Barnes 16 Pines Rd. Greenpoint, Miss. 20376	

18.   Marcel Jean Frontenac   Marcel Jean Frontenac   18._____
                8 Burton On The Water   6 Burton On The Water
                Calender, Me. 01471   Calender, Me. 01471

                J. Scott Marsden   J. Scott Marsden
                174 S. Tipton St.   174 Tipton St.
                Cleveland, Ohio   Cleveland, Ohio

                Lawrence T. Haney   Lawrence T. Haney
                171 McDonough St.   171 McDonough St.
                Decatur, Ga. 31304   Decatur, Ga. 31304

Questions 19-26.

DIRECTIONS: Each of Questions 19 through 26 has two lists of numbers. Each list contains three sets of numbers. Check each of the three sets in the list on the right to see if they are the same as the corresponding set in the list on the left. Mark your answers:
- A.   if none of the sets in the right list are the same as those in the left list
- B.   if only one of the sets in the right list is the same as those in the left list
- C.   if only two of the sets in the right list are the same as those in the left list
- D.   if all three sets in the right list are the same as those in the left list

19.   7354183476   7354983476   19._____
       4474747744   4474747774
       57914302311   57914302311

20.   7143592185   7143892185   20._____
       8344517699   8344518699
       9178531263   9178531263

21.   2572114731   257214731   21._____
       8806835476   8806835476
       8255831246   8255831246

22.   331476853821   331476858621   22._____
       6976658532996   6976655832996
       3766042113715   3766042113745

23.   8806663315   8806663315   23._____
       74477138449   74477138449
       211756663666   211756663666

24.   990006966996   99000696996   24._____
       53022219743   53022219843
       4171171117717   4171171177717

25.   24400222433004   24400222433004   25._____
       5300030055000355   5300030055500355
       20000075532002022   20000075532002022

26. 611166640660001116   611166664066001116   26.____
     7111300117001100733   7111300117001100733
     26666446664476518   26666446664476518

Questions 27-30.

DIRECTIONS: Questions 27 through 30 are to be answered by picking the answer which is in the correct numerical order, from the lowest number to the highest number, in each question.

27.   A.   44533, 44518, 44516, 44547   27.____
       B.   44516, 44518, 44533, 44547
       C.   44547, 44533, 44518, 44516
       D.   44518, 44516, 44547, 44533

28.   A.   95587, 95593, 95601, 95620   28.____
       B.   95601, 95620, 95587, 95593
       C.   95593, 95587, 95601, 95620
       D.   95620, 95601, 95593, 95587

29.   A.   232212, 232208, 232232, 232223   29.____
       B.   232208, 232223, 232212, 232232
       C.   232208, 232212, 232223, 232232
       D.   232223, 232232, 232208, 232212

30.   A.   113419, 113521, 113462, 113588   30.____
       B.   113588, 113462, 113521, 113419
       C.   113521, 113588, 113419, 113462
       D.   113419, 113462, 113521, 113588

KEY (CORRECT ANSWERS)

1.	C	11.	A	21.	C
2.	B	12.	C	22.	A
3.	D	13.	A	23.	D
4.	A	14.	A	24.	A
5.	C	15.	C	25.	C
6.	B	16.	B	26.	C
7.	D	17.	B	27.	B
8.	A	18.	B	28.	A
9.	D	19.	B	29.	C
10.	C	20.	B	30.	D

NAME AND NUMBER CHECKING

EXAMINATION SECTION
TEST 1

DIRECTIONS: This test is designed to measure your speed and accuracy. You are urged to work both quickly and accurately and to do correctly as many lists as you can in the time allowed. The test consists of lists of pairs of names and numbers. Count the number of IDENTICAL pairs in each list. Then, select the correct number, 1,2, 3, 4, or 5, and indicate your choice by circling the corresponding number on your answer paper. Two sample questions are presented for your guidance, together with the correct solutions.

SAMPLE QUESTIONS

CIRCLE
CORRECT ANSWER

SAMPLE LIST A

Adelphi College - Adelphia College   1 2 3 4 5
Braxton Corp. - Braxeton Corp.
Wassaic State School - Wassaic State School
Central Islip State Hospital - Central Isllip State Hospital
Greenwich House - Greenwich House

NOTE that there are only two correct pairs - Wassaic State School and Greenwich House. Therefore, the CORRECT answer is 2.

SAMPLE LIST B
78453694   - 78453684   1 2 3 4 5
784530   - 784530
533   - 534
67845   - 67845
2368745   - 2368755

NOTE that there are only two correct pairs - 784530 and 67845. Therefore, the COR- RECT answer is 2.

LIST 1
Diagnostic Clinic   - Diagnostic Clinic   1 2 3 4 5
Yorkville Health   - Yorkville Health
Meinhard Clinic   - Meinhart Clinic
Corlears Clinic   - Carlears Clinic
Tremont Diagnostic   - Tremont Diagnostic

LIST 2
73526   - 73526   1 2 3 4 5
7283627198   - 7283627198
627   - 637
728352617283   - 728352617282
6281   - 6281

CIRCLE
CORRECT ANSWER
1 2 3 4 5

LIST 3
    Jefferson Clinic   - Jeffersen Clinic
    Mott Haven Center - Mott Havan Center
    Bronx Hospital   - Bronx Hospital
    Montefiore Hospital - Montifeore Hospital
    Beth Isreal Hospital - Beth Israel Hospital

LIST 4
    936271826   - 936371826   1 2 3 4 5
    5271   - 5291
    82637192037 - 82637192037
    527182   - 5271882
    726354256   - 72635456

LIST 5
    Trinity Hospital   - Trinity Hospital   1 2 3 4 5
    Central Harlem   - Centrel Harlem
    St. Luke's Hospital - St. Lukes' Hospital
    Mt.Sinai Hospital   - Mt.Sinia Hospital
    N.Y.Dispensery   - N.Y.Dispensary

LIST 6
    725361552637 - 725361555637   1 2 3 4 5
    7526378   - 7526377
    6975   - 6975
    82637481028 - 82637481028
    3427   - 3429

LIST 7
    Misericordia Hospital - Miseracordia Hospital   1 2 3 4 5
    Lebonan Hospital   - Lebanon Hospital
    Gouverneur Hospital - Gouverner Hospital
    German Polyclinic   - German Policlinic
    French Hospital   - French Hospital

LIST 8
    8277364933251 - 827364933351   1 2 3 4 5
    63728   - 63728
    367281   - 367281
    62733846273 - 6273846293
    62836   - 6283

LIST 9
    King's County Hospital - Kings County Hospital   1 2 3 4 5
    St.Johns Long Island - St.John's Long Island
    Bellevue Hospital   - Bellvue Hospital
    Beth David Hospital - Beth David Hospital
    Samaritan Hospital   - Samariton Hospital

LIST 10
      62836454   - 62836455   1 2 3 4 5
      42738267   - 42738369
      573829   - 573829
      738291627874   - 738291627874
      725   - 735

LIST 11
      Bloomingdal Clinic   - Bloomingdale Clinic   1 2 3 4 5
      Communitty Hospital   - Community Hospital
      Metroplitan Hospital   - Metropoliton Hospital
      Lenox Hill Hospital   - Lonex Hill Hospital
      Lincoln Hospital   - Lincoln Hospital

LIST 12
      6283364728   - 6283648   1 2 3 4 5
      627385   - 627383
      54283902   - 54283602
      63354   - 63354
      7283562781   - 7283562781

LIST 13
      Sydenham Hospital   - Sydanham Hospital   1 2 3 4 5
      Roosevalt Hospital   - Roosevelt Hospital
      Vanderbilt Clinic   - Vanderbild Clinic
      Women's Hospital   - Woman's Hospital
      Flushing Hospital   - Flushing Hospital

LIST 14
      62738   - 62738   1 2 3 4 5
      727355542321   - 72735542321
      263849332   - 263849332
      262837   - 263837
      47382912   - 47382922

LIST 15
      Episcopal Hospital   - Episcapal Hospital   1 2 3 4 5
      Flower Hospital   - Flouer Hospital
      Stuyvesent Clinic   - Stuyvesant Clinic
      Jamaica Clinic   - Jamaica Clinic
      Ridgwood Clinic   - Ridgewood Clinic

LIST 16
      628367299   - 628367399   1 2 3 4 5
      111   - 111
      118293304829   - 1182839489
      4448   - 4448
      333693678   - 333693678

LIST 17
Arietta Crane Farm	- Areitta Crane Farm	1 2 3 4 5
Bikur Chilim Home	- Bikur Chilom Home	
Burke Foundation	- Burke Foundation	
Blythedale Home	- Blythdale Home	
Campbell Cottages	- Cambell Cottages	

LIST 18
32123	- 32132	1 2 3 4 5
273893326783	- 27389326783	
473829	- 473829	
7382937	- 7383937	
362890122332	- 36289012332	

LIST 19
Caraline Rest	- Caroline Rest	1 2 3 4 5
Loreto Rest	- Loretto Rest	
Edgewater Creche	- Edgwater Creche	
Holiday Farm	- Holiday Farm	
House of St. Giles	- House of st. Giles	

LIST 20
557286777	- 55728677	1 2 3 4 5
3678902	- 3678892	
1567839	- 1567839	
7865434712	- 7865344712	
9927382	- 9927382	

LIST 21
Isabella Home	- Isabela Home	1 2 3 4 5
James A. Moore Home	- James A. More Home	
The Robin's Nest	- The Roben's Nest	
Pelham Home	- Pelam Home	
St.Eleanora's Home	- St. Eleanora's Home	

LIST 22
273648293048	- 273648293048	1 2 3 4 5
334	- 334	
7362536478	- 7362536478	
7362819273	- 7362819273	
7362	- 7363	

LIST 23
St.Pheobe's Mission	- St.Phebe's Mission	1 2 3 4 5
Seaside Home	- Seaside Home	
Speedwell Society	- Speedwell Society	
Valeria Home	- Valera Home	
Wiltwyck	- Wildwyck	

CIRCLE
CORRECT ANSWER

LIST 24

63728	- 63738	
63728192736	- 63728192738	
428	- 458	
62738291527	- 62738291529	
63728192	- 63728192	

1 2 3 4 5

LIST 25

McGaffin	- McGafin
David Ardslee	- David Ardslee
Axton Supply	- Axeton Supply Co
Alice Russell	- Alice Russell
Dobson Mfg.Co.	- Dobsen Mfg. Co.

1 2 3 4 5

————

KEY (CORRECT ANSWERS)

1.	3		11.	1
2.	3		12.	2
3.	1		13.	1
4.	1		14.	2
5.	1		15.	1
6.	2		16.	3
7.	1		17.	1
8.	2		18.	1
9.	1		19.	1
10.	2		20.	2

21.	1
22.	4
23.	2
24.	1
25.	2

————

TEST 2

DIRECTIONS: This test is designed to measure your speed and accuracy. You are urged to work both quickly and accurately and to do correctly as many lists as you can in the time allowed. The test consists of lists of pairs of names and numbers. Count the number of IDENTICAL pairs in each list. Then, select the correct number, 1, 2, 3, 4, or 5, and indicate your choice by circling the corresponding number on your answer paper. Two sample questions are presented for your guidance, together with the correct solutions.

CIRCLE
CORRECT ANSWER

LIST 1

82637381028	- 82637281028	1 2 3 4 5
928	- 928	
72937281028	- 72937281028	
7362	- 7362	
927382615	- 927382615	

LIST 2

Albee Theatre	- Albee Theatre	1 2 3 4 5
Lapland Lumber Co.	- Laplund Lumber Co.	
Adelphi College	- Adelphi College	
Jones & Son Inc.	- Jones & Sons Inc.	
S.W.Ponds Co.	- S.W. Ponds Co.	

LIST 3

85345	- 85345	1 2 3 4 5
895643278	- 895643277	
726352	- 726353	
632685	- 632685	
7263524	- 7236524	

LIST 4

Eagle Library	- Eagle Library	1 2 3 4 5
Dodge Ltd.	- Dodge Co.	
Stromberg Carlson	- Stromberg Carlsen	
Clairice Ling	- Clairice Linng	
Mason Book Co.	- Matson Book Co.	

LIST 5

66273	- 66273	1 2 3 4 5
629	- 620	
7382517283	- 7382517283	
637281	- 639281	
2738261	- 2788261	

LIST 6
Robert MacColl   - Robert McColl
Buick Motor   - Buck Motors
Murray Bay & Co.Ltd. - Murray Bay Co.Ltd.
L.T. Ltyle   - L.T, Lyttle
A.S. Landas   - A.S. Landas

LIST 7
627152637490   - 627152637490   1 2 3 4 5
73526189   - 73526189
5372   - 5392
63728142   - 63728124
4783946   - 4783046

LIST 8
Tyndall Burke   - Tyndell Burke   1 2 3 4 5
W. Briehl   - W, Briehl
Burritt Publishing Co. - Buritt Publishing Co.
Frederick Breyer & Co. - Frederick Breyer Co.
Bailey Buulard   - Bailey Bullard

LIST 9
634   - 634   1 2 3 4 5
162837   - 163837
273892223678   - 27389223678
527182   - 527782
3628901223   - 3629002223

LIST 10
Ernest Boas   - Ernest Boas   1 2 3 4 5
Rankin Barne   - Rankin Barnes
Edward Appley   - Edward Appely
Camel   - Camel
Caiger Food Co. - Caiger Food Co.

LIST 11
6273   - 6273   1 2 3 4 5
322   - 332
15672839   - 15672839
63728192637   - 63728192639
738   - 738

LIST 12
Wells Fargo Co. - Wells Fargo Co.   1 2 3 4 5
W.D. Brett   - W.D. Britt
Tassco Co.   - Tassko Co.
Republic Mills - Republic Mill
R.W. Burnham   - R.W. Burhnam

CIRCLE
CORRECT ANSWER

LIST 13

		1 2 3 4 5
7253529152	- 7283529152	
6283	- 6383	
52839102738	- 5283910238	
308	- 398	
82637201927	- 8263720127	

LIST 14

		1 2 3 4 5
Schumacker Co.	- Shumacker Co.	
C.H. Caiger	- C.H. Caiger	
Abraham Strauss	- Abram Straus	
B.F. Boettjer	- B.F. Boettijer	
Cut-Rate Store	- Cut-Rate Stores	

LIST 15

		1 2 3 4 5
15273826	- 15273826	
72537	- 73537	
726391027384	- 72639107384	
637389	- 627399	
725382910	- 725382910	

LIST 16

		1 2 3 4 5
Hixby Ltd.	- Hixby Lt'd.	
S. Reiner	- S. Riener	
Reynard Co.	- Reynord Co.	
Esso Gassoline Co.	- Esso Gasolene Co.	
Belle Brock	- Belle Brock	

LIST 17

		1 2 3 4 5
7245	- 7245	
819263728192	- 819263728172	
682537289	- 682537298	
789	- 789	
82936542891	- 82936542891	

LIST 18

		1 2 3 4 5
Joseph Cartwright	- Joseph Cartwrite	
Foote Food Co.	- Foot Food Co.	
Weiman & Held	- Weiman & Held	
Sanderson Shoe Co.	- Sandersen Shoe Co.	
A.M. Byrne	- A.N. Byrne	

LIST 19

		1 2 3 4 5
4738267	- 4738277	
63728	- 63729	
6283628901	- 6283628991	
918264	- 918264	
263728192037	- 2637728192073	

CIRCLE
CORRECT ANSWER

LIST 20

Exray Laboratories	- Exray Labratories	1 2 3 4 5
Curley Toy Co.	- Curly Toy Co.	
J. Lauer & Cross	- J. Laeur & Cross	
Mireco Brands	- Mireco Brands	
Sandor Lorand	- Sandor Larand	

LIST 21

607	- 609	1 2 3 4 5
6405	- 6403	
976	- 996	
101267	- 101267	
2065432	- 20965432	

LIST 22

John Macy & Sons	- John Macy & Son	1 2 3 4 5
Venus Pencil Co.	- Venus Pencil Co,	
Nell McGinnis	- Nell McGinnis	
McCutcheon & Co.	- McCutcheon & Co.	
Sun-Tan Oil	- Sun-Tan Oil	

LIST 23

703345700	- 703345700	1 2 3 4 5
46754	- 466754	
3367490	- 3367490	
3379	- 3778	
47384	- 47394	

LIST 24

arthritis	- athritis	1 2 3 4 5
asthma	- asthma	
endocrene	- endocrene	
gastro-enterological	- gastrol-enteralogical	
orthopedic	- orthopedic	

LIST 25

743829432	- 743828432	1 2 3 4 5
998	- 998	
732816253902	- 732816252902	
46829	- 46830	
7439120249	- 7439210249	

KEY (CORRECT ANSWERS)

1.	4		11.	3
2.	3		12.	1
3.	2		13.	1
4.	1		14.	1
5.	2		15.	2
6.	1		16.	1
7.	2		17.	3
8.	1		18.	1
9.	1		19.	1
10.	3		20.	1

21.	1
22.	4
23.	2
24.	3
25.	1

_____

PHILOSOPHY, PRINCIPLES, PRACTICES AND TECHNICS
OF
SUPERVISION, ADMINISTRATION, MANAGEMENT AND ORGANIZATION

TABLE OF CONTENTS

Page

I.   MEANING OF SUPERVISION   1

II. THE OLD AND THE NEW SUPERVISION   1

III. THE EIGHT (8) BASIC PRINCIPLES OF THE NEW
     SUPERVISION   1
     1. Principle of Responsibility   1
     2. Principle of Authority   2
     3. Principle of Self-Growth   2
     4. Principle of Individual Worth   2
     5. Principle of Creative Leadership   2
     6. Principle of Success and Failure   2
     7. Principle of Science   3
     8. Principle of Cooperation   3

IV. WHAT IS ADMINISTRATION?   3
     1. Practices commonly classed as "Supervisory"   3
     2. Practices commonly classed as "Administrative"   3
     3. Practices classified as both "Supervisory" and "Administrative" 4

V.   RESPONSIBILITIES OF THE SUPERVISOR   4

VI. COMPETENCIES OF THE SUPERVISOR   4

VII. THE PROFESSIONAL SUPERVISOR—EMPLOYEE RELATIONSHIP   4

VIII. MINI-TEXT IN SUPERVISION, ADMINISTRATION, MANAGEMENT
      AND ORGANIZATION   5
      A. Brief Highlights   5
         1. Levels of Management   5
         2. What the Supervisor Must Learn   6
         3. A Definition of Supervision   6
         4. Elements of the Team Concept   6
         5. Principles of Organization   6
         6. The Four Important Parts of Every Job   6
         7. Principles of Delegation   6
         8. Principles of Effective Communications   7
         9. Principles of Work Improvement   7

TABLE OF CONTENTS (CONTINUED)

10. Areas of Job Improvement   7
11. Seven Key Points in Making Improvements   7
12. Corrective Techniques for Job Improvement   7
13. A Planning Checklist   8
14. Five Characteristics of Good Directions   8
15. Types of Directions   8
16. Controls   8
17. Orienting the New Employee   8
18. Checklist for Orienting New Employees   8
19. Principles of Learning   9
20. Causes of Poor Performance   9
21. Four Major Steps in On-The-Job Instructions   9
22. Employees Want Five Things   9
23. Some Don'ts in Regard to Praise   9
24. How to Gain Your Workers' Confidence   9
25. Sources of Employee Problems   9
26. The Supervisor's Key to Discipline   10
27. Five Important Processes of Management   10
28. When the Supervisor Fails to Plan   10
29. Fourteen General Principles of Management   10
30. Change   10

B. Brief Topical Summaries   11
    I. Who/What is the Supervisor?   11
    II. The Sociology of Work   11
    III. Principles and Practices of Supervision   12
    IV. Dynamic Leadership   12
    V. Processes for Solving Problems   12
    VI. Training for Results   13
    VII. Health, Safety and Accident Prevention   13
    VIII. Equal Employment Opportunity   13
    IX. Improving Communications   14
    X. Self-Development   14
    XI. Teaching and Training   14
       A. The Teaching Process   14
          1. Preparation   14
          2. Presentation   15
          3. Summary   15
          4. Application   15
          5. Evaluation   15
       B. Teaching Methods   15
          1. Lecture   15
          2. Discussion   15
          3. Demonstration   16
          4. Performance   16
          5. Which Method to Use   16

Northport-East Northport Public Library

The following item(s) were checked out on 02/12/2024

Title: **Senior clerk-typist : test preparation study**
Author:
Barcode: 30605004539193
Due: **03-11-24**

Title: **Senior clerk : test preparation study guide,**
Author:
Barcode: 30605004841367
Due: **03-11-24**

Total items checked out: 2

You just saved an estimated $69.90 by using the library today.

Northport
151 Laurel Avenue
Northport, NY 11768
631-261-6930

East Northport
185 Larkfield Road
East Northport, NY 11731
(631) 261-2313

www.nenpl.org

PHILOSOPHY, PRINCIPLES, PRACTICES, AND TECHNICS
OF
SUPERVISION, ADMINISTRATION, MANAGEMENT AND ORGANIZATION

I. MEANING OF SUPERVISION

The extension of the democratic philosophy has been accompanied by an extension in the scope of supervision. Modern leaders and supervisors no longer think of supervision in the narrow sense of being confined chiefly to visiting employees, supplying materials, or rating the staff. They regard supervision as being intimately related to all the concerned agencies of society, they speak of the supervisor's function in terms of "growth", rather than the "improvement," of employees.

This modern concept of supervision may be defined as follows:

Supervision is leadership and the development of leadership within groups which are cooperatively engaged in inspection, research, training, guidance and evaluation.

II. THE OLD AND THE NEW SUPERVISION

TRADITIONAL
1. Inspection
2. Focused on the employee
3. Visitation
4. Random and haphazard
5. Imposed and authoritarian
6. One person usually

MODERN
1. Study and analysis
2. Focused on aims, materials, methods, supervisors, employees, environment
3. Demonstrations, intervisitation, workshops, directed reading, bulletins, etc.
4. Definitely organized and planned (scientific)
5. Cooperative and democratic
6. Many persons involved (creative)

III THE EIGHT (8) BASIC PRINCIPLES OF THE NEW SUPERVISION

1. *PRINCIPLE OF RESPONSIBILITY*
   Authority to act and responsibility for acting must be joined.
   a. If you give responsibility, give authority.
   b. Define employee duties clearly.
   c. Protect employees from criticism by others.
   d. Recognize the rights as well as obligations of employees.
   e. Achieve the aims of a democratic society insofar as it is possible within the area of your work.
   f. Establish a situation favorable to training and learning.
   g. Accept ultimate responsibility for everything done in your section, unit, office, division, department.
   h. Good administration and good supervision are inseparable.

2. *PRINCIPLE OF AUTHORITY*
The success of the supervisor is measured by the extent to which the power of authority is not used.

    a. Exercise simplicity and informality in supervision.
    b. Use the simplest machinery of supervision.
    c. If it is good for the organization as a whole, it is probably justified.
    d. Seldom be arbitrary or authoritative.
    e. Do not base your work on the power of position or of personality.
    f. Permit and encourage the free expression of opinions.

3. *PRINCIPLE OF SELF-GROWTH*
The success of the supervisor is measured by the extent to which, and the speed with which, he is no longer needed.

    a. Base criticism on principles, not on specifics.
    b. Point out higher activities to employees.
    c. Train for self-thinking by employees, to meet new situations.
    d. Stimulate initiative, self-reliance and individual responsibility.
    e. Concentrate on stimulating the growth of employees rather than on removing defects.

4. *PRINCIPLE OF INDIVIDUAL WORTH*
Respect for the individual is a paramount consideration in supervision.

    a. Be human and sympathetic in dealing with employees.
    b. Don't nag about things to be done.
    c. Recognize the individual differences among employees and seek opportunities to permit best expression of each personality.

5. *PRINCIPLE OF CREATIVE LEADERSHIP*
The best supervision is that which is not apparent to the employee.

    a. Stimulate, don't drive employees to creative action.
    b. Emphasize doing good things.
    c. Encourage employees to do what they do best.
    d. Do not be too greatly concerned with details of subject or method.
    e. Do not be concerned exclusively with immediate problems and activities.
    f. Reveal higher activities and make them both desired and maximally possible.
    g. Determine procedures in the light of each situation but see that these are derived from a sound basic philosophy.
    h. Aid, inspire and lead so as to liberate the creative spirit latent in all good employees.

6. *PRINCIPLE OF SUCCESS AND FAILURE*
There are no unsuccessful employees, only unsuccessful supervisors who have failed to give proper leadership.

    a. Adapt suggestions to the capacities, attitudes, and prejudices of employees.
    b. Be gradual, be progressive, be persistent.
    c. Help the employee find the general principle; have the employee apply his own problem to the general principle.
    d. Give adequate appreciation for good work and honest effort.
    e. Anticipate employee difficulties and help to prevent them.
    f. Encourage employees to do the desirable things they will do anyway.
    g. Judge your supervision by the results it secures.

7. *PRINCIPLE OF SCIENCE*

Successful supervision is scientific, objective, and experimental. It is based on facts, not on prejudices.

      a. Be cumulative in results.
      b. Never divorce your suggestions from the goals of training.
      c. Don't be impatient of results.
      d. Keep all matters on a professional, not a personal level.
      e. Do not be concerned exclusively with immediate problems and activities.
      f. Use objective means of determining achievement and rating where possible.

8. *PRINCIPLE OF COOPERATION*

Supervision is a cooperative enterprise between supervisor and employee.

      a. Begin with conditions as they are.
      b. Ask opinions of all involved when formulating policies.
      c. Organization is as good as its weakest link.
      d. Let employees help to determine policies and department programs.
      e. Be approachable and accessible - physically and mentally.
      f. Develop pleasant social relationships.

IV. WHAT IS ADMINISTRATION?

Administration is concerned with providing the environment, the material facilities, and the operational procedures that will promote the maximum growth and development of supervisors and employees. (Organization is an aspect, and a concomitant, of administration.)

There is no sharp line of demarcation between supervision and administration; these functions are intimately interrelated and, often, overlapping. They are complementary activities.

1. *PRACTICES COMMONLY CLASSED AS "SUPERVISORY"*

      a. Conducting employees conferences
      b. Visiting sections, units, offices, divisions, departments
      c. Arranging for demonstrations
      d. Examining plans
      e. Suggesting professional reading
      f. Interpreting bulletins
      g. Recommending in-service training courses
      h. Encouraging experimentation
      i. Appraising employee morale
      j. Providing for intervisitation

2. *PRACTICES COMMONLY CLASSIFIED AS "ADMINISTRATIVE"*

      a. Management of the office
      b. Arrangement of schedules for extra duties
      c. Assignment of rooms or areas
      d. Distribution of supplies
      e. Keeping records and reports
      f. Care of audio-visual materials
      g. Keeping inventory records
      h. Checking record cards and books
      i. Programming special activities
      j. Checking on the attendance and punctuality of employees

3. *PRACTICES COMMONLY CLASSIFIED AS BOTH "SUPERVISORY" AND "ADMINISTRATIVE"*
    a. Program construction
    b. Testing or evaluating outcomes
    c. Personnel accounting
    d. Ordering instructional materials

V. RESPONSIBILITIES OF THE SUPERVISOR

A person employed in a supervisory capacity must constantly be able to improve his own efficiency and ability. He represents the employer to the employees and only continuous self-examination can make him a capable supervisor.

Leadership and training are the supervisor's responsibility. An efficient working unit is one in which the employees work with the supervisor. It is his job to bring out the best in his employees. He must always be relaxed, courteous and calm in his association with his employees. Their feelings are important, and a harsh attitude does not develop the most efficient employees.

VI. COMPETENCIES OF THE SUPERVISOR

1. Complete knowledge of the duties and responsibilities of his position.
2. To be able to organize a job, plan ahead and carry through.
3. To have self-confidence and initiative.
4. To be able to handle the unexpected situation and make quick decisions.
5. To be able to properly train subordinates in the positions they are best suited for.
6. To be able to keep good human relations among his subordinates.
7. To be able to keep good human relations between his subordinates and himself and to earn their respect and trust.

VII. THE PROFESSIONAL SUPERVISOR-EMPLOYEE RELATIONSHIP

There are two kinds of efficiency: one kind is only apparent and is produced in organizations through the exercise of mere discipline; this is but a simulation of the second, or true, efficiency which springs from spontaneous cooperation. If you are a manager, no matter how great or small your responsibility, it is your job, in the final analysis, to create and develop this involuntary cooperation among the people whom you supervise. For, no matter how powerful a combination of money, machines, and materials a company may have, this is a dead and sterile thing without a team of willing, thinking and articulate people to guide it.

The following 21 points are presented as indicative of the exemplary basic relationship that should exist between supervisor and employee:

1. Each person wants to be liked and respected by his fellow employee and wants to be treated with consideration and respect by his superior.
2. The most competent employee will make an error. However, in a unit where good relations exist between the supervisor and his employees, tenseness and fear do not exist. Thus, errors are not hidden or covered up and the efficiency of a unit is not impaired.
3. Subordinates resent rules, regulations, or orders that are unreasonable or unexplained.
4. Subordinates are quick to resent unfairness, harshness, injustices and favoritism.
5. An employee will accept responsibility if he knows that he will be complimented for a job well done, and not too harshly chastised for failure; that his supervisor will check the cause of the failure, and, if it was the supervisor's fault, he will assume the blame therefore. If it was the employee's fault, his supervisor will explain the correct method or means of handling the responsibility.

6. An employee wants to receive credit for a suggestion he has made, that is used. If a suggestion cannot be used, the employee is entitled to an explanation. The supervisor should not say "no" and close the subject.
7. Fear and worry slow up a worker's ability. Poor working environment can impair his physical and mental health. A good supervisor avoids forceful methods, threats and arguments to get a job done.
8. A forceful supervisor is able to train his employees individually and as a team, and is able to motivate them in the proper channels.
9. A mature supervisor is able to properly evaluate his subordinates and to keep them happy and satisfied.
10. A sensitive supervisor will never patronize his subordinates.
11. A worthy supervisor will respect his employees' confidences.
12. Definite and clear-cut responsibilities should be assigned to each executive.
13. Responsibility should always be coupled with corresponding authority.
14. No change should be made in the scope or responsibilities of a position without a definite understanding to that effect on the part of all persons concerned.
15. No executive or employee, occupying a single position in the organization, should be subject to definite orders from more than one source.
16. Orders should never be given to subordinates over the head of a responsible executive. Rather than do this, the officer in question should be supplanted.
17. Criticisms of subordinates should, whoever possible, be made privately, and in no case should a subordinate be criticized in the presence of executives or employees of equal or lower rank.
18. No dispute or difference between executives or employees as to authority or responsibilities should be considered too trivial for prompt and careful adjudication.
19. Promotions, wage changes, and disciplinary action should always be approved by the executive immediately superior to the one directly responsible.
20. No executive or employee should ever be required, or expected, to be at the same time an assistant to, and critic of, another.
21. Any executive whose work is subject to regular inspection should, whever practicable, be given the assistance and facilities necessary to enable him to maintain an independent check of the quality of his work.

VIII. MINI-TEXT IN SUPERVISION, ADMINISTRATION, MANAGEMENT, AND ORGANIZATION

A. BRIEF HIGHLIGHTS

Listed concisely and sequentially are major headings and important data in the field for quick recall and review.

1. *LEVELS OF MANAGEMENT*
Any organization of some size has several levels of management. In terms of a ladder the levels are:

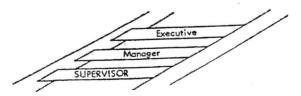

The first level is very important because it is the beginning point of management leadership.

2. WHAT THE SUPERVISOR MUST LEARN

A supervisor must learn to:
(1) Deal with people and their differences
(2) Get the job done through people
(3) Recognize the problems when they exist
(4) Overcome obstacles to good performance
(5) Evaluate the performance of people
(6) Check his own performance in terms of accomplishment

3. A DEFINITION OF SUPERVISOR

The term supervisor means any individual having authority, in the interests of the employer, to hire, transfer, suspend, lay-off, recall, promote, discharge, assign, reward, or discipline other employees or responsibility to direct them, or to adjust their grievances, or effectively to recommend such action, if, in connection with the foregoing, exercise of such authority is not of a merely routine or clerical nature but requires the use of independent judgment.

4. ELEMENTS OF THE TEAM CONCEPT

What is involved in teamwork? The component parts are:

(1) Members	(3) Goals	(5) Cooperation
(2) A leader	(4) Plans	(6) Spirit

5. PRINCIPLES OF ORGANIZATION

(1) A team member must know what his job is.
(2) Be sure that the nature and scope of a job are understood.
(3) Authority and responsibility should be carefully spelled out.
(4) A supervisor should be permitted to make the maximum number of decisions affecting his employees.
(5) Employees should report to only one supervisor.
(6) A supervisor should direct only as many employees as he can handle effectively.
(7) An organization plan should be flexible.
(8) Inspection and performance of work should be separate.
(9) Organizational problems should receive immediate attention.
(10) Assign work in line with ability and experience.

6. THE FOUR IMPORTANT PARTS OF EVERY JOB

(1) Inherent in every job is the *accountability* for results.
(2) A second set of factors in every job is *responsibilities*.
(3) Along with duties and responsibilities one must have the *authority* to act within certain limits without obtaining permission to proceed.
(4) No job exists in a vacuum. The supervisor is surrounded by key *relationships*.

7. PRINCIPLES OF DELEGATION

Where work is delegated for the first time, the supervisor should think in terms of these questions:
(1) Who is best qualified to do this?
(2) Can an employee improve his abilities by doing this?
(3) How long should an employee spend on this?
(4) Are there any special problems for which he will need guidance?
(5) How broad a delegation can I make?

8. *PRINCIPLES OF EFFECTIVE COMMUNICATIONS*
 (1) Determine the media
 (2) To whom directed?
 (3) Identification and source authority
 (4) Is communication understood?

9. *PRINCIPLES OF WORK IMPROVEMENT*
 (1) Most people usually do only the work which is assigned to them
 (2) Workers are likely to fit assigned work into the time available to perform it
 (3) A good workload usually stimulates output
 (4) People usually do their best work when they know that results will be reviewed or inspected
 (5) Employees usually feel that someone else is responsible for conditions of work, workplace layout, job methods, type of tools/equipment, and other such factors
 (6) Employees are usually defensive about their job security
 (7) Employees have natural resistance to change
 (8) Employees can support or destroy a supervisor
 (9) A supervisor usually earns the respect of his people through his personal example of diligence and efficiency

10. *AREAS OF JOB IMPROVEMENT*
The areas of job improvement are quite numerous, but the most common ones which a supervisor can identify and utilize are:

 (1) Departmental layout (5) Work methods
 (2) Flow of work (6) Materials handling
 (3) Workplace layout (7) Utilization
 (4) Utilization of manpower (8) Motion economy

11. *SEVEN KEY POINTS IN MAKING IMPROVEMENTS*
 (1) Select the job to be improved
 (2) Study how it is being done now
 (3) Question the present method
 (4) Determine actions to be taken
 (5) Chart proposed method
 (6) Get approval and apply
 (7) Solicit worker participation

12. *CORRECTIVE TECHNIQUES OF JOB IMPROVEMENT*

Specific Problems	General Improvement	Corrective Techniques
(1) Size of workload	(1) Departmental layout	(1) Study with scale model
(2) Inability to meet schedules	(2) Flow of work	(2) Flow chart study
(3) Strain and fatigue	(3) Work plan layout	(3) Motion analysis
(4) Improper use of men and skills	(4) Utilization of manpower	(4) Comparison of units produced to standard allowance
(5) Waste, poor quality, unsafe conditions	(5) Work methods	(5) Methods analysis
(6) Bottleneck conditions that hinder output	(6) Materials handling	(6) Flow chart & equipment study
(7) Poor utilization of equipment and machine	(7) Utilization of equipment	(7) Down time vs. running time
(8) Efficiency and productivity of labor	(8) Motion economy	(8) Motion analysis

13. A PLANNING CHECKLIST
(1) Objectives
(2) Controls
(3) Delegations
(4) Communications
(5) Resources

(6) Resources
(7) Manpower
(8) Equipment
(9) Supplies and materials
(10) Utilization of time

(11) Safety
(12) Money
(13) Work
(14) Timing of improvements

14. FIVE CHARACTERISTICS OF GOOD DIRECTIONS
In order to get results, directions must be:
(1) Possible of accomplishment
(2) Agreeable with worker interests
(3) Related to mission
(4) Planned and complete
(5) Unmistakably clear

15. TYPES OF DIRECTIONS
(1) Demands or direct orders
(2) Requests
(3) Suggestion or implication
(4) Volunteering

16. CONTROLS
A typical listing of the overall areas in which the supervisor should establish controls might be:
(1) Manpower
(2) Materials
(3) Quality of work
(4) Quantity of work
(5) Time
(6) Space
(7) Money
(8) Methods

17. ORIENTING THE NEW EMPLOYEE
(1) Prepare for him
(2) Welcome the new employee
(3) Orientation for the job
(4) Follow-up

18. CHECKLIST FOR ORIENTING NEW EMPLOYEES

Yes No

(1) Do your appreciate the feelings of new employees when they first report for work?

(2) Are you aware of the fact that the new employee must make a big adjustment to his job?

(3) Have you given him good reasons for liking the job and the organization?

(4) Have you prepared for his first day on the job?

(5) Did you welcome him cordially and make him feel needed?

(6) Did you establish rapport with him so that he feels free to talk and discuss matters with you?

(7) Did you explain his job to him and his relationship to you?

(8) Does he know that his work will be evaluated periodically on a basis that is fair and objective?

(9) Did you introduce him to his fellow workers in such a way that they are likely to accept him?

(10) Does he know what employee benefits he will receive?

(11) Does he understand the importance of being on the job and what to do if he must leave his duty station?

(12) Has he been impressed with the importance of accident prevention and safe practice?

(13) Does he generally know his way around the department?

(14) Is he under the guidance of a sponsor who will teach the right ways of doing things

(15) Do you plan to follow-up so that he will continue to adjust successfully to his job?

19. *PRINCIPLES OF LEARNING*
        (1) Motivation   (2) Demonstration or explanation   (3) Practice

20. *CAUSES OF POOR PERFORMANCE*
        (1) Improper training for job
        (2) Wrong tools
        (3) Inadequate directions
        (4) Lack of supervisory follow-up
        (5) Poor communications
        (6) Lack of standards of performance
        (7) Wrong work habits
        (8) Low morale
        (9) Other

21. *FOUR MAJOR STEPS IN ON-THE-JOB INSTRUCTION*
        (1) Prepare the worker
        (2) Present the operation
        (3) Tryout performance
        (4) Follow-up

22. *EMPLOYEES WANT FIVE THINGS*
        (1) Security (2) Opportunity (3) Recognition (4) Inclusion (5) Expression

23. *SOME DON'TS IN REGARD TO PRAISE*
        (1) Don't praise a person for something he hasn't done
        (2) Don't praise a person unless you can be sincere
        (3) Don't be sparing in praise just because your superior withholds it from you
        (4) Don't let too much time elapse between good performance and recognition of it

24. *HOW TO GAIN YOUR WORKERS' CONFIDENCE*
    Methods of developing confidence include such things as:
        (1) Knowing the interests, habits, hobbies of employees
        (2) Admitting your own inadequacies
        (3) Sharing and telling of confidence in others
        (4) Supporting people when they are in trouble
        (5) Delegating matters that can be well handled
        (6) Being frank and straightforward about problems and working conditions
        (7) Encouraging others to bring their problems to you
        (8) Taking action on problems which impede worker progress

25. *SOURCES OF EMPLOYEE PROBLEMS*
    On-the-job causes might be such things as:
        (1) A feeling that favoritism is exercised in assignments
        (2) Assignment of overtime
        (3) An undue amount of supervision
        (4) Changing methods or systems
        (5) Stealing of ideas or trade secrets
        (6) Lack of interest in job
        (7) Threat of reduction in force
        (8) Ignorance or lack of communications
        (9) Poor equipment
      (10) Lack of knowing how supervisor feels toward employee
      (11) Shift assignments

    Off-the-job problems might have to do with:
        (1) Health   (2) Finances   (3) Housing   (4) Family

26. *THE SUPERVISOR'S KEY TO DISCIPLINE*
There are several key points about discipline which the supervisor should keep in mind:
(1) Job discipline is one of the disciplines of life and is directed by the supervisor.
(2) It is more important to correct an employee fault than to fix blame for it.
(3) Employee performance is affected by problems both on the job and off.
(4) Sudden or abrupt changes in behavior can be indications of important employee problems.
(5) Problems should be dealt with as soon as possible after they are identified.
(6) The attitude of the supervisor may have more to do with solving problems than the techniques of problem solving.
(7) Correction of employee behavior should be resorted to only after the supervisor is sure that training or counseling will not be helpful.
(8) Be sure to document your disciplinary actions.
(9) Make sure that you are disciplining on the basis of facts rather than personal feelings.
(10) Take each disciplinary step in order, being careful not to make snap judgments, or decisions based on impatience.

27. *FIVE IMPORTANT PROCESSES OF MANAGEMENT*
(1) Planning (2) Organizing (3) Scheduling
(4) Controlling (5) Motivating

28. *WHEN THE SUPERVISOR FAILS TO PLAN*
(1) Supervisor creates impression of not knowing his job
(2) May lead to excessive overtime
(3) Job runs itself -- supervisor lacks control
(4) Deadlines and appointments missed
(5) Parts of the work go undone
(6) Work interrupted by emergencies
(7) Sets a bad example
(8) Uneven workload creates peaks and valleys
(9) Too much time on minor details at expense of more important tasks

29. *FOURTEEN GENERAL PRINCIPLES OF MANAGEMENT*
(1) Division of work
(2) Authority and responsibility
(3) Discipline
(4) Unity of command
(5) Unity of direction
(6) Subordination of individual interest to general interest
(7) Remuneration of personnel
(8) Centralization
(9) Scalar chain
(10) Order
(11) Equity
(12) Stability of tenure of personnel
(13) Initiative
(14) Esprit de corps

30. *CHANGE*
Bringing about change is perhaps attempted more often, and yet less well understood, than anything else the supervisor does. How do people generally react to change? (People tend to resist change that is imposed upon them by other individuals or circumstances.

Change is characteristic of every situation. It is a part of every real endeavor where the efforts of people are concerned.

A. Why do people resist change?
People may resist change because of:
(1) Fear of the unknown
(2) Implied criticism
(3) Unpleasant experiences in the past
(4) Fear of loss of status
(5) Threat to the ego
(6) Fear of loss of economic stability

B. How can we best overcome the resistance to change?
In initiating change, take these steps:
(1) Get ready to sell
(2) Identify sources of help
(3) Anticipate objections
(4) Sell benefits
(5) Listen in depth
(6) Follow up

B. BRIEF TOPICAL SUMMARIES

I. WHO/WHAT IS THE SUPERVISOR?
1. The supervisor is often called the "highest level employee and the lowest level manager."
2. A supervisor is a member of both management and the work group. He acts as a bridge between the two.
3. Most problems in supervision are in the area of human relations, or people problems.
4. Employees expect: Respect, opportunity to learn and to advance, and a sense of belonging, and so forth.
5. Supervisors are responsible for directing people and organizing work. Planning is of paramount importance.
6. A position description is a set of duties and responsibilities inherent to a given position.
7. It is important to keep the position description up-to-date and to provide each employee with his own copy.

II. THE SOCIOLOGY OF WORK
1. People are alike in many ways; however, each individual is unique.
2. The supervisor is challenged in getting to know employee differences. Acquiring skills in evaluating individuals is an asset.
3. Maintaining meaningful working relationships in the organization is of great importance.
4. The supervisor has an obligation to help individuals to develop to their fullest potential.
5. Job rotation on a planned basis helps to build versatility and to maintain interest and enthusiasm in work groups.
6. Cross training (job rotation) provides backup skills.
7. The supervisor can help reduce tension by maintaining a sense of humor, providing guidance to employees, and by making reasonable and timely decisions. Employees respond favorably to working under reasonably predictable circumstances.
8. Change is characteristic of all managerial behavior. The supervisor must adjust to changes in procedures, new methods, technological changes, and to a number of new and sometimes challenging situations.
9. To overcome the natural tendency for people to resist change, the supervisor should become more skillful in initiating change.

III. PRINCIPLES AND PRACTICES OF SUPERVISION
1. Employees should be required to answer to only one superior.
2. A supervisor can effectively direct only a limited number of employees, depending upon the complexity, variety, and proximity of the jobs involved.
3. The organizational chart presents the organization in graphic form. It reflects lines of authority and responsibility as well as interrelationships of units within the organization.
4. Distribution of work can be improved through an analysis using the "Work Distribution Chart."
5. The "Work Distribution Chart" reflects the division of work within a unit in understandable form.
6. When related tasks are given to an employee, he has a better chance of increasing his skills through training.
7. The individual who is given the responsibility for tasks must also be given the appropriate authority to insure adequate results.
8. The supervisor should delegate repetitive, routine work. Preparation of recurring reports, maintaining leave and attendance records are some examples.
9. Good discipline is essential to good task performance. Discipline is reflected in the actions of employees on the job in the absence of supervision.
10. Disciplinary action may have to be taken when the positive aspects of discipline have failed. Reprimand, warning, and suspension are examples of disciplinary action.
11. If a situation calls for a reprimand, be sure it is deserved and remember it is to be done in private.

IV. DYNAMIC LEADERSHIP
1. A style is a personal method or manner of exerting influence.
2. Authoritarian leaders often see themselves as the source of power and authority.
3. The democratic leader often perceives the group as the source of authority and power.
4. Supervisors tend to do better when using the pattern of leadership that is most natural for them.
5. Social scientists suggest that the effective supervisor use the leadership style that best fits the problem or circumstances involved.
6. All four styles -- telling, selling, consulting, joining -- have their place. Using one does not preclude using the other at another time.
7. The theory X point of view assumes that the average person dislikes work, will avoid it whenever possible, and must be coerced to achieve organizational objectives.
8. The theory Y point of view assumes that the average person considers work to be as natural as play, and, when the individual is committed, he requires little supervision or direction to accomplish desired objectives.
9. The leader's basic assumptions concerning human behavior and human nature affect his actions, decisions, and other managerial practices.
10. Dissatisfaction among employees is often present, but difficult to isolate. The supervisor should seek to weaken dissatisfaction by keeping promises, being sincere and considerate, keeping employees informed, and so forth.
11. Constructive suggestions should be encouraged during the natural progress of the work.

V. PROCESSES FOR SOLVING PROBLEMS
1. People find their daily tasks more meaningful and satisfying when they can improve them.
2. The causes of problems, or the key factors, are often hidden in the background. Ability to solve problems often involves the ability to isolate them from their backgrounds. There is some substance to the cliché that some persons "can't see the forest for the trees."
3. New procedures are often developed from old ones. Problems should be broken down into manageable parts. New ideas can be adapted from old ones.

4. People think differently in problem-solving situations. Using a logical, patterned approach is often useful. One approach found to be useful includes these steps:

    (a) Define the problem   (d) Weigh and decide
    (b) Establish objectives   (e) Take action
    (c) Get the facts   (f) Evaluate action

VI. TRAINING FOR RESULTS

1. Participants respond best when they feel training is important to them.
2. The supervisor has responsibility for the training and development of those who report to him.
3. When training is delegated to others, great care must be exercised to insure the trainer has knowledge, aptitude, and interest for his work as a trainer.
4. Training (learning) of some type goes on continually. The most successful supervisor makes certain the learning contributes in a productive manner to operational goals.
5. New employees are particularly susceptible to training. Older employees facing new job situations require specific training, as well as having need for development and growth opportunities.
6. Training needs require continuous monitoring.
7. The training officer of an agency is a professional with a responsibility to assist supervisors in solving training problems.
8. Many of the self-development steps important to the supervisor's own growth are equally important to the development of peers and subordinates. Knowledge of these is important when the supervisor consults with others on development and growth opportunities.

VII. HEALTH, SAFETY, AND ACCIDENT PREVENTION

1. Management-minded supervisors take appropriate measures to assist employees in maintaining health and in assuring safe practices in the work environment.
2. Effective safety training and practices help to avoid injury and accidents.
3. Safety should be a management goal. All infractions of safety which are observed should be corrected without exception.
4. Employees' safety attitude, training and instruction, provision of safe tools and equipment, supervision, and leadership are considered highly important factors which contribute to safety and which can be influenced directly by supervisors.
5. When accidents do occur they should be investigated promptly for very important reasons, including the fact that information which is gained can be used to prevent accidents in the future.

VIII. EQUAL EMPLOYMENT OPPORTUNITY

1. The supervisor should endeavor to treat all employees fairly, without regard to religion, race, sex, or national origin.
2. Groups tend to reflect the attitude of the leader. Prejudice can be detected even in very subtle form. Supervisors must strive to create a feeling of mutual respect and confidence in every employee.
3. Complete utilization of all human resources is a national goal. Equitable consideration should be accorded women in the work force, minority-group members, the physically and mentally handicapped, and the older employee. The important question is: "Who can do the job?"
4. Training opportunities, recognition for performance, overtime assignments, promotional opportunities, and all other personnel actions are to be handled on an equitable basis.

IX. IMPROVING COMMUNICATIONS

1. Communications is achieving understanding between the sender and the receiver of a message. It also means sharing information -- the creation of understanding.
2. Communication is basic to all human activity. Words are means of conveying meanings; however, real meanings are in people.
3. There are very practical differences in the effectiveness of one-way, impersonal, and two-way communications. Words spoken face-to-face are better understood. Telephone conversations are effective, but lack the rapport of person-to-person exchanges. The whole person communicates.
4. Cooperation and communication in an organization go hand in hand. When there is a mutual respect between people, spelling out rules and procedures for communicating is unnecessary.
5. There are several barriers to effective communications. These include failure to listen with respect and understanding, lack of skill in feedback, and misinterpreting the meanings of words used by the speaker. It is also common practice to listen to what we want to hear, and tune out things we do not want to hear.
6. Communication is management's chief problem. The supervisor should accept the challenge to communicate more effectively and to improve interagency and intra-agency communications.
7. The supervisor may often plan for and conduct meetings. The planning phase is critical and may determine the success or the failure of a meeting.
8. Speaking before groups usually requires extra effort. Stage fright may never disappear completely, but it can be controlled.

X. SELF-DEVELOPMENT

1. Every employee is responsible for his own self-development.
2. Toastmaster and toastmistress clubs offer opportunities to improve skills in oral communications.
3. Planning for one's own self-development is of vital importance. Supervisors know their own strengths and limitations better than anyone else.
4. Many opportunities are open to aid the supervisor in his developmental efforts, including job assignments; training opportunities, both governmental and non-governmental -- to include universities and professional conferences and seminars.
5. Programmed instruction offers a means of studying at one's own rate.
6. Where difficulties may arise from a supervisor's being away from his work for training, he may participate in televised home study or correspondence courses to meet his self-development needs.

XI. TEACHING AND TRAINING

A. The Teaching Process

Teaching is encouraging and guiding the learning activities of students toward established goals. In most cases this process consists in five steps: preparation, presentation, summarization, evaluation, and application.

1. Preparation

Preparation is twofold in nature; that of the supervisor and the employee.

Preparation by the supervisor is absolutely essential to success. He must know what, when, where, how, and whom he will teach. Some of the factors that should be considered are:

(1) The objectives	(5) Employee interest
(2) The materials needed	(6) Training aids
(3) The methods to be used	(7) Evaluation
(4) Employee participation	(8) Summarization

Employee preparation consists in preparing the employee to receive the material. Probably the most important single factor in the preparation of the employee is arousing and maintaining his interest. He must know the objectives of the training, why he is there, how the material can be used, and its importance to him.

2. Presentation

In presentation, have a carefully designed plan and follow it.
The plan should be accurate and complete, yet flexible enough to meet situations as they arise. The method of presentation will be determined by the particular situation and objectives.

3. Summary

A summary should be made at the end of every training unit and program. In addition, there may be internal summaries depending on the nature of the material being taught. The important thing is that the trainee must always be able to understand how each part of the new material relates to the whole.

4. Application

The supervisor must arrange work so the employee will be given a chance to apply new knowledge or skills while the material is still clear in his mind and interest is high. The trainee does not really know whether he has learned the material until he has been given a chance to apply it. If the material is not applied, it loses most of its value.

5. Evaluation

The purpose of all training is to promote learning. To determine whether the training has been a success or failure, the supervisor must evaluate this learning.
In the broadest sense evaluation includes all the devices, methods, skills, and techniques used by the supervisor to keep himself and the employees informed as to their progress toward the objectives they are pursuing. The extent to which the employee has mastered the knowledge, skills, and abilities, or changed his attitudes, as determined by the program objectives, is the extent to which instruction has succeeded or failed.
Evaluation should not be confined to the end of the lesson, day, or program but should be used continuously. We shall note later the way this relates to the rest of the teaching process.

B. Teaching Methods

A teaching method is a pattern of identifiable student and instructor activity used in presenting training material.
All supervisors are faced with the problem of deciding which method should be used at a given time.

1. Lecture

The lecture is direct oral presentation of material by the supervisor. The present trend is to place less emphasis on the trainer's activity and more on that of the trainee.

2. Discussion

Teaching by discussion or conference involves using questions and other techniques to arouse interest and focus attention upon certain areas, and by doing so creating a learning situation. This can be one of the most valuable methods because it gives the employees 'an opportunity to express their ideas and pool their knowledge.

3. Demonstration

The demonstration is used to teach how something works or how to do something. It can be used to show a principle or what the results of a series of actions will be. A well-staged demonstration is particularly effective because it shows proper methods of performance in a realistic manner.

4. Performance

Performance is one of the most fundamental of all learning techniques or teaching methods. The trainee may be able to tell how a specific operation should be performed but he cannot be sure he knows how to perform the operation until he has done so.

As with all methods, there are certain advantages and disadvantages to each method.

5. Which Method to Use

Moreover, there are other methods and techniques of teaching. It is difficult to use any method without other methods entering into it. In any learning situation a combination of methods is usually more effective than anyone method alone.

Finally, evaluation must be integrated into the other aspects of the teaching-learning process.

It must be used in the motivation of the trainees; it must be used to assist in developing understanding during the training; and it must be related to employee application of the results of training.

This is distinctly the role of the supervisor.

———

ANSWER SHEET

TEST NO. _____ PART _____ TITLE OF POSITION _____

(AS GIVEN IN EXAMINATION ANNOUNCEMENT - INCLUDE OPTION, IF ANY)

PLACE OF EXAMINATION _____ DATE_____

(CITY OR TOWN)   (STATE)

RATING

USE THE SPECIAL PENCIL.   MAKE GLOSSY BLACK MARKS.

	A B C D E		A B C D E		A B C D E		A B C D E		A B C D E
1	:: :: :: :: ::	26	:: :: :: :: ::	51	:: :: :: :: ::	76	:: :: :: :: ::	101	:: :: :: :: ::
2	:: :: :: :: ::	27	:: :: :: :: ::	52	:: :: :: :: ::	77	:: :: :: :: ::	102	:: :: :: :: ::
3	:: :: :: :: ::	28	:: :: :: :: ::	53	:: :: :: :: ::	78	:: :: :: :: ::	103	:: :: :: :: ::
4	:: :: :: :: ::	29	:: :: :: :: ::	54	:: :: :: :: ::	79	:: :: :: :: ::	104	:: :: :: :: ::
5	:: :: :: :: ::	30	:: :: :: :: ::	55	:: :: :: :: ::	80	:: :: :: :: ::	105	:: :: :: :: ::
6	:: :: :: :: ::	31	:: :: :: :: ::	56	:: :: :: :: ::	81	:: :: :: :: ::	106	:: :: :: :: ::
7	:: :: :: :: ::	32	:: :: :: :: ::	57	:: :: :: :: ::	82	:: :: :: :: ::	107	:: :: :: :: ::
8	:: :: :: :: ::	33	:: :: :: :: ::	58	:: :: :: :: ::	83	:: :: :: :: ::	108	:: :: :: :: ::
9	:: :: :: :: ::	34	:: :: :: :: ::	59	:: :: :: :: ::	84	:: :: :: :: ::	109	:: :: :: :: ::
10	:: :: :: :: ::	35	:: :: :: :: ::	60	:: :: :: :: ::	85	:: :: :: :: ::	110	:: :: :: :: ::

Make only ONE mark for each answer.   Additional and stray marks may be
counted as mistakes.   In making corrections, erase errors COMPLETELY.

	A B C D E		A B C D E		A B C D E		A B C D E		A B C D E
11	:: :: :: :: ::	36	:: :: :: :: ::	61	:: :: :: :: ::	86	:: :: :: :: ::	111	:: :: :: :: ::
12	:: :: :: :: ::	37	:: :: :: :: ::	62	:: :: :: :: ::	87	:: :: :: :: ::	112	:: :: :: :: ::
13	:: :: :: :: ::	38	:: :: :: :: ::	63	:: :: :: :: ::	88	:: :: :: :: ::	113	:: :: :: :: ::
14	:: :: :: :: ::	39	:: :: :: :: ::	64	:: :: :: :: ::	89	:: :: :: :: ::	114	:: :: :: :: ::
15	:: :: :: :: ::	40	:: :: :: :: ::	65	:: :: :: :: ::	90	:: :: :: :: ::	115	:: :: :: :: ::
16	:: :: :: :: ::	41	:: :: :: :: ::	66	:: :: :: :: ::	91	:: :: :: :: ::	116	:: :: :: :: ::
17	:: :: :: :: ::	42	:: :: :: :: ::	67	:: :: :: :: ::	92	:: :: :: :: ::	117	:: :: :: :: ::
18	:: :: :: :: ::	43	:: :: :: :: ::	68	:: :: :: :: ::	93	:: :: :: :: ::	118	:: :: :: :: ::
19	:: :: :: :: ::	44	:: :: :: :: ::	69	:: :: :: :: ::	94	:: :: :: :: ::	119	:: :: :: :: ::
20	:: :: :: :: ::	45	:: :: :: :: ::	70	:: :: :: :: ::	95	:: :: :: :: ::	120	:: :: :: :: ::
21	:: :: :: :: ::	46	:: :: :: :: ::	71	:: :: :: :: ::	96	:: :: :: :: ::	121	:: :: :: :: ::
22	:: :: :: :: ::	47	:: :: :: :: ::	72	:: :: :: :: ::	97	:: :: :: :: ::	122	:: :: :: :: ::
23	:: :: :: :: ::	48	:: :: :: :: ::	73	:: :: :: :: ::	98	:: :: :: :: ::	123	:: :: :: :: ::
24	:: :: :: :: ::	49	:: :: :: :: ::	74	:: :: :: :: ::	99	:: :: :: :: ::	124	:: :: :: :: ::
25	:: :: :: :: ::	50	:: :: :: :: ::	75	:: :: :: :: ::	100	:: :: :: :: ::	125	:: :: :: :: ::

MAR – – 2019

ANSWER SHEET

TEST NO. _____ PART _____ TITLE OF POSITION _____
(AS GIVEN IN EXAMINATION ANNOUNCEMENT - INCLUDE OPTION, IF ANY)

PLACE OF EXAMINATION _____ DATE _____
(CITY OR TOWN) (STATE)

RATING

USE THE SPECIAL PENCIL.   MAKE GLOSSY BLACK MARKS.

(Answer grid, questions 1–125, columns A B C D E)

1 … 26 … 51 … 76 … 101 …
2 … 27 … 52 … 77 … 102 …
3 … 28 … 53 … 78 … 103 …
4 … 29 … 54 … 79 … 104 …
5 … 30 … 55 … 80 … 105 …
6 … 31 … 56 … 81 … 106 …
7 … 32 … 57 … 82 … 107 …
8 … 33 … 58 … 83 … 108 …
9 … 34 … 59 … 84 … 109 …
10 … 35 … 60 … 85 … 110 …

Make only ONE mark for each answer.   Additional and stray marks may be
counted as mistakes.   In making corrections, erase errors COMPLETELY.

11 … 36 … 61 … 86 … 111 …
12 … 37 … 62 … 87 … 112 …
13 … 38 … 63 … 88 … 113 …
14 … 39 … 64 … 89 … 114 …
15 … 40 … 65 … 90 … 115 …
16 … 41 … 66 … 91 … 116 …
17 … 42 … 67 … 92 … 117 …
18 … 43 … 68 … 93 … 118 …
19 … 44 … 69 … 94 … 119 …
20 … 45 … 70 … 95 … 120 …
21 … 46 … 71 … 96 … 121 …
22 … 47 … 72 … 97 … 122 …
23 … 48 … 73 … 98 … 123 …
24 … 49 … 74 … 99 … 124 …
25 … 50 … 75 … 100 … 125 …